**A FRIEDMAN GROUP BOOK**

This 1992 edition published by Crescent Books, distributed by
Outlet Book Company, Inc., a Random House Company,
225 Park Avenue South, New York, New York 10003.

ISBN 0-517-07277-7

*AMERICAN COUNTRY LIVING: THE ULTIMATE LIFESTYLE COMPENDIUM*
*Cooking, Design, Gardening, and Entertaining*
was prepared and produced by
Michael Friedman Publishing Group, Inc.
15 West 26th Street
New York, New York 10010

Typeset by Bookworks Plus
Color separations by Excel Graphic Arts Co., Hong Kong
Printed and bound in Hong Kong by Leefung-Asco Printers Ltd.

8   7   6   5   4   3   2   1

# THE ULTIMATE
## AMERICAN
# COUNTRY LIVING
### LIFESTYLE COMPENDIUM

**CRESCENT BOOKS**

New York

# CONTENTS

# PART ONE

COUNTRY

CANNING PRESERVING

TECHNIQUES, RECIPES, USES, AND MORE

LINDA FERRARI

# THE HISTORY OF CANNING

T hroughout history people have tried to think of ways to preserve their food. When they killed large animals, they tried smoking and drying the meat in hopes of preserving it for times when they were not so lucky or game was not so plentiful.

The turning point came in 1795 when the French army offered money to anyone who could discover a way to preserve food for their troops. Times were hard and even though the French were winning battles they were losing their troops to illness and malnutrition. The challenge was accepted by a Frenchman, Nicolas Appert, a chef and scientist who had experimented with preserving foods for many years. He laid out the first principles for food processing and preserving, using heat and closed containers. While Appert's means and lab equipment were meager, he was very organized and scientific in his approach.

Appert filled glass jars with food, corked the jars, and then wired them shut. He was aware that air had to be eliminated from the food to preserve it, but he did not fully understand why this was so important. He put the jars into sacks for cooking. This allowed him to safely lower the jars that may otherwise have broken during the cooking period.

In 1809, after years of tremendous effort and perseverance, Appert won the prize given by the French army for preserving food by heating a hermetically sealed container.

While a few other people had accomplished the feat of preserving food before Appert, he was the first person to apply his principles of preservation on a commercial level. He actually started a commercial cannery but saw it destroyed during the Napoleonic Wars. We are fortunate that Appert went on to write a paper detailing his discoveries.

© Jody Drake/Mutrux & Associates

Today, we are all beneficiaries of his knowledge and still use many of his principles.

Louis Pasteur, the great French scientist, helped us understand how Appert's concept of heat and the elimination of air helped destroy microorganisms that cause the decomposition of foods. Pasteur went on to teach the process of sterilization called pasturization. All of Pasteur's work was made easier by his use of the discoveries Appert had made.

Two other scientists, Samuel Prescott and William Underwood, studied the fundamental principles of bacteriology and their application to the canning process. Their most significant contribution was to let us realize just how important it is to carefully follow specific steps for the safety of our foods.

The final inventions fundamental to canning and preserving were the metal can by Peter Durand in 1810, the glass jar with threaded tops by John Mason in 1858, and the pressure canner by A. K. Shriver in 1874.

The metal can underwent continuous improvements to reach its present state of development, eliminating rusting, which was a serious problem. The last mechanical improvement in canning was the invention of the metal lid for glass jars. This device helped to prolong the life of the preserved food.

All of this knowledge came from the desire to solve a single common problem: The need to have foods available to everyone, everywhere, throughout the year. We have taken the process to such lengths that we now have freeze-dried foods for campers and astronauts. Today, more and more people are taking up canning simply for the pure pleasure it offers, to give as special gifts, and the beauty of having our summer pleasures packed into a jar year round.

© Brian Leatard/Bon Appetit

# CANNING BASICS

There are many reasons people today are returning to the crafts of yesteryear. Quilting, basket weaving, doll making, rug braiding, and canning are just a few of the things our ancestors did. They canned to make a harvest last from one season to another. They made quilts to keep their families warm. They made baskets to carry laundry, fruit, groceries, even children. They wove rugs so they would have something on their floors.

Today we do these things to recall old times, or because we take pride in doing something for ourselves in a world where anything desired can be bought. We think of many of these crafts as a form of art because of the skill they require. I like to can because I take pride in the fact that I can give my family and friends wonderful summer flavors all year long. I love to cook and use my canned goods in many intriguing ways. I can also give my best friend her favorite summertime fruit at Christmas, and it tastes just as fresh as if it was just picked.

## APPROPRIATE FOODS FOR CANNING

The secret to having nice, fresh-tasting fruits and vegetables is starting out with fresh, firm, ripe fruits and vegetables. Most of us don't have an orchard in our backyard and that's why it is a good idea to look for places in your area to buy fresh produce. Remember, as soon as fruits and vegetables are picked they begin to deteriorate. There are farmers in almost every town who bring their produce into the city to sell at either indoor or outdoor farmers' markets. You can buy from trucks on the roadsides, or look for produce terminals or canneries who will sell to people who are willing to buy large quantities. They will sell by the lug, bushel, crate, or box; buying in bulk helps to lower your price.

I am lucky enough to live in an area devoted to fruit growing. There is a place nearby called Apple Hill, which consists of several farms that band together at different times of the year to sell different fruits. For example, in the early summer they sell several varieties of cherries. You can buy by the lug or box if you want. They have desserts made from cherries, and one farm even had a cherry pit spitting contest. At apple time, the farms sell all varieties of apples as well as apple pies, fritters, jams, cider, and even apple dolls. Some of the farms have craft fairs and one even has fishing for the kids and helicopter rides for those with strong stomachs. There are many ways to get your fruit and some are really fun.

If you have a small garden and a few fruit trees, you know that sometimes you have more than enough food to can at home. You may also preserve on the same day for real freshness.

Once you have found a place to buy your produce and know that it must be firm, crisp, and ripe, you want to make sure that you protect the beautiful color of your canned foods. Simply cut the food directly into a gallon of water into which you have added 2 tablespoons each of vinegar and salt. This will give a slight flavor to your food so make sure that you thoroughly rinse it before adding the canning liquid. You could also use a commercial powdered ascorbic acid solution that is added to water, being careful to follow directions on the package.

# CANNING EQUIPMENT

Starting off with the proper equipment will make canning easier and safer. Some of the equipment is absolutely essential for the safety and quality of successfully canned foods. Other equipment listed here is very helpful and makes your job easier. You probably have most of the equipment you will need for canning, but if you do not you can purchase it at most grocery or hardware stores. For hard to find equipment or specialty equipment look at the mail order sources in the back of the book.

**CANNING JARS AND LIDS:** Canning jars are made of high-tempered glass to withstand the changing temperatures that occur in the canning process. Because of the temperature changes, it is not recommended that you ever use commercial jars that were used for mayonnaise, jelly, or other store-bought foods. These jars could easily crack during processing.

Canning jars come with wide-mouth or regular mouth openings. The wide-mouth variety is much easier to use for fruits and vegetables. The regular mouth jars are great for jams, jellies, and preserves.

Jars come in many sizes: ½-pint, pint, 1½-pint (24-ounce), and quart. Choose the size that is most convenient for what you are preparing.

The most common lid is flat, metal, and self seals with a metal screw band. The flat metal lid can only be used once, but you can use the metal screw bands over and over again. Discard metal screw bands if they have become rusty or are bent out of shape.

Make sure you always check your jars before canning, discarding any that are cracked or nicked.

Decorative jars that have wire bails and rubber rings are very tricky to use when processing foods. For one thing, most of the decorative jars with clamp tops are not made of glass strong enough to withstand the heat required to process the food. When you fill the jars with food and liquid you then place the rubber ring (a new one each time you use the jar) around the lid, close the jar and catch the small wire loop on the lid to the clamp. You only catch the lid because if you totally lock it at this stage the seal is too tight and it may explode during the heating process. On most of these jars just "catching the lid" is not a very tight fit, so during processing water can leak into your food. These jars are very pretty and are much better used with jams, jellies, preserves, marmalades, and butters, where processing will not involve the risk of spoilage.

If, however, you have older jars (with the glass dome lids), then you are in luck because the loop of the bail holds the top down tight enough for a good seal before processing in water. Be careful to check these jars carefully for chips on the glass and rust on the bails because of their age.

Always wash the jars in hot soapy water and rinse well. Wash and rinse the metal bands also. The metal lids with sealing compound should be put in boiling water a few minutes before putting on the jar for proper sealing. Follow the manufacturer's directions found on your package of lids. If you use rubber rings, use new, clean rings each time; wash them in hot soapy water and rinse before use, being careful not to stretch the rubber rings.

**CANNERS:** There are basically three kinds of canners: the water bath canner, the pressure canner, and the steam canner.

The water bath canner is used for fruit, tomatoes, butters, pickles, relishes, and anything else high in acid. You can buy the distinctive, large, black-spotted water bath canners in almost any grocery or hardware store. They come with a rack that holds and separates seven jars of food. You can also use any lightweight pot that is at least 12 inches deep and has a lid. In this case you will have to place a rack in the pan to keep the jars from touching the bottom of the pan and to let the air circulate properly. The canner should be at least 4 inches taller than the jars, because you need at least 2 inches of water above the jars plus boiling room. Remember the water bath canner is used only for high-acid foods. The recipes in this book will specify which canning procedure to use for which recipe.

The second canning process is pressure canning. This is used when processing low-acid foods such as vegetables, meat, fish, and poultry. The pressure canner is the only way for us to get heat high enough to insure the safety of low-acid foods. There are many brands of pressure canners, but as they are sometimes hard to find I have given some suggestions where to find them in the mail-order section of this book. A pressure canner is a metal kettle and cover that are clamped together to make them steam tight. There is a weight gauge that usually reads 5, 10, and 15 pounds, plus a vent or petcock, and a pressure safety valve.

On some pressure canners there will also be a dial pressure gauge. Make sure you always carefully follow the instructions that come with your pressure canner. For the safe operation of your pressure canner always make sure your safety valve opening and petcock are clean. Hold it up and look through the safety valve opening to see if you can see through it. If you can't, run a string through it and clean it. Do this often during the canning season.

Last, we have steam canning. It can be used instead of a water bath canner for acid foods such as tomatoes, fruits, and pickles. This is *not* a pressure canner. The food is processed by a flow of steam instead of being submerged in water. You can use the same time schedules that you use with a water bath canner. Most experts on canning prefer water bath canning to this method and consider water bath canning to be safer.

**COLANDERS and STRAINERS:** These are a necessity when cleaning fruits and vegetables. A strainer is also very handy when making jellies. You can put a piece of cheesecloth in a strainer and strain the fruit juices until they are clear. If you do not have a food processor or food mill you can force fruits through a strainer for butters and sauces.

**WIDE MOUTH CANNING FUNNELS:** Wide and small mouth funnels are used to keep the rims of the jars clean. The wide mouth funnel will fit into the canning jar and the small size is great for funneling syrups or vinegars into fancy or decorative bottles.

**JAR LIFTER:** This device has rubber on its ends and makes lifting hot jars out of boiling water much safer.

**LABELS:** Labels are very handy, not only as a reminder of what is inside the jar, but also the date it was canned.

**LADLES:** Ladles are necessary because they make it easy and less messy to pour syrups or hot cooking liquids over the prepared foods. You will have fewer spills or drips, leaving your jars cleaner.

© L & M Photos/FPG International

**LARGE BOWLS:** You will need these to hold fruit, to acidify vegetables, and to use in making freezer jams. Actually, you will find that you use them in hundreds of ways while canning.

**LARGE POTS AND PANS:** These are needed for precooking foods and to make jams and jellies. Large sizes (6 to 10 quarts) are best and allow for boiling room. I also have a large unlined copper pan for making my jellies and I love it; of course, this is not a necessity. The best pots to use are the nonreactive kind that will not discolor or change the flavor of the food. Heavy weight stainless or heavy enamel is probably your best bet.

**LONG HANDLED SPOONS and SLOTTED SPOONS:** Use these to stir boiling substances without burning your hands. Slotted spoons are particularly useful to remove parboiled fruits and vegetables from boiling liquid.

**MEASURING CUPS and SPOONS:** These are absolutely necessary for accurate measuring. One- to four-cup measures are essential, and a one-quart measuring cup is very useful.

**SHARP KNIVES:** A sharp knife is very important for preparing food. In my opinion, stainless steel is the best because it will not discolor the food.

**THERMOMETER:** This is necessary in measuring the jell point of jams and jellies. When the jelly reaches a temperature of 220°F the jelly is ready. This temperature is for sea level. If you are not at sea level boil some water and see what the temperature is when it boils and add 8°F to that and you will have your jell point.

**TIMER:** It is absolutely essential to assure that directions are followed accurately. You want to prevent possible spoilage and assure the right jell to your jams and jellies.

**VEGETABLE BRUSH:** A vegetable brush is a good way to assure that your fruits and vegetables are clean.

## EQUIPMENT THAT IS HELPFUL

**Apple Corer and Peeler:** This is a great gadget and prepares apples quickly for canning, cooking, and making pies.

**Cheesecloth:** This is helpful in straining jellies and juices.

**Cherry Pitter:** This simple device makes an easy job of getting your cherries ready for canning, either in syrup or in brandy. The cherries look beautiful when canned and it is nice not to have to worry about the pits when you eat them. Williams-Sonoma sells a really nice one that makes less mess than most. It is the Leifheit Cherrymat.

**Food Mill:** This is a handheld tool that purees the juice and pulp of fruits and vegetables. This is great for fruit butters, applesauce, and all sorts of sauces. It separates the puree from the seeds and skin.

**Food Processor:** This is one of my favorite tools for any type of cooking. I find it extremely helpful with canning. It chops and cuts vegetables in beautiful, even pieces and purees fruits for jams and jellies. Cuisinart makes a strainer attachment for their processor that is wonderful. It strains so well that you can actually put raspberries in it and produce a beautiful, clear juice perfect for jelly, with no seeds at all. It also makes a great applesauce by separating the pulp from the skin and seeds. You can even make fruit, vegetable, and meat baby foods with this attachment.

**Jelly Bag:** A mesh bag suspended by a metal holder to hold cooked or mashed fruit, allowing the juices to drain.

**Tongs:** These are useful for removing lids from hot water and placing them on the jars, and for arranging foods inside jars that are hard to reach.

**Towels:** You need towels to wipe the rims of your jars; they are also useful as a safe place to put hot, jars.

# PREPARATION METHODS

**COLD or RAW PACK METHOD:** With this method you clean, cut, and prepare raw fresh fruits or uncooked vegetables and put the food into hot, sterilized jars. Boiling liquid or syrup is then poured into the jars. Continue by releasing the air bubbles, cleaning the rims, and sealing the jars. Process according to directions.

**HOT PACK:** Prepare the fruit or vegetables and partially cook them, then pack them hot into hot, sterilized jars and cover with hot liquid or syrup. You can use the same liquid you used to cook the food in. Release the air and add more liquid if necessary; seal and process.

**OPEN KETTLE METHOD:** This is used for jams, jellies, preserves, conserves, marmalades, and butters. First cook the food to the jell point (which is 8°F above the temperature at which water boils), then pour the boiling hot food into hot, sterilized jars and seal. The food does not necessarily need to be further processed; however, I like to process my fruit preserves for 10 minutes in a hot water bath to assure a good seal. You must never use this method on vegetables or meats as microorganisms will assuredly grow and cause contamination.

**OVEN CANNING METHOD:** This is a process that you may remember your mother or grandmother using. *This method is not recommended as the foods simply do not get hot enough to kill microorganisms.* With heat distribution being so uneven and the likely possibility of jars exploding upon removal from the oven, it is best to use another canning method.

**MICROWAVE CANNING:** This is a rather new process for those who don't want to can large amounts of food. If you have a small garden with a small yield then this is a great way to can as your produce becomes ripe.

# MICROWAVE CANNING

Though I am an avid canner, microwave canning has never been my choice. If my tree is brimming with fruit or I have bought several lugs of fruit, I would want to can it all within a few days. However, I can understand how someone with a small garden or a few baskets of fruit really wouldn't want to get out all the equipment to can so little. For these circumstances microwave canning may be for you.

You must still always sterilize your canning jars and lids. You will also have to process your jams and jellies in a water bath, freeze or refrigerate them, or use paraffin to seal them. If you decide to use paraffin, you have to melt it on the top of a double boiler, since paraffin will not melt in a microwave oven, as the microwaves go straight through it.

There is a product that has been out on the market for a couple of years now, called the MICRO-DOME. The MICRO-DOME is a small pressure canner that holds one pint jar or one half-pint jar at a time. When you buy the MICRO-DOME it comes with a booklet full of recipes. They advise you to only use the recipes that have been specially designed to be used in the MICRO-DOME.

To give you an example, if you are canning fresh pineapple you would cut the pineapple and pack it into the jar tightly to extract its own juice. Seal the jar and microwave according to the directions given with the canner. You remove the canner when a little whistle sounds, then put it into a sink full of tepid water to let it cool. After it cools, remove it from the canner and let it cool again, then store it. The jar will lose some liquid during the canning process. However the MICRO-DOME people assure us that this is all right and that the product will still be safe. Make sure you read all the directions before using an appliance like this to insure the safety of the food you produce.

# SEALING METHODS

**LIDS and RINGS:** The safest lid is a flat metal lid with a ring of sealer running around the inner edge of the lid. These are held on the jars with a metal screw band. You must heat the flat lid for 2 to 3 minutes in boiling water before applying it to the jar (see manufacturer's insert). The screw band is then screwed on tightly and the jar can be processed.

**PARAFFIN:** Paraffin can be bought in slabs in grocery or hardware stores. It is used to seal jams, jellies, preserves, marmalades, and fruit butters. You must be very careful when handling paraffin because it could burn you badly. Never melt it over direct heat. Instead, melt the paraffin in a double boiler, keeping it over hot water until ready to use. Cover jelly with ⅛ of an inch of paraffin and tilt the jar to make sure the paraffin touches all sides for a proper seal. If bubbles form you can pop them, but it is not necessary. If you ever have a paraffin fire just put a lid over it. *Never put water on a paraffin fire.*

**FANCY CANNING JARS with BAIL LIDS:** These jars are very pretty and successfully hold jams, jellies, preserves, and the like. However, if you try to put up foods that require processing you could run into trouble. To process you have to close the lid and push down the bail, but do not yet snap it into the lock position. While it is being processed water can easily seep into the jar. Do not totally lock the jar until processing is complete; unfortunately, by then water has seeped into your food. Remember, when using these jars you must always have a new rubber ring for proper sealing.

# COOLING, TESTING, AND STORING CANNED FOOD

Always remove jars from boiling water with a jar lifter, holding a folded cloth under the jar so no hot water drips on you. Let the jars cool on a wooden surface, on a wire rack, or on a folded towel. Separate the jars so air can circulate easily around them. When the jars are cool, test the seals by pressing the lids with your finger. The lids should not give and should have a slight concave appearance.

Foods that don't appear to be sealed properly can be reprocessed or refrigerated and used within a few days. You can remove the screw caps from the jars and store them until the next time you preserve. Store your canned goods in a dark, cool, dry place.

# FOOD SPOILAGE

Microorganisms are present in all fresh foods. Acid helps to inhibit growth, but low-acid foods need the pressure canner to get the heat high enough to destroy microorganisms.

If you are very careful in following the procedures for canning in this book, it is unlikely that any of your canned food will spoil. But if, for some reason, the food was not processed long enough or not sealed properly there is a chance of spoilage. Spoiled canned food can cause a serious illness called botulism. Botulism is caused by the toxin produced by the growth of clostridium botulinum in low-acid foods or foods that have become low acid.

Botulism can be fatal and it is not easily detected. It has no smell. Never taste any canned food which shows gas pressure in the jar, that is mushy, moldy, or has a bad odor.

If you have any question about the food being spoiled, boil it for 30 minutes. Smell it while it is simmering. Any off odor is more detectable by boiling. The odor you should worry about is one that is rancid or somewhat putrid smelling. If there is any doubt about the contents of a jar, do not taste it. If someone has tasted spoiled food call a doctor immediately. It would be a good idea to take the food with you to the doctor's office touching the jar as little as possible and washing your hands with alcohol and water.

© Robert Edwards

# CANNING FRUITS AND TOMATOES

**W**hen summer comes we all love the wonderful fresh tastes of the fruits that become ripe during these months. If you have fruit trees, they are probably brimming with fruit and producing faster than you can eat it. Isn't it great that we are able to preserve these fruits? Even if you don't have your own garden, it is hard to resist the farmers' markets, roadside food vendors, or even the produce your market is displaying.

In this chapter I will not only give fruit recipes, but pie fillings and some great ideas for tomatoes.

You will love preserving all these wonderful tastes for your family and friends.

When canning fruit you must pick firm, ripe fruit that is free of blemishes. Fruit can be left whole, halved, or sliced. Smooth skinned fruit such as plums or cherries can be canned with the skin left on. Be sure to prick the skin before canning so it will not burst during cooking. Other fruits can be easily peeled by putting the whole fruit in boiling water for 30 seconds and then putting it into cold water. The skins will peel right off. This is also how to peel tomatoes for canning.

If sugar content is a concern of yours, it is good to know that all fruit can be canned without the addition of sugar. Syrup is added to make the fruit taste better and to hold the color. You can use the juice of the fruit, water, or commercial juice without sugar, filling the jar to within ½ inch of the top and process the same as if you used a sugar-based syrup.

All fruit and tomatoes are processed in a water bath canner because of the amount of acid in fruit. If the fruit is very ripe you may want to add a couple of tablespoons of bottled lemon juice to each quart of fruit to assure the amount of acid is correct.

# STEP-BY-STEP PROCEDURES FOR CANNING FRUIT

**CHECK AND CLEAN ALL EQUIPMENT:** Check jars for nicks and cracks and make sure screw-on lids are rust-free and not bent. Wash all jars and screw lids in soapy water and sterilize by boiling them right side up on the rack in a boiling-water canner. Make sure you have new flat lids each time you can.

**PREPARE FOOD FOR CANNING:** Pick firm, ripe fruit or tomatoes, making sure it has no bruises or blemishes. Prepare just enough to fill the canner each time. Be sure to protect the fruit color with a commercial anti-darkening solution or ascorbic acid. Follow the package directions.

**PICKING YOUR SYRUP OR LIQUID:** You may can fruit in plain water, although sugar enhances the flavor in high-acid fruits. You can also flavor with artificial sweeteners, but I do not recommend this because they can becom bitter with heating. You could, however, add the artificial sweetener right before serving and avoid the problem of bitterness. On pages 46 and 47 are recipes for low- and no-sugar fruits.

**Sugar Syrups:** light—2 cups sugar, 4 cups water
medium—3 cups sugar, 4 cups water
heavy—4¾ cups sugar, 4 cups water

**Corn Syrup** can replace the sugar or you can use a combination of corn syrup and sugar.

**Honey** can also replace sugar, but don't use a strong flavored honey as it will overpower the flavor of the fruit.

**Fruit Juice** can also cover the fruit. Commercially prepared juices or fresh juice from the fruit may be used. I like to can tomatoes in their own juice.

## FILLING THE JARS
**Raw Pack**—Tightly pack your fruit into the jars and cover with the boiling liquid of your choice. Leave a ¼-inch headspace.

**Hot Pack**—Cook the fruit in the packing liquid for a few minutes before packing it in jars, leaving ½-inch headspace. Cover with boiling liquid and proceed.

**REMOVING AIR BUBBLES:** Use a plastic or rubber knife or spatula and insert on side of jar to release air bubbles. Add more liquid if necessary.

**CLEANING THE RIMS OF THE JARS:** Using a wet cloth, remove drips of syrup or liquid that might prevent the lid from sealing.

**APPLYING THE LIDS:** Follow the manufacturer's directions on the box—they usually recommend putting the lids in boiling water for 2 or 3 minutes to insure a proper seal. Screw on the metal bands immediately.

**PROCESSING METHODS:** All fruits are processed in a water bath canner. Make sure the water will be high enough to cover the jars by 2 inches and that the water has reached a full boil before adding the jars. Carefully lower the jars into the canner. Add boiling water, if necessary, to cover the jars. Cover the canner. When the water returns to a gentle boil, begin counting the processing time. At altitudes above 3,000 feet, add 2 minutes processing time for each additional 1,000 feet.

**PROPER LIFTING OF THE JARS:** Be very careful removing the jars from boiling water. Use a lifter made for this purpose and hold a folded cloth under the jar so hot liquid won't drop on you.

**COOLING JARS:** Allow the jars to cool on a wood surface, metal rack, or folded towels. A cold surface will crack the jars. Place jars in a draft-free spot with space between them to allow a free circulation of air.

**CHECKING THE SEAL:** There is no sweeter sound to a canner than the "pop" of the lid as it sits and cools. When you hear that pop you know that it has properly sealed. If, after the jars have cooled, the lid is not concave in appearance, test the seal by pressing on the lid with your finger. The lid should not move.

**PROPER STORAGE:** Label and date your jars and store them in a cool, dark place.

© Christopher Bain

# SOME COMMON QUESTIONS ABOUT CANNING FRUIT AND TOMATOES

**Why is liquid lost during the canning process and should it be replaced?** Canning liquid is usually lost because of over-packing the jars. If this should happen it will not hurt the quality of the product, but the food above the liquid may darken. There is no need to replace the liquid—if you did you would have to reprocess the food or it will spoil.

**Is it safe to eat the discolored food?** The food should be fine. However, if there is an off odor to the food, discard it.

**Do the black deposits on the underside of lids indicate spoilage?** No, these deposits are harmless if the seal is good. Natural compounds in some foods corrode the metal.

**Why do some fruits turn dark brown after being canned?** Possibly you forgot to protect the color of the fruit while preparing it for processing. Once it turns color there is nothing you can do. It is a good idea to add a tablespoon or two of lemon juice per quart, or two teaspoons per pint, to each jar.

**Why do some fruits float to the top of a jar?** Fruits and tomatoes usually shrink when they are processed, so make sure you have packed the fruit tightly.

© Melabee Miller/Envision

# HOW TO PREPARE FRUIT FOR CANNING

| FRUIT | HOW TO PREPARE | PROCESSING TIME | |
| --- | --- | --- | --- |
| | | Pint | Quart |
| | | minutes | |
| APPLES | Pare, cut in halves or quarters, and trim off core. To keep from darkening, dip in 1 gallon of water that contains 2 tablespoons each of salt and vinegar. Drain. Cook in hot syrup for 2 to 4 minutes according to the variety. Pack hot. Cover with hot liquid and seal. | 15 | 15 |
| APPLESAUCE | Wash, pare, if desired, quarter, and core cooking apples. Simmer, covered, in a small amount of water until tender. Press through sieve or food mill. Sweeten if desired. Reheat to boiling and pack into hot jars. Add 1 tablespoon lemon juice to top of each jar. Seal. | 20 | 20 |
| APRICOTS | Choose firm, well-colored apricots that are not overripe. To peel, dip in boiling water for 1 minute, then plunge into cold water and peel, or can apricots without peeling. Leave whole, or cut in halves and remove pits.<br>**To pack hot:** Bring to a boil in liquid and just heat through or cook about 1 to 3 minutes. Pack hot and cover with hot liquid. Seal.<br>**To pack raw:** Fill the jars with uncooked apricots. Cover with boiling liquid. Seal. | 20<br>25 | 20<br>30 |
| BERRIES OTHER THAN STRAWBERRIES | Drain well after washing. For firm berries, add ½ cup sugar to each quart of fruit. Cover pan, bring to a boil, and shake to keep fruit from sticking. Pack hot and cover with hot liquid. Seal. For red raspberries and other soft berries, fill jars with raw fruit and shake down for a full pack. Cover with boiling syrup made with juice or water (½ cup sugar and about ¾ cup juice for each quart). Seal. | 10<br><br>10 | 10<br><br>15 |
| CHERRIES | Wash, remove stems, sort for size and ripeness, and pit if desired. If left whole, prick to help prevent splitting.<br>**To pack hot:** For pitted cherries, follow directions for firm berries. For cherries with pits, follow directions for firm berries but add a little water to prevent sticking or bring to a boil in hot syrup. Pack hot and seal.<br>**To pack raw:** Pack into hot jars. Cover with boiling syrup or juice. Seal. | 15<br>20 | 15<br>25 |
| FIGS | Use tree-ripened figs that are not overripe. Sort and wash. Bring to a boil in hot water. Let stand in the hot water for 3 to 4 minutes. Drain. Pack hot into hot jars. Add 1 table-spoon of lemon juice to each 1-quart jar. Cover with boiling liquid. Do not use baking soda in preparing figs. Seal. | 90 | 90 |
| FRUIT JUICES | Wash, remove pits, if desired, and crush fruit. Heat to simmering to release juice. Strain through a cloth bag. Some fruits are not normally heated before extracting the juice. Fruits not heated are apples, white cherries, grapefruit, white grapes, lemons, and oranges. (Navel orange juice will be bitter and is not recommended for canning.) Sweeten juice to taste. Immediately heat or reheat juice to simmering.<br>**To pack hot:** Fill hot jars with hot juice to ½ inch of top. Seal. | 15 | 15 |

| FRUIT | HOW TO PREPARE | PROCESSING TIME | |
|---|---|---|---|
| | | PINT | QUART |
| | | minutes | |
| **GRAPEFRUIT** | Use thoroughly ripened fruit. Peel. Separate segments and peel them. Pack segments in jars. Cover with hot syrup. Seal. | 20 | 25 |
| **GRAPES** | Use ripe Muscat or slightly underripe seedless grapes for canning. Remove stems and wash. | | |
| | **To pack hot:** Bring to a boil in a small amount of liquid. Pack hot into hot jars. Cover with the hot liquid and seal. | 15 | 15 |
| | **To pack raw:** Put into hot jars and cover with boiling liquid. Seal. | 20 | 20 |
| **NECTARINES** | Follow directions for freestone peaches. | | |
| **NOPALES** | Remove spines from young, tender cactus leaves. Cut into cubes or strips. Diced or cubed cactus is easier to handle, but either strips or cubes may be used. Rinse diced cactus once or twice in cold water. Place diced cactus in water, bring to a boil, and turn down to simmer. Cook until tender, about 10 to 15 minutes. | | |
| | **To pack hot:** Pack hot into clean jars. Add ½ teaspoon salt and 1 teaspoon lemon juice or vinegar per pint; 1 teaspoon salt and 2 teaspoons lemon juice or vinegar per quart. Add other spices (garlic, cloves, or onion powder, for example) if desired. Cover with water leaving ½ inch headspace. Seal. | 15 | 20 |
| **ORANGES** | For Valencia or Mandarin oranges, follow directions for grapefruit. Other orange varieties are not recommended, because they become bitter. | | |
| **PEACHES** | To peel all except canning varieties of clingstones, dip in boiling water for about 1 minute, plunge into cold water, then slip off skins. Cut into halves and remove pits. To keep from darkening, dip in 1 gallon of water that contains 2 tablespoons each of salt and vinegar. Drain at once. Peel canning varieties of clingstone peaches like you would apples, preferably with a stainless steel knife. Once peeled, a cut around the peach and a twisting motion between the hands will remove one-half of the fruit from the pit. You can remove the pit from the second half with a special spoon-shaped knife or cut it out carefully with a paring knife. | | |
| | **To pack hot:** If fruit is juicy, add ½ cup sugar to each quart of raw fruit. Bring to a boil. Drop less juicy fruit into a medium-thin syrup that is boiling hot. Just heat through. Pack hot. Cover with boiling liquid. Seal. | | |
| |     Clingstone. | 20 | 25 |
| |     Freestone. | 15 | 20 |
| | **To pack raw:** Pack in jars with the cut side down and the edges overlapping. Cover with boiling liquid. Seal. | | |
| |     Clingstone | 25 | 30 |
| |     Freestone | 20 | 25 |

University of California, Davis; Department of Food Technology.

| FRUIT | HOW TO PREPARE | PROCESSING TIME | |
|---|---|---|---|
| | | PINT | QUART |
| | | minutes | |
| **PEARS** | Ripen pears for canning after picking. Do not allow them to become too soft. Pare, cut in halves, and trim out cores. **To pack hot:** Same as for less juicy peaches. Seal. **To pack raw:** Same as for peaches. Seal. | 15 20 | 20 25 |
| **PINEAPPLE** | Pare firm but ripe pineapple. Slice crosswise or cut into wedges. Remove the core and trim the "eye." Simmer pineapple in light syrup or pineapple juice until tender. **To pack hot:** Pack hot slices or wedges (spears) into hot jars. Cover with hot cooking liquid, leaving ½ inch headspace. Seal. | 15 | 20 |
| **PLUMS AND FRESH PRUNES** | Sort, remove stems, and wash. If canning whole, prick to help prevent bursting, or cut into halves. **To pack hot:** Bring to a boil in juice or in a thin to medium syrup. Pack hot. Cover with boiling liquid. Seal. **To pack raw:** Pack the fruit into the jar. Cover with boiling juice or syrup. Seal. | 15 20 | 15 20 |
| **RHUBARB** | Cut into ½-inch lengths. Add ½ cup sugar to each quart of rhubarb and let stand 3 to 4 hours to draw out juice. Bring to a boil. Pack hot. Cover with hot juice. Seal. | 10 | 10 |
| **STRAWBERRIES** | Not recommended because the product is usually not satisfactory. | | |
| **TOMATOES** | Sort, picking out any that are spoiled or green. Do not can overripe tomatoes. They may be too low in acid for safe water bath canning. (If tomatoes are excessively dirty, wash with a solution containing 4 teaspoons chlorine bleach in each gallon water.) Dip in boiling water long enough to crack skins (about 1 minute). Dip in cold water. Peel and remove cores. Save any juice to add to the tomatoes when heating. **To pack hot:** Bring whole, peeled tomatoes to a boil. Pack immediately into hot jars. Cover with the hot liquid in which the tomatoes were heated. Add 1 teaspoon salt and 2 teaspoons vinegar or 2 teaspoons bottled lemon juice to each quart. Seal. **To pack raw:** Pack raw, whole, peeled tomatoes tightly to the tops of hot jars. Press tomatoes down after each two tomatoes are added to release juice and to fill spaces. Add 1 teaspoon salt and 2 teaspoons vinegar or 2 teaspoons bottled lemon juice to each quart. Seal. **Hot pack without lemon juice or vinegar.** **Raw pack without lemon juice or vinegar.** | 15 30 30 45 | 15 30 30 45 |
| **TOMATO JUICE** | Use sound, well-ripened, but not overripe, tomatoes. Peel, core, and cut into pieces. Either cook until soft and strain or extract juice from uncooked tomatoes. Juice from cooked tomatoes is thicker and smoother. Juice from raw tomatoes is thin and watery and tends to separate. Immediately after extracting, heat juice to simmering. Fill hot jars to ½ inch of top. Add 1 tablespoon bottled lemon juice or vinegar to each quart. Add 1 tablespoon salt to each quart or salt to taste. Seal. Process in a gently boiling water bath. | 15 | 15 |

© Guy Marche/FPG International

## APRICOTS

*16 pounds apricots*

*6 cups sugar*

*8 cups water*

*7500 mg vitamin C tablets*

Pick ripe, firm, unblemished apricots. Wash the fruit carefully, cut in half, and remove pits. Put cut fruit into water to which an anti-darkening solution of ascorbic acid has been added.

Put water and sugar into a saucepan and heat until the sugar dissolves and syrup begins to boil. Keep the liquid hot. Add one vitamin C tablet to each quart jar. Pack apricots cut side down into hot jars. Fill the jars with hot liquid to within ½ inch of the top of the jar. Remove the air bubbles and add more liquid if necessary. Wipe the rims and seal. Process in a water bath canner for 30 minutes.

**Makes 7 quarts.**

## CHUNKY APPLESAUCE

My children love applesauce, and with three apple trees we have more than enough apples to fill our pantry with applesauce for the year. I used white sugar in the following recipe so the applesauce would have a lighter appearance, similar to what you buy at the market. However, when I make it for my family I use light brown sugar. My applesauce is darker and it has a rich, maplelike flavor. When adding the sugar, add ½ cup at a time until you reach the sweetness you prefer.

*24 large apples*

*½ cup water*

*2 tablespoons bottled lemon juice*

*½ to 1½ cups sugar*

*3 teaspoons cinnamon*

*½ teaspoon nutmeg*

*1 teaspoon vanilla*

Peel, core, and thinly slice apples. Put apples into a large saucepan with water and lemon juice. Cook covered until tender, about 20 to 25 minutes, stirring occasionally. When apples are tender, chop coarsely with a metal spoon. Add sugar, cinnamon, nutmeg, and vanilla and continue to cook until sugar dissolves. Spoon hot mixture into hot jars, to within ½ inch of top, release air bubbles, clean rims, and seal. Process in a water bath canner for 20 minutes for pints and 30 minutes for quarts.

**Makes 5 pints.**

## BRANDIED CHERRIES

You can brandy any sweet cherry. I have used the Rainier variety because of its beautiful color. It is yellow skinned and just blushed with a hint of red. Rainier cherries are large, sweet, and firm. When I can cherries I always pit them, but brandied cherries are much prettier if they are not pitted.

*10 pounds Rainier cherries*

*2 cups sugar*

*2 cups water*

*2 tablespoons bottled lemon juice*

*3 tablespoons brandy per jar*

Clean cherries and remove stems. Make syrup with sugar, water, and lemon juice. Cook, stirring just until syrup begins to boil. Fill clean, hot jars with cherries packed tightly. Pour hot liquid in, filling jar halfway. Add 3 tablespoons of good quality brandy, then add more hot syrup, filling the jar to within ½ inch of top. Release air bubbles and add more liquid if necessary. Clean rims, seal, and process in a water bath canner. Process pint jars for 20 minutes, 1½-pint jars for 25 minutes, and quart jars for 30 minues.

**Makes 5 1½-pint jars.**

## MIXED FRUIT COCKTAIL

When making this fruit cocktail dice your peaches and pears into large squares. Show them off in a beautiful clear syrup that highlights the fruit's colors. A couple of helpful hints; don't pit the cherries or they will tint the syrup red. However, prick the grapes with a sterilized needle to prevent them from splitting during heating. Since the grape juice is clear it won't discolor the syrup.

*3 pounds peaches (about 6 large)*

*3 pounds pears (about 6 large)*

*1 pound seedless green grapes*

*1 pound Royal Ann cherries*

*4 cups water*

*3 cups sugar*

*2 tablespoons bottled lemon juice*

Peel, core, and dice the pears. Put them in an ascorbic acid solution until all the fruit is prepared. Peel, pit, and dice the peaches. Put them into the same solution as the pears. Stem and wash grapes and cherries. Heat the water, sugar, and lemon juice and cook until it just begins to boil. Drain fruit and mix all of them together. Pack fruit tightly, cut sides down, into hot jars, adding hot syrup to within ½ inch of the top of the jars. Release air bubbles, and add more liquid if necessary. Clean rims, seal, and process in a water bath canner. Process pint jars for 25 minutes and quart jars for 30 minutes.

**Makes 6 pints.**

© Michael Keller/FPG International

## SPICED PEACHES IN PEACH WINE

These peaches are very special and make a wonderful gift.

*12 pounds peaches (about 24 large)*

*4 cups peach wine*

*2 cups granulated sugar*

*1 cup brown sugar*

*¼ cup bottled lemon juice*

*whole stick cinnamon*

*whole cloves*

Peel peaches and leave whole. Put the peaches in an acid solution while you peel all the fruit. Cook the wine, both sugars, lemon juice, and one whole cinnamon stick. Stir constantly until sugar dissolves and liquid begins to boil. Drain and reserve syrup. Rinse peaches if necessary. Stick one or two cloves into each peach. Add the peaches to the syrup and heat just until peaches are slightly softened. Remove pan from stove and let peaches remain in syrup overnight. This will keep them from shriveling. The next day, remove the cinnamon stick and reheat the peaches. When hot, pack the peaches as tightly as you can in hot jars. You can add one cinnamon stick per jar if you want. Cover the peaches with hot syrup, release air bubbles, and add more syrup if necessary. Clean rims and seal. Process quart jars for 20–25 minutes in a water bath canner.

**Makes 6 quarts.**

© Steven Mark Needham/Envision

## PEARS AND RASPBERRIES

This is a great flavor combination and makes a beautiful breakfast compote.

*3 boxes raspberries (about 1½ pounds)*

*9 pounds pears (about 18 large)*

*3 tablespoons bottled lemon juice*

*3½ cups sugar*

*4 cups water*

Carefully rinse and drain the raspberries. Peel, core, and dice the pears, putting diced pears in an anti-discoloration solution until all the fruit is cut. Make the syrup using lemon juice, sugar, and water. Cook the syrup until it just begins to boil. Add the pears, after they have been drained, to the syrup. Cook the pears for 3 minutes. Put pears about one-third of the way up the hot jars, then add some raspberries. Continue adding pears and raspberries until the jars are packed. Add the hot syrup and release air bubbles. Add more syrup if necessary. Clean rims, seal, and process in a water bath canner. Process quart jars for 30 minutes.

**Makes 5 quarts.**

## CINNAMON PEARS

This will make the most beautiful Christmas gift. They are pretty to use on a Christmas fruit platter filled with a mixture of cottage cheese, nuts, and other fruits.

*6 pounds pears (about 12 large)*

*2 cups cinnamon red hot candies*

*5 cups water*

*1 tablespoon powdered fruit protector (like Fruit Fresh™)*

Peel, core, and halve pears. The core can be removed with a melon baller. Put pears into a large bowl of water with an acid solution added to prevent the fruit from darkening, until all fruit is prepared. Put the red hot candies into a large saucepan and add water. Cook and stir until candies have completely melted. Add the powdered fruit protector and stir until dissolved. Add the pears, cover, and cook 3 to 5 minutes, stirring often. Put the pears, cut side down, into hot jars and pack tightly. Fill with hot cooking liquid. Release bubbles and clean rims. Process pint jars for 20 minutes in a water bath canner.

**Makes 6 pints.**

## CREME DE MENTHE PEARS

This is another great pear to use at Christmas time. I love to decorate my turkey platter with these pretty green pears filled with cranberry sauce.

*5 pounds pears (about 10 large)*

*3 cups sugar*

*4 cups water*

*3 drops green food coloring*

*1 tablespoon fruit protector*

*1½ cups creme de menthe*

Peel, core, and halve pears. Bring sugar, water, green food coloring, and fruit protector to a boil. Add crème de menthe and stir well. Add pears and simmer covered over low heat 3 to 5 minutes, just to heat pears through. Put the pears, cut side down, into hot jars and pack. Fill with hot cooking liquid. Release air bubbles and clean rims. Process pint jars for 20 minutes in a water bath canner.

**Makes 5 pints.**

# FRUIT PIE FILLINGS

Canning fruit fillings can be a little tricky. The problem is with the thickening agent you use. Fillings using cornstarch or potato starch will tend to break down in time. Flour will usually become crumbly with time. All of these thickening agents will tend to be very stiff when you use them.

The following recipes have been contributed by the USDA, which has come out with some wonderful pie fillings using a thickening agent called Clear Jel A. This is a fairly new product that is used commercially, but has not yet become well enough known to be stocked in all grocery stores. You can buy it in 400-pound sacks at $1.00 a pound or you can buy it in one pound increments for $2.49. If you wish to order it by the pound, write to Dacus Inc., P.O. Drawer 2067, Tupelo, Mississippi, 38803.

Because these recipes using Clear Jel A are so good, I have included a few of the USDA recipes. For those unable to purchase 400 pounds of Clear Jel A, or don't want to send away for it, I have included an alternative method of making pie fillings.

I prefer to can fruit in a heavy syrup seasoned with lemon and spices. Then, when I want to make a pie, I pour the jar of fruit (a quart will make a nice 8-inch pie) in a pan and thicken it with cornstarch, then let it cool and make the pie. It is easy, not messy, and I can have fresh-tasting pies any time of the year. These fillings are also delicious cooked in breakfast pastries.

## USDA APPLE PIE FILLING

*Quantities of ingredients*
*needed for:*

|  | *1 quart* | *7 quarts* |
|---|---|---|
| *Blanched, sliced fresh apples* | 3½ cups | 6 quarts |
| *Granulated sugar* | ¾ cup + 2 tbsp | 5½ cups |
| *Clear Jel A* | ¼ cup | 1½ cups |
| *Cinnamon* | ½ tsp | 1 tbsp |
| *Cold Water* | ½ cup | 2½ cups |
| *Apple juice* | ¾ cup | 5 cups |
| *Bottled lemon juice* | 2 tbsp | ¾ cup |
| *Nutmeg (optional)* | ⅛ tsp | 1 tsp |
| *Yellow food coloring (optional)* | 1 drop | 7 drops |

**Quality:** Use firm, crisp apples. Stayman, Golden Delicious, Rome, and other varieties of similar quality are suitable. If apples lack tartness, use an additional ¼ cup of lemon juice for each 6 quarts of slices.
**Procedure:** Wash, peel, and core apples. Prepare slices ½ inch wide and place in water containing ascorbic acid to prevent browning. Blanch 2 quarts at a time for 1 minute in boiling water. While blanching other batches of apples, keep those already blanched in a covered pot so they will stay warm. Combine sugar, Clear Jel A, and cinnamon in a large kettle with water and apple juice. If desired, food coloring and nutmeg may be added. Stir and cook on medium-high heat until mixture thickens and begins to bubble. Drain apple slices. Add lemon juice and boil 1 minute, stirring constantly. Fold in apple slices immediately and fill jars with mixture.

## BLUEBERRY PIE FILLING

*4½ quarts blueberries*

*½ cup bottled lemon juice*

*rind of one lemon cut in
    thin strips*

*1 teaspoon nutmeg*

*1 teaspoon mace*

*5½ cups sugar*

*6½ cups water*

Clean blueberries carefully and drain. Combine lemon juice, lemon rind, nutmeg, mace, sugar, and water. Cook until the mixture begins to boil. Fold in berries and cook 1 minute more. Ladle mixture into hot jars. Release air bubbles, clean rims of jars, seal, and process quart jars in a water bath canner for 30 minutes.

**Makes 5 quarts.**

## USDA CHERRY PIE FILLING

*Fresh or thawed sour cherries*

*Granulated sugar*

*Clear Jel A*

*Cold water*

*Bottled lemon juice*

*Cinnamon (optional)*

*Almond extract (optional)*

*Red food coloring (optional)*

**Quality:** Select fresh, very ripe, firm cherries. Unsweetened frozen cherries may be used. If sugar has been added, rinse it off while the fruit is still frozen.

**Procedure:** Rinse and pit fresh cherries, and hold in cold water. To prevent stem end browning, use an ascorbic acid solution. Combine sugar and Clear Jel A in a large saucepan and add water. If desired, add cinnamon, almond extract, and food color-

*Quantities of ingredients needed for:*

| 1 quart | 7 quarts |
| --- | --- |
| 3⅓ cups | 6 quarts |
| 1 cup | 7 cups |
| ¼ cup + 1 tbsp | 1¾ cups |
| 1⅓ cups | 9⅓ cups |
| 1 tbsp + 1 tsp | ½ cup |
| ⅛ tsp | 1 tsp |
| ¼ tsp | 2 tsp |
| 6 drops | ¼ tsp |

ing. Stir mixture and cook over medium-high heat until it thickens and begins to bub-ble. Add lemon juice and boil 1 minute, stirring constantly. Fold in cherries immediately and fill hot jars with mixture without delay, leaving ½ inch headspace. Clean rims, adjust lids, and process in a water bath canner immediately. At altitudes of 0–1,000 feet, process pints and quarts for 30 minutes; add an additional 5 minutes to each 2,000 feet above that.

## RHUBARB AND PEAR PIE FILLING

*5 pounds rhubarb*

*4 cups sugar*

*4 pounds pears (about 8 large)*

*1 cup orange juice*

*1 teaspoon vanilla*

*6 cups water*

*2 tablespoons orange peel, thinly sliced*

*1 teaspoon mace*

*1 teaspoon cinnamon*

Slice rhubarb in ½-inch slices. Add 2 cups of the sugar, the orange juice, and vanilla to the rhubarb in a heavy saucepan. Mix well and set aside while you prepare the pears.

Peel, core, and dice pears. Place cut pears into water containing ascorbic acid, until all pears are diced. Add the rest of the sugar, water, orange peel, mace, and cinnamon to rhubarb mixture. Stir well and bring to a boil. Drain pears and add to rhubarb mixture, cooking for 3 minutes longer. Ladle hot mixture into

© Jay Brenner/FPG International

hot jars. Release air bubbles, clean rims of jars, and seal. Process quart jars in a water bath canner for 25 minutes.

**Makes 5 quarts.**

## PEACH PIE FILLING

*6 pounds peaches (about 12 large)*

*1 cup plus 2 tablespoons bottled lemon juice*

*3¾ cups water*

*5 cups sugar*

*2 teaspoons cinnamon*

*¾ teaspoon cloves*

*1 teaspoon nutmeg*

Peel, pit, and slice peaches. To loosen skin, dip peaches in boiling water for 30 seconds, then submerge in cold water. The peaches will now peel easily. Place peach slices in water containing ascorbic acid, until all peaches are sliced. Combine lemon juice, water, sugar, cinnamon, cloves, and nutmeg in a large saucepan. Stir and cook over medium heat until mixture boils. Drain peaches and add to syrup mixture. Cook for 3 minutes. Ladle into hot jars, release air bubbles, clean jar rims, and seal. Process quart jars in a water bath canner for 30 minutes.

**Makes 5 quarts.**

# TOMATOES

If you grow tomatoes, you know what a high-yielding fruit they are. Tomatoes are easy to preserve but must be processed at the height of flavor. They are very easy to can. All you do is peel them and pack them tightly into jars, adding salt and lemon juice. If they are packed tightly, they have plenty of their own juice for the canning liquid. Tomatoes are processed in a boiling water bath. To insure that they are acid enough and won't support the growth of botulism, add 2 tablespoons of bottled lemon juice to each quart. This not only guarantees acidity, it enhances flavor as well. I usually put up about seventy-five quarts of tomatoes a year and have great, fresh-tasting tomatoes for cooking all year long.

At this time there is some controversy over the processing time used in canning tomatoes. However, the USDA has come out with the standard safety time of processing tomatoes as being 85 minutes. It is possible that the reason for the lengthy time period for these tomatoes is because the USDA was using a very thick-skinned (like Italian tomatoes) unpeeled tomato. This particular type of thick-skinned tomato, with the skin left on, would take 85 minutes to penetrate the heat needed to safely process.

## TOMATO SAUCE

*21 pounds tomatoes (about 63)*

*2 onions*

*1 large green bell pepper*

*2 stalks celery*

*½ cup bottled lemon juice*

*1 tablespoon sugar*

*1 tablespoon salt*

*1½ teaspoons black pepper*

*⅓ cup chopped parsley*

Peel tomatoes and puree in a tomato press or in batches in a food processor. Put into a large pan. Process onions, bell pepper, and celery together and mince finely. Add to tomatoes. Add the rest of the ingredients and mix well. Cook over medium heat, stirring occasionally, until mixture thickens and has reduced by almost half. Ladle hot mixture into hot jars. Clean rims of jars, seal, and process in a water bath canner for 35 minutes.

**Makes 7 pints.**

## FANCY KETCHUP

This ketchup has a wonderful taste; the apple lends a nice sweetness. I used a great tomato press I bought from Williams-Sonoma. Put the tomatoes in the press, crank it, and the seeds and skins come out one spout, while the puree comes out another. The Cuisinart strainer attachment also works well for this purpose.

*25 to 30 tomatoes*

*4 apples*

*1 onion*

*1 cup cider vinegar*

*3 tablespoons brown sugar*

*1 teaspoon oregano*

*½ teaspoon chili powder*

*3 whole bay leaves*

Peel and core tomatoes. Puree in a processor or push the tomatoes through a strainer into a large 6- to 8-quart enamel or stainless steel pan. Peel, core, and slice apples. Put them in a pan with 1 cup of water. Cover and cook for 15 to 20 minutes until soft. Process (or use the tomato press) the apples to a fine puree. Add to the tomatoes. Add all the rest of the ingredients and cook on low heat stirring often, for 2 hours or until proper consistency of ketchup is reached. Ladle hot ketchup into hot jars. Clean rims of jars, seal, and process in a water bath canner for 45 minutes for ½-pint jars or pint jars.

**Makes 4 half-pints.**

## CANNED TOMATOES

These are the tomatoes I use in cooking sauces and soups all year. Because they are canned at the peak of their flavor, they are far superior to the tomatoes available most of the year.

*35 to 40 large tomatoes*

*1 teaspoon sugar per quart (optional)*

*1 teaspoon salt per quart (optional)*

*2 tablespoons bottled lemon juice*

Peel the tomatoes by dropping them into boiling water for 15 seconds. Core each tomato and leave it whole. Put salt, sugar, and lemon juice into hot jars. Pack tomatoes tightly into the jars. You should have plenty of juice to cover the tomatoes by pressing them down. Remove air bubbles and clean the rim of the jars. Seal and process in a water bath canner. Process quart jars for 45 minutes.

**Makes 7 quarts.**

## FRESH BASIL TOMATO SAUCE

This is one of my family's favorites. It is light and low in calories, but full of spicy flavor.

*3 tablespoons olive oil*

*3 onions, minced*

*3 garlic cloves, minced*

*2 tablespoons fresh basil, chopped or 1 tablespoon dried basil*

*3 tablespoons minced parsley*

*25 to 30 tomatoes*

*2 teaspoons salt*

*2 teaspoons pepper*

*1½ teaspoons sugar*

*1 tablespoon plus 1 teaspoon beef bouillon*

Add oil to a 6-quart pot. Mince onions and garlic in food processor and sauté in oil until transparent. Add basil and parsley. Peel tomatoes (dip in boiling water 15 seconds and peel) and process until like juice. Add to pot with onions and herbs. Add the rest of the ingredients and blend well. Cook on low heat for 1½ hours, stirring often. When sauce is done, ladle into hot jars to within ½ inch of the top of the jar. Clean rims and seal. Process for 45 minutes in a water bath canner.

**Makes 6 quarts.**

# CHAPTER THREE

# JAMS, JELLIES, AND PRESERVES

I n the summer, my favorite time of day is the early morning, when the sun is shining and casting shadows across my kitchen. The French doors are open and sweet smells sweep through the house, while on my stove is a copper jelly pan full of softly boiling, beautifully colored fruit.

There is nothing nicer than starting your day with a wonderful homemade jam spread on a fresh baked biscuit. When you start preserving you will be excited with all the fruit combinations you can create. Once you have started feeding your family and friends these homemade preserves it will be hard to go back to store bought.

Many different kinds of preserves can be made with fruit. They change by adding ingredients to the fruit, or as with jelly, extracting the juice from the fruit. You can have lots of fun with your imagination and can easily create your own recipes.

The many types of preserves are defined below.

**FRUIT BUTTERS:** Butters are made from purees of fruit to which sugar and spices have been added. Butters are cooked very slowly on the stove, in the oven, or in a crock pot, stirring often so that it won't burn. The mixture is cooked until it is very thick and spreadable.

**CONSERVES:** Combinations of two or more fruits, cooked to a jamlike consistency, usually adding nuts or raisins to the mixture.

**JAMS:** Crushed or chopped fruit cooked to a smooth, thick consistency that is easily spread.

**JELLIES:** Clear and beautifully colored, jellies are made from the juice of the fruit. It is not as thick as jam and should quiver (shake like partially set jello) when spooned.

**MARMALADES:** Like bright jellies with suspended fruit and slivers of citrus.

**PRESERVES:** Brightly colored, having tender chunks of the fruit or a combination of fruits. If the consistency is correct, the fruit pieces are beautifully suspended in the jar.

Following are recipes for all these different categories of preserves, as well as a few jam and jelly recipes that have little or no sugar. These no-sugar recipes have been devised at the University of California at Davis, by the Division of Agricultural Sciences.

© Peter Johansky/FPG International

# METHODS FOR MAKING JAMS, PRESERVES, MARMALADES, AND CONSERVES

Prepare your jars and lids; wash and sterilize jars and rings.

Prepare your fruit by washing, peeling, pitting, cutting, or leaving whole.

Decide if you will use pectin or the long boil method. If you use pectin, follow my directions for the short boil method or follow the directions that come with the pectin. If you use the long boil method cook until the jell point is reached. (Measure the temperature of water at a full boil and add 8°F more for the jell point. It is 220°F at sea level.)

Remove from heat and wait 5 minutes, skimming off any foam that forms. This 5-minute wait also helps the fruit to cool just enough so it will suspend nicely in the jar and not all rise to the top.

Fill hot, sterilized jars with your preserves. Wipe the rims and seal the jars.

Process the jars in a boiling water bath for 10 minutes. This will insure a good seal.

Check your seal by pressing down on the lid about 2 hours after processing. The lid should not move. If it does, open it, clean the rims, reseal with a new lid, and reprocess. You can also refrigerate and use the jam if it didn't seal. But if you follow directions, you should have a great seal.

You can also seal with paraffin, melting it in a metal cup in a pan of water. Pour about ⅛ inch in the jar and turn the jar so the paraffin touches all sides for a good seal. Wait a couple of minutes and add ⅛ inch more.

Store your preserves in a cool, dry, dark place. If juices and fruit preserves are stored in a sunlit area the color may darken over time.

# JELLIES

Jellies are clear and beautifully colored. They are made from the juice of fruit. You can use commercially bought juices (like grape, apple, or cranberry) to make jellies or you can prepare and cook your fruit then strain out the juice. You can also use frozen fruit. Mash it and add sugar to draw the juice out. Let it set for an hour or so before straining it.

Begin by picking out your fruit. Then peel, pit, and slice it, or chop it in a food processor. You are trying to get as much juice from the fruit as possible. It is best not to dilute your fruit juice, but when you are cooking apples or plums they tend to burn if some water is not added when cooking. Add ¼ cup of water per pound of fruit when cooking. Cook the fruit until it is soft, 10 to 20 minutes. Then pour the mixture into a suspended jelly bag and let the juice drip. You could also use cheesecloth or muslin folded in a strainer or colander and let it drip into a bowl. Never squeeze the jelly bag or cheesecloth to get more juice. You will have cloudy jelly. Plan to have enough time to let it drip. You can always refrigerate or freeze the juice to make jelly at another time.

With berries you can add some sugar and mash them. Letting them sit for an hour or so before straining will help to draw the juice out.

Once you have the juice you can use the short boil method or the long boil method.

The **Short Boil** method is when you use pectin as your jelling agent. Bring the fruit or juice to a boil, add lemon juice if called for, and pectin. Bring the fruit to a rolling boil again. Never add sugar first if you use pectin. You must add the pectin first, before the sugar, or it will not jell. Add the required amount of sugar and bring back to a boil that cannot be stirred down. Boil 1 minute more. Remove from heat and skim any foam that has formed. Pour into hot jars and seal. It is always a good idea to read all directions that come with your pectin.

The **Long Boil** method is when no pectin is used. If you are unsure of the pectin level of the fruit, add some lemon juice. This method allows you to use less sugar than the short boil method. Combine all your ingredients and boil until your jell point is reached (8°F above the point at which water will boil.) The jell point is 220°F at sea level.

| PROBLEMS YOU MAY HAVE WITH JAMS AND JELLIES | |
|---|---|
| Jam or jelly too hard. | Cooked too long and/or too much pectin added. |
| Jam or jelly too soft. | You did not cook long enough or you did not follow the recipe and use the right amount of sugar or pectin. Also never try to make too much at once. Make only one recipe at a time. |
| Cloudy jelly. | You may have squeezed your jelly bag to extract juice. |
| Fruit at top of jars. | Be sure to cool the jam or preserves 5 minutes before putting in the jar. This will let the fruit suspend nicely in the jar. |
| Darkening of jam or jelly. | You may have stored your preserves in too light of a place. They need to be stored in a dark, dry, cool place. |
| Weeping (liquid on the top) jam. | Too much acid in the juice or too thick a layer of paraffin. |
| Sugar crystals. | You may have used too much sugar or you may have cooked the jelly too long. Try to follow the recipes as close as possible. |

## MINT APPLE JELLY

*4 cups apple juice*

*1 cup mint leaves*

*1 package (2 ounces) powdered fruit pectin*

*3½ tablespoons bottled lemon juice*

*3½ cups sugar*

*3 or 4 drops green food coloring*

Bring apple juice to a boil. Chop mint leaves in a food processor and add to apple juice. Boil 1 minute. Remove saucepan from heat and let stand covered for 15 to 20 minutes. Return to heat and bring to a boil again. Boil 30 seconds more. Pour apple juice and mint into a jelly bag and strain the juice. Do not squeeze the jelly bag. Return the apple juice to the pan and stir in the lemon juice and pectin. Bring to a boil again, stirring constantly. Add sugar all at once and stir well to dissolve. Bring back to a rolling boil and boil hard for 1 minute, stirring constantly. Remove from heat and add food coloring. Skim off any foam and ladle into hot jars leaving ¼-inch headspace. Clean rims, seal, and process in a hot water bath for 10 minutes.

**Makes 5 half-pint jars.**

## CURRANT JELLY

*3 pounds red currants*

*2 cups water*

*3⅓ cups sugar*

Wash currants in a strainer. When clean, put currants and 2 cups of water into a heavy saucepan. Boil for 5 minutes. Stir to slightly crush berries. Remove from heat and pour into a jelly bag to strain. You should get about 4 cups of juice. Put juice in a heavy pan and add sugar. Cook, stirring often, and skim foam as it accumulates. When the jell point is reached, remove from heat and skim the foam again. Ladle into hot jars. Clean rims and seal. Process in a water bath canner for 10 minutes.

**Makes 4 half-pint jars.**

## POMEGRANATE JELLY

This jelly is a beautiful clear color. It makes a wonderful Christmas present. Before I owned a food processor this jelly took forever to make; trying to extract the juice from those little seeds drove me crazy. Now that I have the Cuisinart strainer attachment it is really easy. A little hint: If you use the strainer attachment, cover the top with a paper towel so you don't get any juice stains on you.

*10 pomegranates*

*⅓ cup bottled lemon juice*

*1 package (2 ounces) powdered fruit pectin*

*5 cups sugar*

© Maggie Oster

To extract the juice from pomegranates, first score each piece of fruit about five times and pull apart under water. You do this because the juice will stain clothing. After you have removed the seeds, swirl them in a food processor, using the metal blade, until the fruit is juicy. Put into a jelly bag and let it strain overnight. Put the juice (you'll have about 4 cups), lemon juice, and pectin into a pan. Stir and bring to a rolling boil. Stirring constantly, add the sugar all at once and continue to stir while the jelly boils hard for 1 minute. Remove from heat and skim any foam that has formed. Ladle the hot mixture into hot jars, clean rims, and seal. Process in a water bath canner for 10 minutes.

**Makes 5 half-pint jars.**

## WHITE ZINFANDEL JELLY

This is a very pretty jelly. It could be made with any wine, but I love the color of the jelly when you use a deep-colored zinfandel.

*2 cups white zinfandel wine*

*3 cups sugar*

*1 pouch liquid pectin*

Mix the wine and sugar in the top of a double boiler. Heat, stirring until all the sugar melts; this will take 4 to 5 minutes. Remove from heat and stir in liquid pectin. Pour into hot jars to within ⅛ inch of the top. Clean rims and seal with a thin layer of paraffin.

**Makes 4 or 5 half-pint jars.**

## PEPPER JELLY

A very good friend of mine, Samone August, gave me this recipe for a pepper jelly. It is really different and tastes great. She got it from a friend of hers years ago, and it is well worth passing on. Try serving it on top of crackers that have been spread with cream cheese, or on a grilled turkey or chicken sandwich. It's a great treat with champagne or any before-dinner drink.

*2 medium-size green
   bell peppers*

*½ cup fresh hot chili peppers
   or ½ cup canned chilis*

*1½ cups cider vinegar*

*6 cups sugar*

*6 ounces (2 envelopes)
   liquid pectin*

Remove stems and seeds from peppers. Grind peppers in a food processor until liqui-fied. Measure ¾ cup into a heavy saucepan. Grind the hot chilis in the same way and add to the pan with the peppers. Add the vinegar and sugar. Bring to a full rolling boil, stirring constantly. Add pectin and stir until well blended. Bring back to a full rolling boil and boil for 1 minute. Remove from heat and skim foam with a metal spoon. Ladle into hot jars and seal. Process in a water bath canner for 5 minutes.

**Makes 7 half-pint jars.**

# JAMS

Jams are made from crushed fruits. Once you have mastered making jams you will love making preserves, marmalades, and conserves. These all really only add ingredients, but use the same cooking process as jams.

Jams are made by using the short boil or long boil method described in the jelly section (see page 40). However, jams can also be made with the no-cook method.

The no-cook method, which is often called freezer jam, uses pectin. Prepare your fruit. Crush it or spin it in your food processor. Add the sugar and lemon juice and let it stand for 20 to 30 minutes to draw the juices out. Then put your box of pectin in 1 cup of cold water and stir to dissolve. Bring to a boil and boil for 1 minute. Stir into the fruit mixture that has been standing at room temperature; stir thoroughly for another 2 minutes. Pour into sterilized jars and seal. Check for consistency after a few hours. If it has jelled nicely you can put it in the freezer. If it has not yet jelled, leave in the refrigerator for 2 to 3 days before freezing. This will let it set. Jam prepared this way can be stored in the refrigerator 2 to 3 weeks or in the freezer for a year.

The no-cook method uses the most sugar, 2 cups to one cup of fruit. The jam will be very fresh tasting and sugar does enhance the flavor of jams. So, even though this method requires quite a lot of sugar, there are only about 50 to 60 calories a tablespoon. The long boil method uses the least sugar, cooking the mixture until the desired thickness is reached. With the short boil method you must use the required amount of sugar—usually 1½ cups sugar to 1 cup of fruit—along with the pectin or it will not jell properly.

© Priscilla Connell/Photo/Nats

## PEACH-RASPBERRY JAM

3 large peaches

1 cup raspberries

¼ cup bottled lemon juice

6 cups sugar

1 package (2 ounces) powdered fruit pectin

Peel, pit, and slice peaches. Whirl peaches in the food processor until coarsely chopped. Clean raspberries carefully. Put peaches, raspberries, lemon juice, and pectin into a large saucepan. Bring to a boil, stirring constantly. Add sugar all at once and stir until mixture comes to a rolling boil. Boil rapidly for 1 minute. Let jam sit for 5 minutes while you skim off any foam. Ladle into hot jars, clean rims, seal, and process in a water bath canner for 10 minutes.

**Makes 7 half-pints.**

## RHUBARB-PEACH JAM

*1½ pounds rhubarb*

*½ cup water*

*¼ cup bottled lemon juice*

*1 pound peaches (about 2 large)*

*4½ cups sugar*

*1½ tablespoons crystallized ginger, finely diced*

Wash and cut rhubarb into ½-inch pieces. Put rhubarb, water, and lemon juice into a saucepan and bring to a boil. Remove from heat, stir well, and let stand for 1 hour. Peel, pit, and dice peaches. Add peaches, sugar, and ginger to rhubarb mixture. Bring mixture to a boil, stirring constantly. Cook over medium heat until jam is thick and clear, or reaches the jell point on a thermometer. Skim foam as jam cooks. Remove from heat and let sit 5 minutes. Skim off any more foam that rises. Ladle into hot, sterilized jars, clean rims, seal, and process in a water bath canner for 5 minutes.

**Makes 6 half-pints.**

© Bruce Byers/FPG International

## PEACH JAM

*4 pounds peaches (about 8 large)*

*2 tablespoons bottled lemon juice*

*5 cups sugar*

*½ teaspoon nutmeg*

Prepare peaches by peeling, pitting, and cutting into quarters. Chop in a food processor or cut into small pieces. Put peaches, lemon juice, sugar, and nutmeg in a saucepan and cook over medium heat, stirring to dissolve all the sugar. Boil rapidly and stir constantly until the jam is thick or has reached the jell point on a thermometer. Remove from heat and let stand 5 minutes, skimming off any foam. Ladle into hot jars, clean rims, seal, and process in a water bath canner for 10 minutes.

**Makes 5 half-pint jars.**

© Amy Reichman/Envision

© Jeffry W. Myers/FPG International

## APRICOT-PINEAPPLE JAM

Heat this jam with soy sauce and white wine and baste a pork tenderloin with the mixture in the oven or on a grill.

*7 pounds apricots*

*2 cans (8¾ ounces each) crushed pineapple in heavy syrup (do not drain)*

*⅓ cup bottled lemon juice*

*6 cups sugar*

*1 teaspoon cinnamon*

*¾ teaspoon nutmeg*

Wash and pit apricots. Dice in a food processor. Put apricots, undrained pineapple, lemon juice, sugar, cinnamon, and nutmeg into a large saucepan. Over low heat, stir until sugar melts. Bring to a boil and boil softly, stirring often, until jam is thick and clear, or registers 220°F on the thermometer. Skim off foam while cooking. Remove from heat and let sit 5 minutes. Skim off any foam. Ladle into hot, sterilized jars, clean rims, seal, and process in a water bath canner for 5 minutes.

**Makes 5 pints.**

## CHERRY-BLUEBERRY JAM

*3 cups cherries, pitted*

*3 cups blueberries*

*1 tablespoon lemon rind, thinly sliced*

*2 tablespoons bottled lemon juice*

*4½ cups sugar*

*½ teaspoon nutmeg*

Clean and pit cherries. Clean blueberries. Put cherries, blueberries, lemon rind, and lemon juice, sugar, and nutmeg into a large saucepan. Cook the mixture, stirring constantly until sugar melts. Boil mixture softly until it thickens or reaches the jell point. Ladle into hot jars, clean rims, seal, and process for 10 minutes in a water bath canner.

**Makes 5 half-pint jars.**

# COOKING JAMS AND JELLIES WITH LITTLE OR NO SUGAR

In today's diet-conscious society, less sugar is very important. Also, many medical diets call for less sugar. I have included a few recipes devised by the University of California at Davis, using much less sugar than most jams and jellies. The University of Davis suggests removing excess liquid from the fruit before making the jam. By doing this and cooking the pulp you will have a much thicker jam, naturally.

To remove the excess liquid:

1. Wash and prepare your fruit. Remove pits, stems, or seeds, and peel if necessary.
2. Cut or chop your fruit in a processor or mash with a fork.
3. Cook the fruit in a pan for a few minutes to release the juices.
4. Pour the fruit into a jelly bag and let the juice drain for 15 minutes.
5. Save the juice for jelly or fruit juice.
6. Measure the solid fruit and use for making jams with little or no sugar.

When using less sugar or no sugar, you can freeze the jam or process it. Processed jam with little or no sugar may change color slightly over time; if it is frozen, however, it will retain its color better. If gelatin is used as a thickening agent in the jam or jelly it must not be processed. All jams and jellies should be refrigerated and used within a month.

If you wish to use artificial sweeteners they need to be added after cooking the jam or jelly or it will have a bitter taste. Some people prefer to wait until the jam is opened and then stir in the artificial sweetener.

## LOW-SUGAR PEACH-PINEAPPLE JAM

This first recipe is from the University of California at Davis, and they have given the calorie count for the different levels of sugar used. You can determine what calorie intake is best for you and what tastes best. You can then figure out the other recipes accordingly.

| | Little sugar 1 level tbsp. 22 calories (per level tbsp.) | Less sugar 1 level tbsp. 15 calories (per level tbsp.) | No sugar 1 level tbsp. 8 calories (per level tbsp.) |
|---|---|---|---|
| Drained peach pulp | 4 cups | 4 cups | 4 cups |
| Drained unsweetened crushed pineapple | 2 cups | 2 cups | 2 cups |
| Bottled lemon juice | ¼ cup | ¼ cup | ¼ cup |
| Sugar | 2 cups | 1 cup | 0* |

Place drained cooked peaches, drained crushed pineapple, lemon juice, and sugar in a 4-quart saucepan. Mix well to dissolve sugar. Bring to a boil, stirring constantly. Boil to the desired thickness, 10 to 15 minutes, stirring occasionally to prevent scorching.

**To freeze jam:** Remove from heat. Add calorie-free sweetener if desired. Continue to stir about 2 minutes. Pour into freezer containers, leaving ½-inch headspace. Seal. Chill in refrigerator, then store in freezer. Keep in refrigerator after opening.

Whereas low-sugar jams will retain color better if stored in a freezer, it is safe to can them by the boiling water bath method.

To can jam: Pour boiling hot jam into clean, hot pint or half-pint canning jars to ¼-inch from top of jar. Seal and process in boiling water bath, 15 minutes for half-pint jars, 20 minutes for pint jars. Cool and store in cool, dry, dark place. After opening, store in refrigerator.

*You may wish to add a powdered calorie-free sweetener. Equivalents will be stated on the box.

Makes 4 or 5 half-pint jars, depending on how much sugar is used.

## LOW-SUGAR PLUM-PEACH JAM WITH PECTIN

*3 cups firm, ripe Santa Rosa plums (about 1½ pounds), chopped*

*2 cups firm, ripe peaches, peeled and sliced (about 4 large)*

*1 package (1¾ or 2 ounce) powdered fruit pectin*

*1 cup sugar (for a more tart jam use only ½ cup sugar)*

Grind fruit with medium blade of food processor. If any juice is released drain before making jam. Stir ground fruit, pectin, and sugar in saucepan to dissolve sugar. Bring to a boil and boil 10 to 15 minutes until thickened. Stir constantly.

To freeze: Remove from heat. Pour into clean, hot freezer jars, leaving ½-inch headspace. Cover, chill, and freeze. Thaw before using. Store in refrigerator after opening.

To can: Pour boiling hot jam into clean, hot canning jars to ¼ inch from top of jar. Seal and process in a boiling water bath. Process half-pint jars for 15 minutes. Process pint jars for 20 minutes. Cool and store in a cool, dark, dry place. After opening, store in the refrigerator.

1 tablespoon = 15 calories.

**Makes 4 half-pint jars.**

## SPICED NO-SUGAR APPLE JELLY

*2 envelopes unflavored gelatin*

*4 cups apple juice*

*2 whole sticks cinnamon*

*4 whole cloves*

*2 tablespoons bottled lemon juice*

*2 drops yellow food coloring*

*From 1 teaspoon to 1 tablespoon liquid calorie-free sweetener (depending on sweetness desired)*

Soften gelatin in apple juice in medium-sized saucepan. Add cinnamon sticks, cloves, and lemon juice. Bring slowly to rolling boil, stirring to dissolve gelatin. Boil 2 minutes. Remove from heat. Remove spices. Stir in calorie-free sweetener and food coloring. Pour into hot jelly jars. Seal. Chill and store in refrigerator. This jelly will keep well in refrigerator from 4 to 6 weeks. Do not freeze.

1 tablespoon = 9 calories

**Makes 3 half-pint jars.**

## NO-SUGAR PEACH JAM WITH PECTIN

*4 cups peeled, sliced, firm, ripe peaches (about 3 large)*

*1 package (1¾ or 2 ounces) powdered fruit pectin*

*1 tablespoon bottled lemon juice*

*½ teaspoon liquid calorie-free sweetener (more or less according to taste)*

*½ teaspoon ascorbic acid*

Grind peaches in a food grinder with medium or coarse blade or crush peaches with fork. If peaches are juicy, drain to remove some liquid before making jam. In a saucepan, stir fruit pectin, lemon juice, and ascorbic acid into ground peaches. Bring to a boil and boil 1 minute, stirring constantly. Remove from heat, add calorie-free sweetener, and stir thoroughly.

To freeze jam: Continue to stir for 2 minutes. Pour into clean, hot freezer jars leaving ½-inch headspace. Seal, chill, and freeze. Thaw before serving. Store in refrigerator after opening.

To can jam: Pour hot jam into clean, hot, canning jars to ¼ inch from the top. Seal and process in boiling water bath. Process pint jars for 20 minutes, half-pint jars for 15 minutes. Cool and store in a cool, dark, dry place. After opening, store in the refrigerator.

1 tablespoon = 8 calories

**Makes 2 half-pint jars.**

## NO-SUGAR GRAPE JELLY

*1 envelope unflavored gelatin*

*2 cups unsweetened grape juice (any other unsweetened juice can be used)*

*1 tablespoon bottled lemon juice*

*1¾ teaspoons liquid calorie-free sweetener (use more or less according to taste)*

Add gelatin to grape juice and lemon juice in a saucepan. Place over low heat. Stir constantly until gelatin dissolves. Bring to a boil and boil 1½ to 2 minutes. Remove from heat. Add calorie-free sweetener. Stir well to mix. Pour into clean hot jars. Seal. Cool and store in refrigerator. This jelly will keep well in a refrigerator 4 to 6 weeks. Do not freeze.

1 tablespoon = 10 calories

**Makes 2 half-pint jars.**

# PRESERVES

Preserves, marmalades, and conserves are basically made like jams; however, you add other ingredients. Preserves are closest to jams except that they use large pieces or even whole pieces of fruit instead of mashed or crushed fruit like jam. Marmalades are like a nice jelly but have slivers of citrus peel in them. Conserves, like jam, can use a combination of more than one fruit. Conserves also contain nuts, raisins, or dried fruit.

Preserves, marmalades, or conserves can be cooked the short boil or long boil method just like jam. The equipment needed and procedures for cooking are the same as for jams.

© Burke/Triolo

# PROPER EQUIPMENT FOR FRUIT PRESERVES

A **deep, flat-bottomed pan** large enough so the mixture can boil without boiling over the pan. Enamel, stainless steel, or an unlined copper jelly pan are best to use.

A **jelly thermometer** is helpful in checking for the jelling point, which is 8°F higher than the point of boiling water.

A **food processor** or **food mill** helps so much when you chop or grind the fruit. Also, the Cuisinart strainer attachment makes butters and jellies a snap.

A **jelly bag** for extracting the juice from fruits. You can also use cheesecloth or muslin in a suspended strainer.

A **timer** is very important especially if you are using pectin as a thickener.

**Funnels** will really help to keep your jars clean and make less mess.

**Measuring spoons** and **cups** are a necessity for proper measuring of ingredients.

A **scale** is helpful in measuring the amount of fruit, and it will help you to determine the correct amount of sugar needed.

**Jars** and **lids.**

**Metal cup** or **small pan** if you use paraffin.

A **boiling water canner** or **large kettle** for processing.

A **jar lifter.**

© Bruce Byers/FPG International

## PEACH PRESERVES

This preserve gives you a wonderful summer taste all year.

*3½ pounds peaches (about 7)*

*¼ cup bottled lemon juice*

*5 cups sugar*

*¾ teaspoon almond extract*

Peel, pit, and coarsely dice peaches. Cut peaches into water that has ascorbic acid added until all peaches are cut. Rinse peaches and put them into a heavy saucepan. Add lemon juice and sugar. Heat to boiling, stirring constantly, until sugar is dissolved. Reduce heat so you have a slow boil and cook until fruit is translucent and thick, stirring occasionally. Stir in almond extract. Remove from heat and skim off any foam that rises. Ladle into hot jars, clean rims, seal, and process for 10 minutes in a water bath canner.

**Makes 6 to 7 pints.**

## STRAWBERRY-PEACH PRESERVES

*4 baskets strawberries (2 quarts)*

*2 pounds peaches (4 large)*

*3 tablespoons bottled lemon juice*

*5½ cups sugar*

Clean strawberries. Cut large ones into quarters and small ones in half. Peel and pit peaches and cut into small pieces. Put fruit, lemon juice, and sugar into a large heavy saucepan. Stir over medium heat until all sugar is dissolved. Bring to a boil and cook at a slow boil, stirring often until the preserves are thick and have a transparent look. Ladle into hot jars, clean rims, and seal. Process in a water bath canner for 10 minutes.

**Makes 7 half-pints.**

## PEACH-PINEAPPLE PRESERVES

I remember my Mom and Dad making this recipe every year. We all loved it and it was great on our Thanksgiving ham. Try it on a pork loin roast done on the barbecue. You'll love it.

*5 pounds peaches (about 10 large)*

*2 cans (8¾ ounces each) crushed pineapple (do not drain)*

*⅓ cup bottled lemon juice*

*5 cups sugar*

*1 teaspoon cinnamon*

*½ teaspoon nutmeg*

*¼ teaspoon mace*

Peel, pit, and large dice peaches. Put cut peaches into water containing ascorbic acid so that peaches don't change color, until all peaches are cut. Rinse peaches and put into a heavy saucepan. Add undrained pineapple, lemon juice, sugar, cinnamon, nutmeg, and mace. Bring to a boil, dissolving the sugar. Turn heat down and cook at a slow boil until preserves are thick and translucent. Remove from heat, remove any foam with a metal spoon, ladle into hot jars, clean rims, and seal. Process in water bath canner for 10 minutes.

**Makes 5 to 6 pints.**

© John Mutrux

## STRAWBERRY PRESERVES

I just love strawberry preserves because they are so versatile. They are delicious when used in a trifle, baked in the middle of a breakfast pastry, or dabbed in the center of your favorite sugar cookie.

*8 cups strawberries*

*2 tablespoons bottled lemon juice*

*5 cups sugar*

Clean and stem strawberries. Cut strawberries in half. Put berries, lemon juice, and sugar into a large heavy saucepan. Stir, bringing the mixture to a boil. Cook the mixture on medium heat until the preserves thicken and become transparent. Remove pan from heat. Skim off foam that has formed, and ladle into hot jars. Seal and process in a water bath canner for 10 minutes.

**Makes 7 half-pint jars.**

## CHERRY PRESERVES

Put a teaspoon of these preserves into your Christmas thumbprint cookies.

*6 cups sweet cherries (3 pounds)*

*4 cups sugar*

*3 tablespoons bottled lemon juice*

*½ teaspoon almond extract*

Wash and pit cherries, or cut in half and remove pits. Put cherries, sugar, and lemon juice in a heavy saucepan. Mix well and warm on stove 5 minutes, stirring constantly. Remove from heat and let stand 1 hour. This is to draw the juice out. Return to heat, add almond extract, and cook, stirring occasionally until thick and glossy. Continue cooking until the jell point is reached (220°F at sea level). Skim foam as necessary. Remove from heat, ladle into hot jars, clean rims, seal, and process for 10 minutes in a water bath canner.

**Makes 5 to 6 half-pints.**

## APPLE-PEAR PRESERVES

*2½ pounds pears (about 5 large)*

*2½ pounds apples (about 5 large)*

*¼ cup bottled lemon juice*

*6 cups sugar*

*1 teaspoon cinnamon*

*¼ teaspoon ground allspice*

*2 teaspoons ground ginger*

Peel, core, and coarsely chop pears. Put cut pears into water containing ascorbic acid, until all fruit is prepared. Peel, core, and coarsely chop apples. Add to pears in water until all fruit is diced. Rinse fruit and put in a heavy saucepan. Add lemon juice, sugar, cinnamon, allspice, and ginger to fruit. Stir well, heating to dissolve sugar. Bring mixture to a boil, reduce heat, and cook at a slow boil. Remove foam as it forms. Cook, stirring and skimming until preserves have thickened and become translucent. Mash fruit slightly with a potato masher. Remove from heat and let sit 5 minutes. While it rests skim off any foam that has formed. Ladle into hot jars, clean rims, seal, and process 10 minutes in a water bath canner.

**Makes 4 half-pints.**

# MARMALADES

Marmalades are so pretty. They look like a beautiful jelly with floating slices of citrus peel or small fruits. To make the peels and fruits float throughout the marmalade (and not rise to the top), make sure to let the marmalade cool slightly before ladling into jars.

### LIME MARMALADE

*4 limes*

*1 pound pears (about 2 large)*

*4 cups water*

*¼ cup bottled lemon juice*

*6 cups sugar*

*¼ teaspoon salt*

Peel the limes—I used a lemon zester for this recipe. If you don't have a lemon zester, then just peel the limes and cut the peel into thin slices. Put the peel into a saucepan with water to cover and boil for 15 minutes. Drain and repeat. Remove the white flesh from the limes and cut the pulp into thin slices. Remove the seeds and membranes. Put the peel and pulp into a heavy pan. Now peel, core, and tiny dice the pears. Add the pears to the lime and add water, lemon juice, sugar, and salt. Stir over high heat until sugar is dissolved. Turn the heat down and cook over low heat, stirring occasionally, until the marmalade reaches the jell point. Remove from heat and let the marmalade sit for 5 minutes. If any foam has formed skim it off with a metal spoon. Stir and ladle into hot jars, wipe rims, seal, and process in a water bath canner for 10 minutes.

**Makes 5 to 6 half-pints.**

Courtesy Ball Jar Corporation

### PINK GRAPEFRUIT MARMALADE

*3 pink grapefruit*

*4 cups unsweetened grapefruit juice*

*¼ cup bottled lemon juice*

*1 package (2 ounces) powdered fruit pectin*

*6½ cups sugar*

*1 teaspoon vanilla*

Peel grapefruit and put peel in a saucepan with 1 cup of water. Boil 5 minutes, drain, and put in a pan with 1 more cup of water; boil 5 more minutes. Drain and repeat one more time. Slice peel into thin slivers. Put peel into a pan with a cup of water again and boil; this time cover and leave overnight. The next day, put the drained peel in a heavy saucepan, add the unsweetened grapefruit juice, lemon juice, and pectin. Stir and bring to a rolling boil. Make sure the pectin has dissolved. With the juice at a rolling boil, add the sugar all at once. Bring the mixture back to a boil that can not be stirred down. Boil hard for 4 minutes. Remove foam as it cooks. After 4 minutes remove from heat and let the mixture sit 5 minutes or so to cool slightly. Stir in the vanilla and ladle into hot jars. Wipe rims, seal, and process in a water bath canner for 10 minutes.

**Makes 7 half-pint jars.**

### ORANGE-PINEAPPLE MARMALADE

I like to add one jar of this to my fruitcake recipe. It gives your fruitcake a beautiful shine when it's done.

*peel of 3 oranges*

*pulp of 6 oranges*

*2 cans (20 ounces each) crushed pineapple (do not drain)*

*¼ cup bottled lemon juice*

*5 cups sugar*

*½ teaspoon ground ginger*

Peel three oranges. Put peel in a saucepan with 1 cup of water and boil 40 minutes. Remove from heat and drain. Slice into slivers. Peel other oranges, remove white flesh, and slice orange pulp, removing seed and membrane. Put peel, pulp, undrained pineapple, lemon juice, sugar, and ginger into a pan. Bring to a boil over high heat, stirring constantly to dissolve sugar. Continue cooking over medium heat, stirring occasionally until the marmalade thickens and turns a beautiful amber color. Remove from heat and let sit to cool 5 to 7 minutes. Remove any foam that has formed. Ladle into hot jars, wipe rims, seal, and process in a water bath canner for 10 minutes.

**Makes 6 half-pints.**

# CONSERVES

Conserves are much like jams and preserves. They usually combine one or more fruits and contain nuts and raisins or other diced fruits.

### FIG CONSERVE

*3 pounds figs or 4½ cups puree*

*½ cup bottled lemon juice*

*4 cups sugar*

*½ cup slivered almonds*

*1 teaspoon vanilla*

Peel figs and mash. Put figs, lemon juice, sugar, almonds, and vanilla into a heavy saucepan. Stirring, bring mixture to a slow boil. Boil slowly and stir often until the mixture thickens and becomes transparent. Remove from heat and skim off any foam that has formed. Leave off heat for 5 minutes and then ladle into hot jars. Wipe rims, seal, and process in a water bath canner for 10 minutes.

**Makes 6 to 7 half-pints.**

## PLUM-APPLE CONSERVE

*3½ pounds plums (about 20 medium-size)*

*1½ cups water*

*4 tablespoons bottled lemon juice*

*2 pounds apples (about 6 medium-size)*

*¾ cup slivered almonds*

*½ cup golden raisins*

*1 package (2 ounces) powdered fruit pectin*

*8 cups sugar*

Wash and pit plums. Put in a saucepan with ½ cup water and 2 tablespoons lemon juice. Cook for 10 minutes. Puree in a food mill or a food processor. Peel, core, and slice apples and cook them in a pan with 1 cup water and 2 tablespoons of lemon juice. Cook for about 20 minutes. Puree apples. Combine purees, almonds, and raisins, and bring to a boil. Add pectin and stir to blend, bring back to a boil and add sugar all at once. Stirring constantly, bring mixture back to a rolling boil and boil for 1 minute. Remove from heat, skimming any foam that has formed. Ladle into hot jars, wipe rims, and seal. Process for 10 minutes in a water bath canner.

**Makes 6 half-pint jars.**

## CHERRY-BLUEBERRY CONSERVE

*3½ cups cherries*

*3½ cups blueberries*

*Peel from 1 orange*

*4½ cups sugar*

*1 cup walnuts, chopped*

Pit cherries and cut in half. Wash blueberries and, if large, whirl in the food processor once or twice. Put the fruit into a heavy saucepan, then add orange peel and sugar. Heat mixture until sugar dissolves. Add walnut bits and bring mixture to a slow boil. Cook for 20 to 30 minutes or until the mixture begins to thicken and reaches the jell point (which is 220°F at sea level). Remove from heat, skim off any foam that has formed. Ladle into hot jars, wipe rims, and seal. Process for 10 minutes in a water bath canner.

**Makes 7 to 8 half-pint jars.**

### LEMON-CRANBERRY CONSERVE

This is a great tasting conserve, especially if you like lemon. The blend of flavors and textures is nice. I love black walnuts so I used them because of their distinct flavor, but if you can't find them, any regular walnut will do. Almonds are also nice.

*1 pound cranberries*

*1 cup water*

*zest of 2 lemons*

*pulp of 2 lemons*

*6 cups sugar*

*¾ cup lemonade concentrate*

*1 cup dried apples*

*1 cup black walnuts*

Wash cranberries and put into a heavy saucepan with 1 cup water, lemon zest, lemon pulp, sugar, and lemonade concentrate. Bring to a boil, stirring constantly. Remove from stove and let mixture sit 30 minutes. Chop dried apples and add to cranberry mixture after it has sat for 30 minutes. Return mixture to a boil and add chopped walnuts. Boil the mixture slowly, stirring occasionally until it becomes thick and shiny. Remove conserve and let sit 5 minutes, skimming foam if necessary. Ladle into hot jars, wipe rims, seal jars, and process in a water bath canner for 10 minutes.

**Makes 7 to 8 half-pint jars.**

# BUTTERS

Butters are fruit purees that can be made with one or more fruits. They are cooked slowly until they are of a good spreading consistency. You can add any spices you want to and you can use white or brown sugar. Brown sugar will darken the butter, but it gives it a nice flavor.

You can cook fruit butter on top of the stove, in a slow oven, or in a crockpot. I prefer cooking mine in the oven only because I can busy myself around the house and keep an eye on it while it cooks. Meanwhile, my house smells wonderful. Make sure you stir often so you don't end up burning it on the bottom or edges.

## APRICOT BUTTER

4 pounds apricots or 8 cups puree

½ cup water

3 tablespoons bottled lemon juice

4 cups sugar

1 teaspoon cinnamon

¼ teaspoon ground allspice

¼ teaspoon nutmeg

¼ teaspoon salt

Clean and pit apricots. Put apricots, water, and lemon juice in a saucepan and cook for 15 to 20 minutes until apricots are soft. Remove the apricots and puree in a food mill, food processor, or with the strainer attachment to the Cuisinart. Put puree in a heavy pan and add sugar, cinnamon, allspice, nutmeg, and salt. Bring to a boil, stirring, until all sugar is dissolved. When sugar is dissolved put the mixture into a roasting pan. Put in a 300°F oven and cook until thick and clear, about 1½ to 2½ hours. Stir often or it will burn on the bottom and sides. The butter is done when a sample is put on a plate and there is no rim of liquid around it. When done, ladle into hot jars, wipe rims, and seal. Process in a water bath canner for 10 minutes.

**Makes 5 to 6 half-pint jars.**

## LOQUAT BUTTER

I love the tart taste of this butter spread on a sweet bread.

4 pounds loquats

¾ cup bottled lemon juice

1 cup water

1 lemon, cut in half

2 whole sticks cinnamon

3 cups sugar

Wash loquats, remove stem and flower ends, remove seeds, and cut in half. Put cut fruit into a heavy saucepan with the lemon juice and water. Add halved lemon and the whole cinnamon sticks. Bring to a boil, stirring occasionally, and cook for 30 minutes. Remove the lemon and cinnamon sticks. Continue cooking until mushy. Use a food mill or food processor, and puree. Put the puree into a heavy pan and add sugar. Stir occasionally for 15 to 20 minutes until the puree is thick and spreadable. Put into hot jars, clean rims, and seal. If you like a tart butter add 1 cup less sugar. Process in a water bath canner for 10 minutes.

**Makes 4 half-pint jars.**

## CARRIE'S FAVORITE APPLE BUTTER

6 pounds apples

1 cup water

¼ cup bottled lemon juice

3 cups granulated sugar

3 cups light brown sugar

½ cup apple shnapps liquor

1 teaspoon cinnamon

½ teaspoon nutmeg

¼ teaspoon ground allspice

¼ teaspoon ground cloves

¼ teaspoon salt

1 teaspoon vanilla

Peel, core, and slice apples into water containing ascorbic acid, until all fruit is prepared. Drain the fruit and cook the apples with 1 cup water, in a heavy, covered saucepan, for 10 to 15 minutes. When apples are soft, process until smooth or grind in a food mill. Put puree in a heavy pan and add lemon juice, granulated and brown sugars, liquor, the spices, salt, and vanilla. Stir well to blend and heat to a boil, stirring to dissolve the sugars. Turn heat to low and continue to cook until very thick and spreadable. Stir occasionally so the butter doesn't burn on the bottom or sides. To test if butter is done, put a spoonful on a plate and make sure there is no liquid around the edges. When done, ladle into hot jars, clean rims, seal, and process in a water bath canner for 10 minutes.

**Makes 4 pints and 1 half-pint.**

## PLUM-APPLE BUTTER

2½ pounds plums (about 15)

½ cup bottled lemon juice

1 cup water

2½ pounds apples (about 5)

5½ cups sugar

1 teaspoon cinnamon

¼ teaspoon ground cloves

¼ teaspoon nutmeg

½ teaspoon salt

Wash, then depending on size, cut plums in halves or quarters. Remove pits. Cook with ¼ cup of the lemon juice and ½ cup of the water for 20 to 30 minutes. Stir often so they do not burn. When soft, puree in a food mill or with the strainer attachment to the Cuisinart. Peel, core, and slice apples. Cook apples, ¼ cup lemon juice, and ½ cup water in a covered pan. Cook for 10 minutes or until apples are soft. Puree apples in a food mill or food processor. Combine purees, sugar, spices, and salt. Cook, stirring constantly until mixture boils and sugar dissolves. Put mixture in a heavy roasting pan and put into a 300°F oven. Stir occasionally so it does not burn on the bottom or sides. Continue cooking until thick. Test by putting some on a saucer—if no liquid is on the edges it is done. Ladle into hot jars, clean rims, and seal. Process in a water bath canner for 10 minutes.

**Makes 6 to 7 half-pint jars.**

# CANNING VEGETABLES

## INTRODUCTION TO VEGETABLES

Summer is here and our gardens are overflowing with vegetables. I love a vegetable garden and can hardly wait for spring to start mine. But when my family says they have seen enough peas or beans for awhile, I know it is time to start canning this bounty so we can enjoy them later in the year when fresh vegetables are only a memory.

Vegetables are best canned as fresh as possible, before they start losing their flavor and nutritional value. You want your vegetables crisp not limp, or you won't have a good finished product.

All vegetables except tomatoes require high temperatures because of their low-acid content. To reach this high of a temperature you must use steam under pressure. That is why we use a pressure canner. The only time vegetables are processed in a boiling water canner is if vinegar is used in the recipe. You will find several vegetables in my pickling chapter.

If you carefully follow directions and the timing schedules (making altitude adjustments where necessary), your food should be safe. But as you open each jar make sure you hear the pop of a good seal and that the food looks and smells good. Some food poisoning toxins are not easily detected. So if you are using vegetables someone else has canned and you are not sure just how well they followed directions, it would be a good idea to boil the vegetables for 15 to 20 minutes before serving. Never hesitate to discard vegetables about which you have the slightest doubt—food poisoning can be fatal.

# THE PRESSURE CANNER

A pressure canner is a metal kettle and cover that are clamped together to make them steam tight. It will have a weight gauge from 5 pounds to 15 pounds, a vent or petcock, and a safety gauge. To safely work your pressure canner always follow the directions given with your canner. Also, always check to see that the safety valve opening and petcock are clean. Hold up the lid and look through the safety valve and make sure you see through it. If you can't, run a string through the hole and clean it. You may have to do this several times during the canning season.

Make sure you have a rack in the bottom of the canner so the steam can circulate. If you are processing half-pints or pints you can use a normal-size pressure cooker and not buy the large one.

© Robert Edwards

## PROCESSING TIMES AT 15 POUNDS PER SQUARE INCH AT VARIOUS ALTITUDES FOR PINT AND QUART MASON JARS PROCESSED IN 12-, 16-, OR 21-QUART PRESSURE CANNERS (HOT OR COLD PACK PROCEDURE).

| PRODUCT* | PROCESSING TIME (MINUTES) AT ALTITUDES— | | |
| --- | --- | --- | --- |
| | Less than 3,000 feet | 3,000 to 7,000 feet | Over 7,000 feet |
| Asparagus | 15 | 25 | 35 |
| Beans, lima | 30 | 60 | 85 |
| Beans, snap or wax | 15 | 30 | 45 |
| Beets, whole or sliced | 15 | 30 | 45 |
| Carrots | 15 | 30 | 45 |
| Corn, whole kernel | 50 | 90 | 135 |
| Mushrooms | 20 | 40 | 60 |
| Okra | 15 | 30 | 45 |
| Parsnips | 15 | 30 | 45 |
| Peas, green | 30 | 60 | 85 |
| Peas, black-eye | 30 | 60 | 85 |
| Potatoes, new-whole | 20 | 40 | 60 |
| Rutabagas, sliced or diced | 30 | 60 | 85 |
| Squash, cubed | 20 | 40 | 60 |
| Sweet potatoes | 50 | 90 | 135 |
| Turnips, cubed | 15 | 30 | 45 |

*Processing times at 15 pounds per square inch have not been established for all vegetables.
University of California, Davis; Department of Food Technology

# STEP-BY-STEP PROCEDURES FOR CANNING VEGETABLES

**CHECK AND CLEAN ALL EQUIPMENT:** Check jars and lids for nicks and cracks and wash them in hot, soapy water. Sterilize jars by boiling and have them hot before filling them with food. Always check to see that you have new flat metal lids before you start canning.

**PREPARE YOUR FOOD:** Use very fresh, crisp vegetables. Wash vegetables carefully, using a vegetable brush when needed. Cut food according to the directions given in the recipe. Precook or blanch your vegetables. You may want to raw-pack asparagus and whole beans because they will retain their shape and color better.

**FILLING THE JARS:** If you have precooked the vegetables you can use the cooking liquid for the canning liquid. If you have not precooked the vegetables use boiling water for the canning liquid. You can add salt to jars or, if you are on a salt-free diet, omit it. The salt will enhance the taste of your vegetables. Add salt to your jar, fill with boiling liquid (look at the vegetable chart for each vegetable to see how much headspace to leave). Release any air bubbles and add more liquid if needed. Wipe the rims clean and seal.

**PROCESSING PROCEDURES:** Look at the recipe or table to see timing and at what weight to process vegetables. Make sure you check the time for the size of jar you are using. Always read the directions given with your pressure canner.

Add 2 to 3 inches of boiling water in the canner. Make sure the rack is in place and add the jars to the canner. Clamp on the lid following manufacturer's directions and vent the canner by leaving the petcock open or the vent pipe uncovered and let a stream of steam escape for at least 10 minutes. After venting, close the petcock or put on a weighted gauge and bring the canner to the right pressure. Start timing when the pressure is correct and process for the length of time in each recipe. Regulate the heat to keep it at the right pressure. Don't let the pressure fall.

After processing remove the canner from the heat (do not tilt) and wait until the pressure drops to zero. Open the petcock and remove the weighted gauge. Be very careful not to burn yourself with steam. Open the canner, lifting the side facing away from you and let the steam out slowly and then, carefully, totally remove the lid.

Leave the jars in the kettle until they cool a little (15 to 20 minutes). Then remove them with a jar lifter to a draft-free place to cool completely. When cool test for seal and store in a cool, dry, dark place.

| PROBLEMS YOU MAY HAVE WITH VEGETABLES | |
|---|---|
| Loss of liquid. | Jars are too full or you did not leave enough headspace. Also with a pressure canner, the pressure rate can cause this problem. This does not mean that the food is necessarily spoiled. |
| Foods change color. | The vegetable was overcooked or the liquid in the jar did not cover the food. |
| Mold on food. | The jar was not sealed or the seal was not tight enough and food has spoiled. **Throw out the food.** |
| Cloudy vegetables. | Hard water (if your area has hard water you can use bottled water) or you used vegetables which were too old. The vegetables may be spoiled; check for a bad smell and throw out. |
| Sediment on bottom of jar. | Hard water used or table salt used. |
| Discolored lid on jar. | Caused by certain compounds found in foods. The food is still good. The discoloration is harmless. |

# HOW TO PREPARE VEGETABLES FOR CANNING

| VEGETABLES | HOW TO PREPARE | PROCESSING TIME (10 pounds pressure) | |
| --- | --- | --- | --- |
| | | PINT | QUART |
| | | minutes | |
| **ARTICHOKES** | Use small artichokes. Trim to 1¼ to 2 inches in length. Pre-cook 5 minutes in water to which ¾ cup of vinegar per gallon has been added. Drain. Pack hot into hot jars. Do not overfill. Cover with a boiling brine prepared by adding ¾ cup vinegar or lemon juice and 3 tablespoons salt to 1 gallon water. Fill to within ¾ inch of tops of pint or quart jars. Seal. | 25 | 25 |
| **ASPARAGUS** | Sort, wash, and cut in lengths ¾ inch shorter than the jar or cut into 1- or 2- inch pieces. Cut off scales (bracts). Pre-cook in boiling water for 1 to 3 minutes to wilt. Then plunge quickly into cold water. | | |
| | **To pack whole:** Gather a bundle of stalks with the ends down and fill jar. Do not pack tightly. Add ½ teaspoon salt for pints, 1 teaspoon salt for quarts. Cover with boiling water to ¾ inch of top of jar. Seal. | 28 | 32 |
| | **To pack cuts:** Fill to ¾ inch from top of jar with cuts. Add ½ teaspoon salt for pints, 1 teaspoon salt for quarts. Cover with boiling water to within ¾ inch of top of jar. Seal. | 28 | 32 |
| **BEANS, FRESH LIMA** | **To pack hot:** Proceed as directed for peas. Process as directed for lima beans. **To pack raw:** Use ½ teaspoon salt for pint jars; 1 teaspoon salt for quart jars. **Small beans:** Pack pint jars loosely to within 1 inch of tops; quarts to 1¼ inches. **Large beans:** Pack pint jars loosely to within ¾ inch of tops; quarts to 1¾ inches. Add salt. Fill to ¾ inch of top with boiling water. Seal. | 40 | 50 |
| **BEANS, STRING** | Sort and snip off string if necessary. Use ½ teaspoon salt for pint jars; 1 teaspoon salt for quart jars. For mature beans, see *Peas, mature.* | | |
| | **To pack hot:** Cut in 1-to 1½-inch lengths. Pre-cook in boiling water until pliable, about 2 to 5 minutes. Pack hot into hot jars. Add salt. Cover to within ¾ inch of jar tops with the boiling liquid in which the beans were pre-cooked. Add boiling water if needed. Seal. | 20 | 25 |
| | If beans are left whole, pack beans standing on ends. Seal. | 25 | 30 |
| | **To pack raw:** Cut into 1-inch pieces. Pack tightly to within ¾ inch of jar tops. Add salt. Cover with boiling water to within ¾ inch of top. Seal. | 20 | 25 |
| **BEETS** | **To pack hot:** Leave on roots and 1 to 1½ inch of stems. Boil until skins slip off (about 15 minutes). Dip in cold water. Peel, trim, and slice. Discard woody beets. Reheat in small amount of water. Pack hot into hot jars. Add ½ teaspoon salt to pint jars; 1 teaspoon salt to quart jars. Cover to within ½ inch of jar tops with the boiling liquid in which the beets were reheated. Add boiling water if needed. Seal. *Raw packing of beets is not recommended.* | 35 | 40 |

| VEGETABLES | HOW TO PREPARE | PROCESSING TIME (10 pounds pressure) | |
|---|---|---|---|
| | | PINT | QUART |
| | | minutes | |
| **CARROTS** | **To pack raw:** Wash and scrape or peel. Pack cold, sliced, or asparagus style to within 1 inch of tops of pint or quart jars. Add ½ teaspoon salt to pint jars; 1 teaspoon salt to quart jars. Add boiling water to within ¾ inch of top. Seal. | 30 | 30 |
| **CELERY** | Prepare and slice. Use ½ teaspoon salt for pint jars; 1 teaspoon for quart jars. **To pack hot:** Pre-cook 1 to 3 minutes depending on size and tenderness. Pack hot into hot jars. Add salt. Cover to within ¾ inch of jar tops with boiling liquid in which the celery was pre-cooked. Add boiling water if needed. Seal. | 35 | 35 |
| | **To pack raw:** Slice or cut asparagus style. Pack loosely to within ¾ inch of jar tops. Add salt. Cover with boiling water to within ¾ inch of tops. Seal. | 30 | 30 |
| **CORN, WHOLE KERNEL** | **To pack hot:** Can very soon after harvest. Use a sharp knife to cut raw corn from cob at two-thirds of the total depth of the kernels. Do not scrape the cobs. Cover well with brine (1 level tablespoon salt to 1 quart water). Heat to boiling point. Pack hot into hot jars to within 1 inch of jar tops. Seal. *Raw pack is not recommended.* | 55 | 70 |
| **CORN, CREAM STYLE** | **To pack hot:** Prepare as for whole kernel corn, but scrape the cobs (do not scrape off any of the cob material). Proceed as directed for whole kernel corn. Leave 1½ inch headspace. Seal. *Quart jars are not recommended.* *Raw pack is not recommended.* | 85 | not rec. |
| **CORN, HOMINY** | Cover hominy well with brine, as directed for whole kernel corn. Heat to boiling point. Pack hot into hot jars to within 1 inch of tops. Seal. *Raw pack is not recommended.* | 75 | 90 |
| **GREENS** | Spinach, swiss chard, beet greens, other greens. *Home canning is not recommended.* | 15 | 15 |
| **MUSHROOMS** | NOTE: Trim stems and discolored parts. Rinse in cold water. Leave small mushrooms whole; cut larger ones into halves or quarters. Blanch in simmering hot water or steam for 4 minutes. Pack hot mushrooms into hot jars. Add ½ teaspoon salt and ½ teaspoon of lemon juice to pints. Add boiling cooking liquid or water to cover mushrooms, leaving ½ inch headspace. *Mushrooms will be overcooked if processed enough to be safe.* Apply lids and ring bands. | 30 | Don't use |
| **OKRA** | **To pack hot:** Use young, tender pods. Wash and trim. Leave pods whole or cut into 1-inch pieces. Boil for 1 minute. Pack hot into hot jars, leaving 1 inch headspace. Add ½ teaspoon salt to pints, 1 teaspoon to quarts. Add boiling water to 1 inch of top. Seal. | 25 | 40 |

| VEGETABLES | HOW TO PREPARE | PROCESSING TIME (10 pounds pressure) | |
|---|---|---|---|
| | | PINT | QUART |
| | | minutes | |
| ONIONS, SMALL WHITE | Follow directions for artichokes. | | |
| PEAS, FRESH GREEN | **To pack hot:** Can only young, tender peas. Hull and pre-cook for 1 to 4 minutes in a small amount of water until the skins wrinkle. Pack hot into hot jars to within 1¼ inches of tops. Add salt. Cover to within 1 inch of jar tops with the boiling liquid in which the peas were cooked. Add boiling water if needed. Seal. | 40 | 45 |
| | **To pack raw:** Pack loosely to within 1 inch of jar tops. Add ½ teaspoon salt for pint jars; 1 teaspoon salt for quart jars. Cover with boiling water to within 1 inch of top. Seal. | 40 | 45 |
| PEAS, FRESH BLACK-EYE | **To pack hot:** Follow directions for green peas. *Raw pack is not recommended.* | 50 | 55 |
| PEPPERS, BELL-GREEN, RED, AND PIMENTO | **To pack hot:** Cut out the stem end of each pepper, and remove the core and seeds. Peel peppers by heating in a gas flame or roasting in a very hot oven until the skins separate. Chill at once in cold water. Pack into jars. Cover with boiling water to within ½ inch of jar tops. Add ½ teaspoon salt to pint jars; 1 teaspoon salt to quart jars. It is also necessary to add 1½ teaspoons bottled lemon juice to pint jars; 1 tablespoon lemon juice to each quart jar. *(Process at only 5 pounds pressure; higher pressures affect texture and flavor.)* Seal. | (5 lb pressure) 50 | 60 |
| POTATOES, NEW | Peel new potatoes. Leave small ones whole; cut larger ones in halves. Pack cold without pre-cooking. Add boiling brine made with 1½ to 2 tablespoons salt to 1 quart water. Fill to within ¾ to 1 inch of jar tops. Seal. | 35 | 40 |
| POTATOES, SWEET | Wash and remove any blemishes. **To pack dry:** Place in steamer over boiling water or boil in a small amount of water until crisp-tender. Peel and cut into pieces. Pack tightly into jars, pressing to fill spaces. Add no salt or liquid. Apply lids and ring bands. | 65 | 95 |
| | **To pack wet:** Steam or boil as for dry pack, but remove as soon as skins slip off easily. Peel, cut into pieces, and pack into jars to within 1 inch of tops. Add ½ teaspoon salt to quarts. Cover with boiling water or a syrup of 1 part sugar to 2 parts water, leaving ¾ inch headspace. Apply lids and ringbands. | 55 | 90 |
| PUMPKIN OR MATURE SQUASH, CUBED | **To pack hot:** Wash, remove seeds, and peel. Cut into 1-inch cubes. Add enough water to cover; bring to a boil. Pack hot cubes to ½ inch of the top. Add ½ teaspoon salt to pints; 1 teaspoon to quarts. Cover with hot cooking liquid, leaving ½ inch headspace. Seal. *Raw pack is not recommended.* | 55 | 90 |

University of California, Davis; Department of Food Technology.

| VEGETABLES | HOW TO PREPARE | PROCESSING TIME (10 pounds pressure) | |
|---|---|---|---|
| | | PINT | QUART |
| | | minutes | |
| **PUMPKIN OR MATURE SQUASH, STRAINED** | Scrape out fibrous material and cut flesh and rind into strips. Boil in water, or steam, until flesh is soft. Scrape flesh from rind and press through a colander. Bring to a boil. Pack hot into hot jars to within ¾ to 1 inch of tops. Add ½ teaspoon salt to pint jars; 1 teaspoon salt to quart jars. Seal. *Raw pack is not recommended.* | 85 | 115 |
| **SQUASH, SUMMER CROOKNECK, ZUCCHINI, PATTYPAN** | *Canning summer squash produces a soft to mushy product.* Wash and trim ends; do not peel. Cut into ½-inch thick slices. **To pack hot:** Put into a pan, add water to just cover, and bring to boiling. Pack hot into hot jars, filling loosely up to jar shoulders. Add ½ teaspoon salt to pints, 1 teaspoon to quarts. Cover with boiling cooking liquid, leaving ½ inch headspace. Apply lids and ring bands. | 30 | 40 |
| | **To pack raw:** Pack slices tightly into jars to within 1 inch of tops. Add salt as for hot pack, then fill jars with boiling water, leaving ½ inch headspace. Apply lids and ring bands. | 25 | 30 |
| **TURNIPS** | Follow directions for carrots. | | |

© Hanson Carroll/FPG International

## ASPARAGUS

*11 pounds asparagus (about 200 stalks) per pint jar*

*1 garlic clove*

*1 piece red bell pepper, ½ inch long*

*½ teaspoon salt*

Wash and cut asparagus ¾ inch shorter than your jar. Scrape off scales. Put garlic clove, bell pepper, and salt into hot jars. Loosely pack asparagus, stem end down. Add boiling water, leaving ½-inch headspace. Release air bubbles, wipe rims, and seal. Process in a pressure canner at 10 pounds. Pints take 30 minutes and quarts take 40 minutes.

**Makes 7 pints.**

## GREEN BEANS TIED WITH CARROTS

These look so pretty in the jar and make a really nice gift. Tell whoever is the recipient of these beans to remove them carefully from the jar. A bundle of these drizzled with dressing placed on the side of a chicken salad makes a very impressive sight.

*5½ pounds beans*

*2 to 3 carrots*

*½ teaspoon salt for pints or ¾ teaspoon salt for quarts*

Pick beautiful small beans. Wash and remove stem end and string if necessary. Cook beans in boiling water for 3 to 4 minutes. Do not cover pan—the beans will stay greener. Plunge beans into cold water. Use the deepest orange carrots you can find. Wash and peel carrots. Using a vegetable peeler, peel strips of carrot lengthwise. Cook in boiling water until carrots bend easily but do not break. Take 5 to 6 beans and wrap one piece of carrot around the beans. Repeat this until all beans are used. Take hot jars and add salt. Lay jars on their sides and put several bundles of beans in each jar. Don't pack too tightly. Stand jars up and add boiling water to within ¾ inch of the top of the jar. Carefully remove air bubbles, clean rims, and seal. Process in a pressure canner at 10 pounds, 30 minutes for quarts, 25 minutes for pints.

**Makes 6 to 7 pints.**

## MELANGE OF PEPPERS

These peppers can be served warm with grilled chicken breast and warm flour tortillas.

*8 green bell peppers*

*8 red peppers*

*8 yellow peppers*

*In each jar:*

*1 teaspoon salt*

*1 clove garlic*

*a sprig of fresh tarragon*

*2 tablespoons tarragon vinegar*

Roast peppers in a 400°F oven, turning frequently until they are partially brown and start to bubble. Remove from oven and peel. Cut peppers open and remove white membrane and seeds. Cut each pepper lengthwise into six strips and then in half. Mix peppers for color and interest. Using an 8 to 10 quart pot (the kind with a strainer inside) or a pan large enough to hold a strainer, boil water and add peppers for 2 to 3 minutes, just long enough to soften slightly, so the peppers will fit into the jars more easily. Plunge immediately into cold water to stop the cooking. Put 1 teaspoon salt, 1 clove garlic, a sprig of fresh tarragon, and tarragon vinegar into each hot jar. Fill jar with boiling water, leaving ½-inch headspace. Remove air bubbles, clean rims, and seal. Process in a pressure canner at 10 pounds, for 35 minutes.

**Makes 5 to 6 quarts.**

## MIXED VEGETABLES

This is very pretty in the jar.

*4 cups red bell pepper, cut in 1½-inch pieces*

*4 cups yellow bell pepper, cut in 1½-inch pieces*

*2 pounds green beans, stem end cut and bean stringed, if necessary*

*4 cups carrots cut on the diagonal in ¼-inch slices*

*3 cans (8 ounces each) water chestnuts*

*In each jar: 1 teaspoon salt, one slice yellow onion*

Wash and prepare vegetables. Boil water in a large pan and dip peppers in for 2 minutes (just to soften). Use an 8 to 10 quart pot or larger with a strainer in it or a large pan a strainer will fit in. This will let you use the same water for all vegetables. Remove peppers and add beans; parboil for 5 minutes. Drain beans. Cook carrots in water for 3 minutes; drain. Drain the water chestnuts. To each hot jar add salt and one slice of onion. Carefully add vegetables with water chestnuts, layering them so they look pretty in the jar. Fill the jar with boiling water to within ½ inch of the top. Release air bubbles and seal. Process in a pressure canner at 10 pounds for 30 minutes for quarts, 10 pounds for 25 minutes for pints.

**Makes 4 to 5 quarts or 8 to 10 pints.**

## CARROTS WITH MINT

*8 pounds baby carrots*

*In each jar:*

*1 clove garlic*

*1 sprig mint, about 2 inches
long*

*1 teaspoon lemon juice*

*½ teaspoon salt*

Wash and scrape carrots. Put 1 garlic clove, a sprig of mint, 1 teaspoon lemon juice, and ½ teaspoon salt in each pint. Add carrots and fill jar with boiling water to within ½ inch of tops of jars. Release air bubbles, clean rims, and seal. Process in a pressure canner at 10 pounds for 30 minutes.

**Makes 5 to 6 pints.**

© AGE FotoStock/FPG International

# PICKLES, RELISHES, AND CHUTNEYS

Fruits and vegetables can become crisp, tangy, sweet and sour, or sour with the process of pickling. The flavor changes easily by varying the amount of vinegar, salt, sugar, or seasonings. That is the fun of making these products at home. You can have things as spicy or as mild as you want. You must taste as you go through the recipe so it becomes distinctively yours. Then serve with meat, fish, or poultry, or as an accompaniment to curry.

## TYPES OF PICKLES

**Vegetable Pickles:** I have given a few quick pickle recipes using vinegar and salt brines. The favorite vegetable for pickling is the cucumber and the small variety is the most favorable. Do not use waxed cucumbers from your market; you won't like the result. I have also used beans, asparagus, and beets.

**Fruits** are also wonderful pickled. I use a spicy, sweet-sour syrup. Cloves and cinnamon are common spices used with fruit. You can use many different fruits, but the more popular fruits to pickle are peaches, crabapples, figs, plums, pears, and apples.

**Relishes** are also included in the pickling chapter because we use vinegar and spices and blend different vegetables and fruit to make a piquant blend.

**Chutneys** are another type of relish, again using a variety of chopped fruit and vegetables and blending them with seasonings like onion, garlic, ginger, and turmeric.

## EQUIPMENT FOR PICKLING

If you have canning equipment you are set for pickling. You want to be careful to use containers made of glass, enamel, high-grade plastic, or stainless steel. Other utensils may chemically react with the brine mixture or high-acid solutions.

You will need colanders, long spoons, cheesecloth for packaging spices, and a food grinder or a food processor. The processor will slice your pickling vegetables perfectly and chop your vegetables for relishes or chutneys in no time. You will need jars and lids that are in good shape and new flat metal lids. Pickles, relishes, and chutneys are processed in a water bath because of the high acidity of all these products, so you will need a water canner or a large pan that will hold enough water to cover the jars with water by 2 inches.

## INGREDIENTS FOR PICKLING

Choose firm, fresh vegetables and fruits. Put up as soon as possible after picking or purchasing. The small pickling cucumber is best to use for making crisp pickles. The salad varieties are not as crisp and, if used, it is best to cut them into chunks or slices.

Fruit is best when it is slightly underripe. It will hold its shape better. Try to pick uniformly-sized fruit.

Pickling salt, called for in some of the recipes, can be found in most grocery stores in the summer. Look for it next to ice-cream-making salt.

Fresh spices are preferred and lend wonderful flavor, but dried pickling spices and other ground spices are fine to use.

Granulated beet sugar or brown sugar can both be used. Brown sugar will give a darker color syrup and a little stronger flavor. You may also use half sugar and half honey for sweetness.

Another ingredient so important to the outcome of good crisp pickles is the water. Soft water is great, but hard water can make your pickles cloudy. Hard water will not affect the taste, but if you want you can boil hard water or use distilled water.

Vinegar is one of the main ingredients used in pickling. Pick a good standard vinegar, 40 to 60 grains strength, that is free from sediment. Cider and distilled wine vinegars are good choices. Never overboil vinegar solutions or you may lose the acidity essential for pickling.

Powdered alum is sometimes used to make pickles crispy. But if you have fresh, firm produce and follow directions closely you really don't need it. If you must use it, don't exceed ⅛ teaspoon per quart of liquid plus pickles. Alum can cause digestive problems, so be very careful.

I use pickling lime in a few recipes. You can purchase it from your local nursery. It will not hurt you, but make sure you rinse the food you use it on very well. It makes really nice crisp pickles.

© Burke/Triolo

## A FEW PICKLING RULES

You can have a great time with your ingredients when making pickles, relish, or chutney. But make very sure that you follow directions correctly. If you speed up some processes, like adding your vinegar and sugar syrup to the pickles before the brine solution has worked, you will end up with tough, shriveled pickles. Also, the wrong brine solution can work against you. If the brine is too weak it will give you soft pickles and if too strong it will wilt the pickles.

You must also be careful to follow vinegar amounts. You can choose which kinds but not how much or you may end up with an unsafe product.

## PROCESSING YOUR PICKLES, RELISHES, AND CHUTNEYS

All pickles, relishes, and chutneys are processed in a boiling water canner. Processing time will vary, but each recipe states the proper time required. If you wish to omit the boiling processing step you can keep your goods refrigerated for a few weeks, but not much longer. Surface yeast or mold is the most common problem of refrigerated foods.

Check your jars and lids to make sure that they are safe to use. Wash in hot, soapy water. Make sure you have new flat metal lids and follow manufacturer's directions on preparing them for use.

Put your food into the hot jars and pour in the liquid to within ½ inch of the rim of the jar. Remove air bubbles and wipe the rim of the jar clean. Seal and place jars in a boiling water bath, adding enough water to cover the jars by 2 inches. Begin counting the processing time when the water returns to a gentle boil. Cool your jars on a wooden block or on folded towels, leaving room for air to circulate around the jars. When the jars are cool test the seal by pressing down on the lid. It should not move. You can then remove the screw band and store in a dark, cool, dry place.

Do not be too anxious to try your wares. The flavor of pickles, relishes, and chutneys all improve when stored for several weeks.

| COMMON PROBLEMS WITH PICKLES | |
|---|---|
| Shriveling pickles. | This could be caused by using old vegetables or too strong a vinegar or salt solution. Could also be overprocessed. |
| Soft or slippery pickles. | You may have used too weak a brine or too little vinegar. Not removing scum as it forms on brine, or using cucumbers with the blossom attached will also make pickles soft. |
| Hollow pickles. | You probably have old cucumbers. You may have kept them in the brine too long or had faulty growth. |
| Dark pickles. | Too much spice or cooked too long with spices added. Improper equipment, especially if you used iron. |
| White sediment on bottom of the jar. | Failure to kill bacteria and spoilage is setting in. |
| Dull or faded color. | Vegetables are old, or your vinegar is not a good quality or the proper strength (40 to 60 grain is a good strength). |

## MARY'S SWEET PICKLES

Mary Allison is a favorite teacher of two of my children, and I think she is just wonderful. My youngest son, T. J., said Mrs. Allison made the best sweet pickles. Well, taste these and see what you think. They are so crisp and have a wonderful flavor. You can get the pickling lime from a garden nursery and it will last you a long time. Be sure you rinse the cucumbers thoroughly after soaking them in the lime.

*8 pounds cucumbers*

*½ cup pickling lime*

*3 quarts water*

*2 quarts cider vinegar*

*9 cups sugar*

*3 tablespoons salt*

*2 tablespoons each celery seed, whole cloves, and mixed pickling spices*

Wash and slice cucumbers. Soak the cucumbers in lime and water for 24 hours. Then, drain the cucumbers and rinse well. Soak for 3 hours in enough cold water to cover. Drain again and rinse well. Mix the vinegar, sugar, salt, and spices together and pour over the cucumbers. Let stand overnight. In the morning, bring to a boil and boil on low for 35 minutes. Fill hot jars to within ½ inch of the tops, release air bubbles, wipe the rims, and seal.

**Makes 6 quarts or 12 half-pints.**

## SWEET CHIPS

*5 pounds small cucumbers*

*⅓ cup salt*

*6 cups vinegar*

*7 to 8 cups sugar*

*1 tablespoon pickling spice*

*1½ teaspoons celery seed*

*¾ teaspoon turmeric*

*1 whole stick cinnamon*

*1 teaspoon vanilla (optional)*

Wash and slice cucumbers. Put in a non-metallic container and pour enough boiling water to cover. You may want to lay a plate on top of the cucumbers as a weight so all the cucumbers are in the water. Eight hours later, drain cucumbers and cover again with boiling water, adding the salt. The next day drain cucumbers. Make a syrup of 3 cups of the vinegar and 3 cups of the sugar, the pickling spice, celery seed, turmeric, and cinnamon stick.

Bring the syrup to a boil and pour on cucumbers. Let stand 8 hours or overnight. Drain, saving the syrup. Add 2 cups vinegar and 2 cups sugar to syrup and bring to a boil. Pour on pickles and let stand 12 hours. Remove the cinnamon stick, drain, and add 1 cup vinegar and 2 to 3 cups sugar (to taste). Bring to a boil and add vanilla. Pack the pickles in the jars and cover with the boiling syrup to within ½ inch of the top. Remove air bubbles, clean rims, and seal. Process in a water bath canner for 10 minutes.

**Makes 7 to 8 12-ounce jars.**

## BREAD AND BUTTER PICKLES

*4 quarts pickling cucumbers (about 6 pounds)*

*4 large onions*

*½ cup salt*

*4 cups vinegar*

*4 cups sugar*

*1 tablespoon celery seed*

*2 teaspoons turmeric*

*2 tablespoons mustard seed*

*1 teaspoon mixed pickling spices*

Slice cucumbers and onions and alternately layer in a strainer covering each layer with salt. Cover with ice and let drain 3 hours. Add ice as needed. Drain and rinse thoroughly. Combine vinegar, sugar, and spices and bring to a boil. Boil 10 minutes. Add cucumbers and onions and bring to a boil again. Fill hot jars with cucumber and onions. Add hot liquid to within ½ inch of the tops of the jars. Release air bubbles, clean the rims of the jars, and seal. Process in a water bath canner for 10 minutes.

**Makes 7 to 8 pints.**

© Amy Reichman/Envision

## BETTY KEECH'S DILL PICKLES

This recipe really reaches back into my past. Until I was seven years old, I lived on a ranch and Betty lived a couple of houses away. According to her daughter, Donna, she would can just about anything she could get her hands on. So I am sharing her recipe for Dill Pickles, which everyone I know feels are the best dill pickles around. Betty never processes her pickles and says they are great even after a year. However, if you want to be assured a seal you can process for 10 minutes. I also tried soaking the pickles in food-grade pickling lime, bought at a local nursery, overnight and had really crispy pickles. Put pickles in 3 quarts of water with ½ cup pickling lime and leave for 24 hours. Rinse the pickles thoroughly and proceed with Betty's recipe.

*10 to 12 pounds small*
*cucumbers*

*1½ gallons vinegar*

*1½ gallons water*

*1 cup salt*

*Put in each jar:*

*1 clove garlic*

*1 tablespoon pickling spices*

*several sprigs of fresh dill and*
*1 tablespooon dill seed*

*a pinch of alum (do not use if*
*you used lime)*

You can keep your pickles whole or slice them. Wash the pickles and cut stems off if left whole or slice with your food processor. Stir the vinegar, water, and salt, and let it just come to a boil. Have hot jars ready and put in garlic, pickling spices, dill, dill seed, and alum (if you did not use lime). Pack the jars with cucumbers. Ladle the hot vinegar mixture over to within ½ inch of the tops of jars. Remove the air bubbles, wipe the rims of the jars, and seal. Process in a water bath canner for 10 minutes.

**Makes 9 to 10 quarts.**

© Lynn Karlin

## ZUCCHINI PICKLES

These pickles are so tasty and crispy. They also are such a pretty color that they look beautiful on a bed of lettuce with many other vegetables.

6 cups sliced green zucchini

6 cups sliced yellow zucchini

2 large onions

1 each yellow, red, and green peppers

½ cup salt

2 cups sugar

4 cups water

4 cups vinegar

2 tablespoons mustard seed

2 tablespoons celery seed

2 teaspoons turmeric

Wash and cut vegetables. (I slice my onions thin and make the zucchini about ½ inch thick.) Cover zucchini, onion, and peppers with water to which salt has been added. Let stand for 2 hours. Drain and rinse the vegetables. Combine the sugar, water, vinegar, and spices and bring to a boil. When it boils add the vegetables and cook 2 to 3 minutes. Pack vegetables into hot jars and fill with the hot liquid, leaving ½-inch headspace. Release air bubbles, clean rims, and seal. Process in a water bath canner for 10 minutes.

**Makes 6 to 7 pints.**

## PICKLED BEETS

8 pounds beets

2 cups sugar

2 cups water

4 cups cider vinegar

2 whole sticks cinnamon

6 whole allspice

8 whole cloves

2 large onions, sliced thin

1 lemon, sliced thin

Wash beets. Cook until just tender—about 20 minutes—and plunge into cold water and slip off skins. Shred beets. Combine sugar, water, and vinegar. Put spices in a piece of cheesecloth, tie them, and add to the vinegar mixture. Bring the mixture to a boil, then lower heat and simmer for 5 minutes. Remove spices. Fill hot jars with beets and onions. Add a lemon slice to each jar and fill with the hot liquid to within ½ inch of the top of the jar. Release air bubbles, clean rims, seal, and process in a water bath canner for 30 minutes.

**Makes 4 pints.**

## MICHELLE'S PICKLED CARROTS

4 pounds baby carrots

2 quarts water

½ cup salt

4 cups water

4 cups vinegar

2 cups sugar

In each pint:

¼ teaspoon celery seed

3 or 4 peppercorns

1 sprig fresh thyme or ½ teaspoon dried thyme

1 garlic clove

½-inch piece of red pepper

¼ teaspoon mixed pickling spices

2 teaspoons olive oil

Scrape and clean carrots. Remove ends. If you do not have baby carrots, cut long carrots into chunks. Put 2 quarts water and salt into a bowl and stir to dissolve salt. Add carrots. Cover carrots and water with ice. Refrigerate for 2 hours. Rinse the carrots well and drain. Rinse again and drain. Bring water, vinegar, and sugar to a boil. Put spices and oil into each pint jar. Fill jars with carrots and then with boiling liquid to within ½ inch of the top. Release air bubbles, clean rims, and seal. Process in a water bath canner for 20 minutes.

**Makes 4 to 5 pints.**

## DILLY BEANS

If you need a quick salad, these beans are wonderful on red-leaf lettuces. Use the liquid for your dressing.

2 pounds green beans

2½ cups water

2½ cups vinegar

¼ cup salt

In each jar put:

1 garlic clove

⅛ teaspoon dried dill

small sprig of fresh dill

3 or 4 peppercorns

1 bay leaf

¼ teaspoon red pepper flakes

Cut ends off of beans and wash thoroughly. If the beans are small (I prefer small beans) leave them whole, otherwise cut into 1-inch lengths. Bring water, vinegar, and salt to a boil, then add beans and cook 2 minutes. Remove beans to a paper-towel-lined cookie sheet, making sure you save the liquid the beans were cooked in. Add all the spices to each hot jar. If whole, stand the beans in the jars and fill to within ½ inch of the rim with the cooking liquid. Release the air bubbles, clean rims, and seal. Process in a water bath canner for 10 minutes.

**Makes 4 pints.**

# RELISH

Relishes are great fun to make and are not just used for hot dogs anymore. Relish makes a good accompaniment for many meats and fish. Some are so tasty you may just want to eat them by the spoonful. Relishes are made from combinations of fruits, vegetables, spices, and good quality vinegars.

### AUNT ROSE'S RELISH

This recipe was given to me by my very good friends, Jeff and Patti Coupe. Frances Coupe, Jeff's 95-year-old grandmother, still makes this relish. I hear Jeff eats it by the spoonful so it must be great. Aunt Rose fits in here somewhere, but when you get recipes that have been passed down for so many years you lose track.

*6 ripe red tomatoes, cored and quartered*

*6 green tomatoes, cored and quartered*

*5 sweet peppers*

*3 hot peppers*

*6 medium onions*

*1 quart cider vinegar*

*1 pound brown or granulated sugar*

*1 tablespoon salt*

*1 tablespoon cinnamon*

*1 teaspoon ground allspice*

*1 teaspoon nutmeg*

*1 teaspoon ground cloves*

Add 2 tablespoons of salt to a large bowl of water and add cored and quartered tomatoes to salted water. Remove seeds and membrane from peppers, quarter, and add them to salted water. Peel and quarter onions and add them to salted water. Drain all the vegetables and grind in a food processor or food grinder. Put into a heavy saucepan and add the vinegar, sugar, salt, and spices. Cook over low heat, stirring occasionally, for 2½ to 3 hours. Ladle into hot jars leaving ½-inch headspace, wipe rims, seal, and process in water bath canner for 15 minutes.

**Makes 10 half-pints.**

### PEPPER RELISH

*2 green bell peppers, chopped*

*2 red peppers, chopped*

*2 onions, chopped*

*¾ pound green tomatoes, chopped*

*3 cups vinegar*

*1½ cups sugar*

*1 tablespoon salt*

*2 teaspoons celery seed*

*1 teaspoon mustard seed*

*2 teaspoons turmeric*

*1 teaspoon tarragon*

Prepare peppers, onions, and tomatoes. Put vegetables in a large, heavy saucepan and add the rest of the ingredients. Bring to a boil and cook until slightly thickened. Stir occasionally. Pack into hot jars, wipe rims, and seal. Process in a water bath canner for 10 minutes.

**Makes 4 to 5 pints.**

## CORN RELISH

*4 cups corn (about 10 ears, or use canned niblets corn)*

*1 cup red peppers, chopped*

*1 cup green peppers, chopped*

*1 cup celery, chopped*

*1 cup carrots, shredded*

*½ cup green onions, chopped*

*2½ cups vinegar*

*1½ cups sugar*

*1½ teaspoons salt*

*1 teaspoon turmeric*

*1 tablespoon mustard seed*

*1 teaspoon white pepper*

*1 teaspoon celery seed*

Cook fresh corn 5 minutes in boiling water. Remove corn and put in cold water. Cut corn from cob. If you use canned corn, rinse and drain. Put corn and all other ingredients into a large saucepan and bring to a boil. Simmer for 5 minutes, stirring constantly. Ladle into hot jars, wipe rims, and seal. Process in a water bath canner for 15 minutes.

**Makes 7 to 8 pints.**

## WILMA'S GREEN RELISH

Wilma Casey is a family friend who says she has wonderful childhood memories of making this relish with her mother. It is really easy to make and takes no time at all if you use a food processor for all the chopping.

*4 large onions*

*½ small head cabbage*

*4 cups green tomatoes*

*12 green peppers*

*6 sweet red peppers*

*½ cup salt*

*6 cups sugar*

*1 tablespoon celery seed*

*2 tablespoons mustard seed*

*1½ teaspoons turmeric*

*4 cups cider vinegar*

*2 cups water*

Coarsely grind all vegetables with the steel blade of your food processor or with a food grinder. Sprinkle vegetables with ½ cup salt and mix well. Let stand overnight. The next day, rinse the vegetables well and drain. Put vegetables into a large, heavy saucepan and add sugar, spices, vinegar, and water. Mix well and bring mixture to a boil. When a boil is reached, turn heat down and simmer for 3 minutes. Ladle into hot jars leaving ½-inch headspace, wipe rims, and seal. Process in a water bath canner for 10 minutes.

**Makes 8 to 9 pints.**

© Burke/Triolo

# CHUTNEYS

Chutneys are spicy preserves that combine fruits and vegetables with nuts and dried fruits. They are served with cur-
ries and as accompaniments to many other meat, fish, and
chicken dishes.

© Michael Grand

## MANGO CHUTNEY

2 cups mango, diced

2 cups apple, diced

1 onion, diced

½ cup green pepper, diced

½ cup golden raisins

½ cup sliced almonds

1 cup sugar

1 cup apple cider vinegar

¼ teaspoon ground allspice

¼ teaspoon ground cloves

1 teaspoon cinnamon

½ teaspoon salt

Prepare fruit and vegetables. Put all other ingredients into a large, heavy saucepan. Bring to a boil, stirring constantly. Add fruits and vegetables and cook about 30 minutes or until desired consistency, stirring occasionally. Ladle into hot jars leaving ½-inch headspace. Clean rims of jars and seal. Process in a water bath canner for 10 minutes.

**Makes 5 or 6 half-pints.**

## RUSTY'S CHUTNEY

Rusty Ball is a family friend and this recipe is from her great grandmother's family cookbook. This one goes way back and it is really good.

5 pounds tomatoes, cubed

2 large onions, chopped

½ cup salt

1 pound green apples, peeled and chopped

2 cups cider vinegar

6 cups brown sugar

1 teaspoon cinnamon

1 teaspoon ground cloves

1 teaspoon ground allspice

1 teaspoon white pepper

1 teaspoon ground ginger

1 tablespoon mustard seed

¼ teaspoon cayenne pepper

Prepare tomatoes and onions. Sprinkle with ½ cup of salt and let stand overnight. The next day, rinse and drain the tomatoes and onions. Add all ingredients to a heavy, large saucepan and mix well. Bring to a boil. Reduce heat to a simmer and cook until vegetables are soft and appear clear. Ladle into hot jars, leaving ½-inch headspace, clean rims, and seal. Process in a water bath canner for 10 minutes.

**Makes about 7 pints.**

## APPLE-PEAR CHUTNEY

2 cups pears, diced

3 cups apples, diced

2 cups green tomato, diced

1 medium onion, minced

1 red pepper, minced

3 cups cider vinegar

1½ cups sugar

1½ teaspoons salt

½ teaspoon white pepper

¾ teaspoon cinnamon

¼ teaspoon cayenne pepper

1¼ cups golden raisins

Combine all ingredients in a heavy saucepan and bring to a boil stirring constantly. Reduce heat to a simmer and continue cooking until thickened. Ladle into hot jars, wipe rims, and seal. Process in a water bath canner for 10 minutes.

**Makes about 7 pints.**

## PEACHY GINGER CHUTNEY

Spoon this chutney into a cooked, miniature pumpkin that has been scooped out. This is beautiful alongside your Thanksgiving table.

3½ pounds peaches, diced (about 7 large)

1 large onion, minced

1 yellow pepper, diced

1 hot red pepper, diced

½ cup crystallized ginger, chopped

2 cups cider vinegar

3 cups sugar

1 teaspoon cinnamon

¼ teaspoon ground cloves

¼ teaspoon mace

Prepare fruit and vegetables. Put in a heavy saucepan and add the remaining ingredients. Bring to a boil, stirring constantly. Turn heat to a simmer, and cook until desired consistency. Ladle into hot jars leaving ½-inch headspace, wipe rims, and seal. Process in a water bath canner for 10 minutes.

**Makes 4 to 5 half-pints.**

© Brian Leatart

# CHAPTER SIX

# VINEGARS AND OILS

This section will give you recipes for many of the things you buy in gourmet gift shops. You will be surprised how easy they are to make.

Flavored vinegars and oils are wonderful to cook with and lend themselves to making creative and exciting flavored dishes. Those of you on weight-reducing diets or special medical diets will be surprised at how much flavor these vinegars will add to so many foods. They are great on salads, nice to marinate meat in, and will enhance your vegetables without using butter.

I hope you will enjoy these and think of many great ways to decorate and present them as gifts. There is nothing more appreciated than something homemade. All gifts that you are sending in a bottle or jar—or any other fragile container—must be packed very carefully so that they won't break. If you are shipping more than one bottle or jar in a box, be sure you allow ample room around each—at least three inches. Wrap each container in a layer of newspaper. It is a good idea to cover the bottom of these containers with shredded foam to absorb any shock. Always fill any empty spaces in the box with newspapers or foam. Always label the package as FRAGILE.

If you are shipping many different kinds of goodies in one box, wrap each one individually in plastic or foil. This way, if one breaks, the other will still be protected from absorbing the liquid or odors.

# VINEGARS

Vinegars are really easy to make and fun to use. You can make them look so beautiful in all the interesting bottles that are available in food shops today.

Make sure you start off with very good vinegar and add spices, fresh herbs, or fruits—even citrus peels. Store the vinegar in a cool dark place for several weeks and then strain it into pretty bottles. Add some fresh herbs, peppers, or peels and it will make a lovely gift.

© Michael Grand

### LEMON-THYME VINEGAR

Try tossing some cooked baby shrimp and scallops in a vinaigrette made with this vinegar. Serve on a bed of bibb and radicchio.

*1 quart white wine vinegar*

*1 bunch fresh thyme*

*peel of one lemon*

*2 garlic cloves*

*6 or 7 whole peppercorns*

*6 or 7 whole coriander seeds*

Heat the vinegar until it boils, but do not boil the vinegar. Put all other ingredients into a big glass container with a tight-fitting lid. Pour in the warm vinegar, seal tightly, and store in a cool, dark place. It is best to leave for at least 2 to 3 weeks. At that time, strain the vinegar into a large container. Then pour it into a decorative bottle through a funnel. Add a few new sprigs of fresh thyme and a lemon peel that you have cut in a spiral.

**Makes 1 quart of vinegar.**

### BLACKBERRY VINEGAR

Use fruit vinegars, a little sweet butter, and salt and pepper to deglaze a pan after sautéeing chicken or pork cutlets.

In this vinegar recipe I use rice vinegar. It is a mild, wonderful vinegar often overlooked. You will find it in the Chinese foods section of your grocery store.

*6 cups rice vinegar*

*¼ cup sugar*

*2 cups fresh blackberries, mashed*

Heat the vinegar and sugar until the sugar dissolves. Do not boil. Pour the vinegar over the mashed berries and cover the glass jar with a tight-fitting lid. Leave in a dark, cool place for 2 to 3 days. Strain through a jelly bag or cheesecloth. Pour into a pretty bottle with a tight fitting top.

**Makes 1½ quarts of vinegar.**

### TARRAGON VINEGAR

*8 cups white wine vinegar*

*1 teaspoon sugar*

*1 large bunch fresh tarragon*

*1 large piece of red pepper*

*½ teaspoon whole black pepper*

*1 teaspoon celery seed*

*2 garlic cloves*

Warm vinegar and sugar. Add all other ingredients to a large glass jar with a tight-fitting lid. Pour warm vinegar into the jar and put the lid on tight. Store in a dark, cool place for 3 to 4 weeks. Then strain vinegar and put into a bottle with a tight screw top or a tight cork. Add a sprig of fresh tarragon, 1 garlic clove, and a new piece of red pepper. It will look pretty and taste great.

**Makes 1½ quarts of vinegar.**

## DILL VINEGAR

I like to use this vinegar to make a homemade mayonnaise to use on cold salmon. Just eliminate the lemon juice from your mayonnaise recipe and add this vinegar in place of it.

*6 cups red wine vinegar*

*1 teaspoon sugar*

*½ lemon, quartered, seeds removed*

*1 bunch fresh dill*

*2 garlic cloves*

*1 teaspoon peppercorns*

*1 teaspoon pepper flakes*

*1 teaspoon celery seed*

*½ teaspoon whole mustard seed*

Heat red wine vinegar and 1 teaspoon sugar until warm. Put dill and other ingredients into a glass jar. Pour warm vinegar over and put on a tight-fitting lid. Store at room temperature in a dark, cool place for at least 2 weeks. At the end of this time, strain vinegar and put into a decorative bottle with a tight cork or a screw top. Add a fresh garlic clove and a fresh sprig of dill.

**Makes 1½ quarts of vinegar.**

## BASIL VINEGAR

I always have this vinegar on hand for making pasta salad.

*6 cups white wine vinegar*

*¼ of a fresh red pepper*

*1 cup fresh basil leaves, left whole*

*2 garlic cloves*

*½ teaspoon whole mustard seed*

*½ teaspoon whole white pepper*

*1 teaspoon celery seed*

Heat vinegar, but do not boil. Put all other ingredients into a large glass jar with a tight-fitting lid. Pour warm vinegar into the jar, cover tightly, and set in a dark, cool place for at least 2 weeks. After 2 or more weeks, strain vinegar into a large container. Pour vinegar into pretty bottles, using a funnel to help. Add a new garlic clove and a fresh sprig of basil. Put on a tight cork or screw top.

**Makes 1½ quarts of vinegar.**

## RASPBERRY VINEGAR

Try fruit-flavored vinegars on salads or sprinkle on your favorite cooked vegetables.

*3 cups fresh raspberries, mashed*

*6 cups white wine vinegar*

*¼ cup sugar*

Heat the vinegar and sugar until the sugar dissolves, but do not boil. Pour vinegar over raspberries in a large glass jar. Put in a dark, cool place for 3 or 4 days. Strain the vinegar through a jelly bag so it is very clear. Do not squeeze the bag. Pour through a funnel into a decorative jar and seal with a tight lid or cork.

**Makes 7 cups of vinegar.**

© Brian Leatart

# FLAVORED OILS

Flavored oils are fun to use. If you have ever sautéed chicken in grape oil or used walnut oil on bibb lettuce, you know how good these can be. For the easiest spiced oils pick your favorite oil (be it olive, corn, or any other variety). Add fresh herbs like basil, tarragon, dill, rosemary, or thyme. You can be very imaginative. Just add what you want to a pretty bottle with a tight-fitting top or cork, add oil, and let sit at least two weeks before using. The longer it sits the more pronounced the flavor. Shake the bottle every couple of days to help the flavor spread. Use these oils for sautéeing, dressing, or spreading on a turkey or chicken before baking.

Try olive oil flavored with rosemary or fresh sage to baste on a turkey or chicken before roasting. Use grapeseed oil flavored with dill to sauté red snapper or salmon fish cakes. Try olive oil flavored with fresh basil lightly drizzled over your next homemade pizza, before baking. Chicken sautéed in olive oil flavored with fresh tarragon gives a wonderful flavor to the chicken. If you are adding garlic to the oil, it is best to soak the garlic in vinegar overnight, drain it, and then add it to the oil. Flavored oils are fun to experiment with and they look beautiful in clear fancy bottles to give as gifts.

© Burke/Triolo

# PART TWO

COUNTRY

# FLOWERS AND GARDENS

GROWING AND USING FLOWERS, HERBS, AND VEGETABLES

BARBARA RANDOLPH

# THE COUNTRY GARDEN

Every country garden has a special feeling, a freedom and exuberance, whether it grows old roses and delphinium, herbs and vegetables, or cutting flowers and ornamental grasses. A country garden isn't pretentious, clipped into fussy hedges, or arranged formally into elaborately shaped beds. And yet some of the world's loveliest country gardens sit in sculptured terraces among the manicured lawns of stately English homes. Within these more formal settings, each bed has the space and freedom that characterize a country garden.

There is no single feature that distinguishes a country garden from all others. It isn't its size, setting, or location. A country garden can flourish in a very small space or a very large one.

A country garden looks as if it had always grown there. It feels part of its surroundings—the buildings, the stone walls, the forests, the landscape, the scenery. Not only is it a delight to look at, it is intended for use: It can be strolled through, or cut and brought indoors for a quick bouquet, or snipped as garnish for a sandwich or a glass of lemonade.

In the pages that follow, you'll find gardens for a variety of settings and climates and suggestions for making these plantings work in a good many other environments as well. You can adapt and combine ideas to suit your own taste; you can create a country garden that is uniquely yours. The country gardener who is sensitive to the land will be rewarded with a beautiful landscape.

# PLANNING A GARDEN

**B**efore deciding where to put your garden, you must understand the basic needs of the plants that will grow there. Most garden plants need sunlight and moisture. While some flowers will tolerate shade—and a few woodland flowers thrive in it—nearly all do better with direct sunlight for at least a few hours a day. Choosing the sunniest site for your garden allows you more options in both flowers and vegetables. If the only space available is in the shade, you have two options: You can make the best of it by growing plants suited to that environment, or you can clear the surrounding land of trees to admit more sun.

Although plants need moisture to thrive, very few do well in soggy soil. Avoid marshy areas or low places where water habitually gathers and stays. Plants need water, but most also need good drainage.

When planning which perennial flowers to grow, consider each one's height, since taller plants will often shade lower ones and inhibit their growth. Some plants multiply so quickly that they choke out less vigorous neighbors.

If you are fairly new at gardening, you will most probably be tempted to try to grow everything at once. Each plant you see or smell or read about will interest you, and it may seem impossible to narrow your selection to just a few. It is even harder to choose if you have visited a few well-established gardens and seen how lovely they look with their full clumps and abundant cascades.

The first rule of thumb to remember is that most perennials take a season or two, or even more, to spread into those nicely shaped clumps and mounds. The second is that plants can be moved. Instead of planning a half-acre flower garden, begin with a small layout and alternate spreading perennials with annuals and biennials so there is room for growth but still a good variety of plants.

The same is true for a vegetable plot. Begin small, and don't feel that you must plant every seed in the packet. It is better to have a few plants of each variety than to wear yourself out trying to take care of more than you can handle.

# PREPARING THE SOIL

Although sometimes skipped over by hasty gardeners, proper soil preparation is very important to the success of a garden.

Unless you are working in an established garden plot, you will need to remove all grasses, weeds, roots, seedlings, and other growing things from the soil. If you are planting a garden where grass has grown, do *not* rototill the lawn into the soil. Instead, remove the turf (grass and roots) in squares cut with the sharp edge of a spade. By removing the entire growing layer, you prevent existing roots from filling your garden with persistent grass. (You can use the cut blocks of turf to replace a section of poor lawn elsewhere; keep well watered until the turf is established.) To prevent the surrounding lawn from reinvading the plot, use an edging of metal or plastic. Simply push it into the soil along the edges of the bed. Its top should be even with the soil, so it doesn't show.

Once your garden bed is protected from encroachment, prepare the soil by digging it up and loosening it to a depth of six to eight inches. This is easy to do with a spade or a fork. As you work, remove any roots or runners that might remain, and dig out any deep-rooted weeds such as dandelion or chicory (both respected salad greens, but probably unwelcome in your new garden!). Remove rocks, and if your soil is sandy or heavy clay, work in some well-composted manure or other organic material. The ideal soil for most plants contains enough sand for good drainage, but enough organic matter to hold moisture, nutrients, and air.

The ideal soil texture is crumbly and slightly granular, with spaces between the soil particles and the tiny bits of organic matter. When you squeeze a handful of good soil, it neither compacts into modeling clay consistency nor runs in a fine stream like sand through your fingers.

The nutrient content of your soil can be determined by a soil test done by your county extension office. The test will tell if your soil is low in any of the three main nutrients (nitrogen, phosphorous, potassium). You can add any of the missing nutrients through a fertilizer rich in those elements. Testing will also tell you the pH balance. The pH can be adjusted by digging in wood ashes (alkaline) or peat moss (acid) around the individual plants.

A little time and energy spent on the soil will repay you amply during many years of gardening. Healthy, weed-free soil not only produces better plants, but it resists disease and new weed growth. Free of underground runners of weed grasses, your soil will grow only those weeds whose seeds land on top of it. These are easy to remove as tiny seedlings.

Most beginning gardeners use perennial plants purchased from nurseries or shared by friends. Although perennials can be raised from seed, they are very slow to establish and often take two years before they are more than spindly, single-stemmed specimens. Save your windowsill space for the seedlings of annual plants.

When purchasing nursery plants, look for those that are healthy and field-grown, if possible. These will be in large pots and have well-developed roots. While smaller greenhouse plants may also do well, field-hardy plants are more suited to the rigors of outdoor life. Some nurseries simply take a shovel into the garden and dig you a clump, while others have pots of field-grown plants already dug up. Either type is ready to plant immediately; freshly dug plants must be replanted at once, before the newly bared rootlets dry out.

When buying tender perennials—those that have been propagated in the greenhouse—look for sturdy plants with strong stems and branches and good root growth. A very gentle tug on the stem right above the soil line will tell you if they have just been potted or if they have a good, developed root system. The risk of losing newly potted plants is much higher, and although you may be willing to try your luck with one in order to obtain a rare variety, you should be prepared to give it special care.

Tender greenhouse plants will need to "harden off" for about a week before they are planted outside. Water them well and set them outdoors for about two hours in the late afternoon, extending the time for about an hour each day for two or three days, then by two hours a day. Bring them in at night for the first week, then leave them out, still potted, for two nights before transplanting to the garden. Be sure to check them for water on hot, sunny, or windy days; the pots hold very little moisture and the plants shouldn't be allowed to dry out. If it's windy, set the plants in a protected place until they have developed strong stems that won't get damaged.

When the plants have become used to outdoor life, dig holes in the garden about twice the depth and diameter of the pot and mix in some rich humus or potting soil. Fill the hole with water to which you have added a small amount of liquid fertilizer. Stir this rich mud well and make a depression in its center large enough for the roots of your new plant. If it has become pot-bound, tap the pot to loosen its roots slightly, holding the plant over the hole so any loose potting soil will fall in.

The best time to transplant is on a cloudy, fairly warm day, when plants will suffer the least shock. On a sunny day, transplant late in the afternoon or very early in the morning. Check the plants during the hottest part of the first few days, giving them a little shade if necessary.

## STARTING ANNUALS FROM SEED

If you have a sunny window or a glassed-in porch on the sunny side of the house, you might enjoy growing at least some of your annual plants from seed.

Start the seeds in long plastic trays divided into inch-wide rows, and set in deeper solid plastic trays that hold water. Or, if you are starting only a few plants, use individual peat pots or small flowerpots. Use a sterile starting medium—such as Jiffy-Mix—that is fine and light in texture and can hold necessary moisture without becoming soggy and drowning tiny sprouts. A fine-grained starter mix also makes it easier to separate the tender roots and move them to individual pots later.

Pour the dry soil mix into the long trays, filling each to within one-quarter inch of the top. Shake the trays gently to settle, but not pack, the mix, then add more if needed. Tap the seeds gently onto the soil, trying to avoid clumping, and spread with your fingers until there are about eight to

Separate pots allow each seedling to grow without interference from others.

ten to the inch or three or four to a pot. Some seeds are so tiny, it is almost impossible to get them evenly spread, so don't fuss.

To meet the lighting needs of each type of plant—read the packets carefully to learn what these are—cover the seeds with as much as one-half inch of starter mix. Set the seed trays into solid trays half-filled with lukewarm water. Be sure to label each section so you can tell the seedlings apart when they sprout. Set the trays in a warm place where they will get as much sun as possible.

When the seedlings are about one inch tall, transfer them to individual pots, carefully separating the roots. Put two or three in each pot, unless the seeds are very precious or the germination is poor. In these instances, it is better to use a single pot for a weak seedling than to lose a possible plant. When plants are well started and have developed true leaves, cut off all but the strongest plant in each pot, clipping with scissors instead of pulling, to avoid disturbing the roots of the remaining plant.

By the time they are well established in individual pots, these annuals may be hardened off and planted into the garden whenever the weather conditions are right, just as you would purchased plants.

Once plants are established in the garden, they are quite easy to care for. Weeds can be removed easily if they are pulled before they have a chance to develop deep roots.

# PROTECTING PLANTS
# IN WINTER

Many perennials die back to ground level each winter, springing up again the following year with no particular effort on your part. But others, such as lavender, retain woody growth over the winter, and form new leaves on these existing plants in the spring. If left untrimmed, woody stems are likely to form new spring growth at their outer tips, leaving bare, straggly center stems. These plants should be pruned back in the fall, but not so far back as to remove all the leaves, which continue to support the plant until it is completely dormant.

Black plastic helps keep rows weed-free during the growing season, but should not be used as winter mulch.

The root systems of such plants are fairly fragile, and the alternate freezing and thawing of the ground breaks the tiny root hairs that channel nourishment and moisture to the plant in the spring. To prevent root damage, mulch woody plants lightly with a layer of pine boughs or salt hay or straw once the ground has frozen. (Don't use stable straw; the last thing your plants need as they enter winter is a high-nitrogen fertilizer.) Leaves are not a good mulch, since they pack down and hold too much moisture, which can damage the roots. Some gardeners fear that pine needles will add acidity to the soil, but this is not the case. Pine trees thrive in acid soil and tend to grow there, but they do not make the soil acidic with their needles. In any event, the branches will be removed, and the ground raked in the spring before the needles will have a chance to compost into the soil.

Before the vegetation on nonwoody perennials dies back to the ground, mark their locations with sticks or other durable markers. Markers will help you avoid digging up the plants by mistake in the spring as you clean out the beds for early planting.

In the spring, remove the mulch from woody perennials as the ground begins to thaw—about the time the first tulip leaves emerge. Clean up the perennial beds and tidy up any unwanted spreading growth in preparation for the new season.

While annual plants do not need winter protection, they do need some attention before they are left for the winter. As plants stop producing or are blackened by frost, pull them up by the roots. Remove these dead plants from the garden so that any disease or hardy insect will not be able to lie in wait for next year's crops.

## COPING WITH DROUGHT

1. Use a soaker hose to water slowly and deeply directly into the soil. Sprinklers may cover a broader area at one time, but a great deal of their water is lost to evaporation in the air and on plant foliage. Spraying also waters the area between rows and encourages weeds to grow, taking precious water away from plants.

2. Mulch with organic material, such as straw or shredded bark, to keep moisture in the soil. Black plastic holds in water, but it also holds in heat, which may damage roots if severe drought accompanies a heat wave.

3. Use shade netting to protect plants from direct sun. While plants need sunlight for growth, scorching sun causes them to shrivel and use up more water. By shading lightly during the hottest part of the day, you can prevent this trauma and allow the plants to make more efficient use of the moisture they have.

4. Protect plants from the drying effects of wind with netting or windbreaks. A windbreak can be as simple as brush piled against the garden fence on the side of the prevailing wind.

5. Water plants in the evening, especially if you must use a spray system, to prevent evaporation and to cut down the shock of cold water on hot, sun-drenched plants.

6. Water plants thoroughly twice a week, instead of daily. Water will have a chance to soak downward into the root area where it's needed. Shallow watering encourages roots to grow upward in search of surface water and subjects them to even more damage when the ground dries out.

7. Water the most precious and the least drought-resistant plants first. Lawns, especially established ones, can withstand a dry year; they may turn brown but will not be lost. Juicy vegetables, such as cucumbers, tomatoes, and melons, need the most water. Root vegetables are able to go deeper into the soil for moisture.

8. Use water from the bathtub for watering the garden. If you are recycling bathwater, be sure not to use bath oils or bubble bath products. A little soap, however, is actually good for plants by keeping soft-bodied insects off the leaves.

9. If you must set out new plants during a drought, do so in the evening and mix plenty of organic material into the soil to retain moisture.

© Joanne Pavia

# A VEGETABLE GARDEN

To anyone who loves good food, there is no substitute for fresh-picked produce. The green beans are snappier, the tomatoes sweeter, the corn more tender. The vegetable gardener can, moreover, choose varieties on the basis of flavor, not how well they ship or how long they stay looking fresh on the grocer's shelf. There are no special secrets to a vegetable garden, but if you follow a few general practices, you can help it to grow better and faster. Begin by planting only as much as you can handle. A small, well-tended garden will produce more than a larger garden gone to neglect.

Clearing land of weeds and roots before you plant makes a garden much easier to keep weed-free later. If your soil is sandy, enrich it with compost or other organic material and dig it in well. Be sure you have a source of water if summer drought is a problem. Fence your garden if it is close to the woods or in a wild area. Mowing a wide swath around it will also help discourage small animals from marauding it while you sleep.

Planting times vary with each climate and terrain; the best way to find out when to plant different vegetables in your area is to ask a gardening neighbor or your local county extension office. In general, root crops, peas, and early greens are planted as soon as the ground can be worked. Squash, cucumber, and other fast-growing but frost-sensitive vegetables are planted about two weeks before the last expected frost. Vegetables started indoors or in greenhouses are set out into the garden only after the danger of frost is past. In southern and central states, many vegetables can be planted directly in the garden, while in the North those same vegetables must be started indoors in order to mature during the short growing season.

Most gardeners prefer to plant in a traditional pattern of rows. Sometimes two rows are planted quite close with a wider space between each pair of rows. Double rows use space more efficiently, but still allow the gardener enough room to reach the plants easily. They work well for medium-sized compact plants such as peppers, broccoli, and green beans. Crops such as carrots, beets, radishes, and loose salad greens work well in wide rows, where seeds are scattered in an area about twelve inches wide. As plants sprout, they can be thinned to the distance directed on the seed package.

For most of us, the reward of gardening is in the harvest. To make the best of all the work, it is important to know just when to pick each vegetable. Bigger isn't always better, and most vegetables are the most tender, sweet, and delicious when they are picked quite small. There is no comparison, for example, between a succulent, tender zucchini, hardly larger than your thumb, and the tough, tasteless baseball bats of a week or so later.

Leaf lettuces provide one of the garden's earliest crops in the spring.

**A full basket of greens and vegetables fresh from the garden is the reward of a summer's work.**

Peas should be picked when they are firm and round inside, but while the pods are still firm and deep green. As the pod matures, the peas lose their flavor as well as their tender texture. Green beans are tender and flavorful while pencil-sized and should barely begin to show the bumps of the seeds inside.

You will soon begin to recognize each vegetable at its own peak of perfection. Picking young vegetables encourages new ones to grow, whereas leaving them on the vine to mature causes the plant to stop producing. Use or refrigerate vegetables soon after picking to retain flavor and nutrients.

# VEGETABLES TO GROW

**BROCCOLI** grows well in the North, yielding an especially abundant harvest if you choose varieties that produce secondary side shoots after the main head has been picked. Be sure to harvest while the florets are tight and deep green, before they have overbloomed.

**CARROTS** have the advantage of a long harvest. Plant seeds a few inches apart, directly in the garden, early in the spring. Harvest sweet baby carrots early, large carrots in the fall.

**CHINESE GREENS** are among the special joys of a home garden, since many varieties are hard to find. These "cut and come again" vegetables continue to produce from a few plants. They vary from mildly aromatic to quite pungent. Most do best in the cooler weather of spring and fall and should be harvested before they are overgrown, since most bolt (go to seed) quite quickly.

**CHINESE PEAS** are grown for the whole pods, which can be eaten raw or stir-fried. The dwarf varieties are best for munching raw, while mammoth varieties freeze well. Like English peas, these need to be planted early and harvested daily.

**CORN** tastes dramatically different when eaten fresh from the garden. In New England, there's an old saying that you don't pick the corn until the pot's boiling. But corn does require space and is not the right crop for a little kitchen garden. Plant it in a block of several short rows, side by side instead of one long row.

**CUCUMBERS** can be planted directly in the garden or started indoors for earlier yield. The vines grow quickly and need plenty of space to ramble. Choose slicing varieties for salads and sliced pickles, smaller pickling varieties for dills and gherkins. Cucumbers need a lot of water and should be picked before they become fat or even slightly yellow. To water cucumbers in a dry climate, plant them around a gallon plastic milk jug that is pierced with holes. Leave the neck of the jug above ground and fill it daily from the garden hose. The water seeps into the ground, giving the roots the moisture they need to produce high-quality cucumbers.

**ENGLISH PEAS** are easy to grow, especially in the North. Plant them very early so they can mature before the hot weather sets in. They need a wire fence to climb on and should be harvested daily since they become overgrown very quickly. Among the first vegetables to harvest, English peas are also among the easiest and most reliable to freeze.

**PEPPERS** come in such an enormous variety of sizes, colors, and flavors that it would be possible to plant a whole row with no two the same. All have similar growth habits. Peppers need warmth in order to blossom, so a mulch of black plastic is a good idea in the North. Lay a plastic sheet along the row, bury its edges, and cut holes for plants about a foot apart. Peppers do best if the leaves of neighboring plants are touching slightly. They are usually started indoors or purchased from nurseries to give a longer growing season.

**PUMPKINS** are great for the gardener with lots of room. No crop will bring you more friends among the neighborhood children than a patch of glowing orange pumpkins. Plant large varieties for jack-o'-lanterns and sweet small pumpkins for pies. Be prepared to give the sprawling vines a lot of space, or plant the new bush varieties.

**RADISHES,** either the round red ones or the peppery white icicle varieties, enliven salad and relish trays. Easy to grow and early to harvest, a continuous crop is easily maintained if you drop a seed in the hole each time you pick a radish. Don't plant too many at once.

**SNAP BEANS** come in green, wax, or purple varieties (the latter turn green when cooked). Pole, or climbing, beans take up less garden space and are easier to harvest, but bush beans survive early fall frosts better. Choose stringless varieties and pick beans when they are still very small and tender.

**TOMATOES** are everyone's favorite fresh garden vegetables, perhaps because the difference between fresh-picked and shipped tomatoes is so obvious. Choose round varieties for eating, plum or Italian types for sauces. Be sure they have plenty of fertilizer, and keep them well watered. Tomatoes are usually started indoors or bought as nursery plants for longer yield.

## OLD-FASHIONED VEGETABLES

While vegetables may not go out of style as fast as rock groups and hemlines, they are still subject to the whims of fashion. Grocers' shelves are full of a wide variety our grandparents never saw, but our grandparents grew and loved a number of vegetables that are rarely found today in supermarkets *or* gardens. Fortunately, many of the seeds for old-fashioned varieties are still available, although they are sometimes hard to find.

Some of these forgotten vegetables are among the easiest to grow. Kohlrabi is a good example. Once a staple of New England gardens, it is now a curiosity when found on the "gourmet" vegetable shelf. How our great grandmothers

Winter squash varieties can be harvested late in the fall and stored for several months.

would laugh to see it there! Kohlrabi is a member of the cabbage family, whose main stem enlarges into a bulb just above the ground. Its leaves stick out all over it on short stems, and it looks like no other vegetable on earth. It is planted early in the spring and is best sown at one week intervals to provide a continuous crop. Kohlrabi grows fairly quickly in cold weather. Thin to about four inches apart when the plants are about three inches tall; you can use the thinnings sliced raw in salads or stir-fried.

Harvest kohlrabis when they are about the size of golf balls, and boil them whole and unpeeled. The top leaves can be added at the last minute. Let a few grow until they are about three inches in diameter and hollow out the centers using a melon baller. Parboil them a few minutes and stuff with ground pork or veal that has been sautéed and mixed with some bread crumbs, a little thyme, and an egg. Bake them until they are tender but not mushy.

Swiss chard and kale should be in every beginner's garden, just because they are so encouraging. They grow quickly and abundantly and look so nice in the garden that they give the novice a great sense of success. Neither one goes to seed, and one planting will provide results all summer. Simply keep harvesting the outer stalks of chard and the bottom leaves of kale.

Try cooking chard as the Swiss do, separating the stalks and leaves. Boil or steam the stalks and serve in a light cream sauce. Steam the chopped leaves and serve as a separate dish with a touch of butter and a dash of vinegar. Kale can also be used all summer, either as a cooked green or cut into thin strips to add color, flavor, and nutrients to soups. Its flavor improves after the first heavy frost. When the rest of the garden is a memory, it is still deep green and delicious. That's the time to make a hearty soup of kale with beef broth, potatoes, onions, and sliced smoked sausage.

Salsify is so nearly forgotten that few garden books even mention it. Sow it early in the spring and thin to seven or eight inches apart when it is about three inches tall. It will withstand drought and is shunned by pests, so your crop has a good chance of making it to harvest in October. Dig up the roots, scrape them, and boil in water to which a

© Joanne Pavia

**Kohlrabi should be harvested when it is no larger than a golf ball.**

little vinegar has been added. A favorite way of serving salsify was baked in a casserole mixed with bread crumbs and butter; or they were parboiled, then rolled in egg and bread crumbs before deep frying. In either case, they were so often described as tasting like oysters that they were known as "vegetable oysters."

Parsnips must be the world's most misunderstood vegetables. They would never have gone out of style if everyone had kept picking them fresh from the garden. The woody, tasteless remnants of them that are found in the grocery store are a sorry substitute for their sweet tender fresh roots.

Parsnips require patience to grow, since they are not harvested until they have spent the winter frozen under the snow. Prepare the soil as deep as you would for carrots and plant the seeds in April. Plant thickly and use all the seeds, since germination is often poor and the seeds won't keep until next year. Thin to about four inches apart. Be sure to avoid the plants if you plow in the fall; dig them as soon as the ground thaws in the spring. Slice and boil or stir-fry with a slice of gingerroot, and serve with plenty of butter.

The Jerusalem artichoke—also called the "sunchoke"—is really a perennial sunflower. It resembles a small, lumpy potato and has a crispy texture that is not lost with cooking Don't plant it in your flower bed, even though its yellow flowers are very attractive, since it will take over very quickly. Plant it alongside the barn or a shed, where its tall stems will have some support. Plant in the spring and you should be able to dig a few the first fall. They don't store well, so dig only what you need for a few days at a time. Always leave enough to keep the bed growing. Slice the roots raw in salads, boil whole, or roast with lamb, pork, or beef.

**The Jerusalem artichoke is a member of the sunflower family.**

## ZUCCHINI SURPLUS? NIP IT IN THE BUD

If you wonder how to stem the tide of zucchini that floods your garden from only a few plants, you can literally nip it in the bud! The blossoms are a delicious vegetable in their own right, providing you with innovative dinners and a clear conscience.

The American Indians were probably the first to try the flowers as food; the Zuni of the Southwest fried them separately and also used them to flavor other dishes. Although they are now a great favorite in the cuisines of many European countries, the squash is an indigenous American vegetable.

To harvest the blossoms, clip them with scissors just as they are about to open. Although the male blossoms (those with the long thin stems) are larger and easier to use for some dishes, the female blossoms (the ones with little squashes beginning to form at the base) are just as tasty. If zucchini population control is not your purpose, use the male blossoms. If you use female blossoms, clip out the pistil in the center of the flower and clip the stems as close as possible on all blossoms.

If you don't plan to use the blossoms immediately, place them in a plastic bag and seal it closed, including a lot of air space, like a balloon. The air cushion will protect the blossoms in the refrigerator. Wash them very carefully just before you use them and drain on paper towels. They are very fragile, so it is best not to pile them in layers when you harvest or put them in storage.

Stuffed squash blossoms are a good main dish, and are a perfect use for leftover chicken, ham, or any other meat. Add a few slivers of salami or pepperoni for extra flavor.

© Lynn Karlin

# A FRAGRANT GARDEN

Planting a garden especially for fragrance was a popular pastime of Victorians, a delightful custom that deserves revival. In an olitory (the name for such a garden), plants should be placed within easy reach, since many release their fragrance only when the foliage is brushed against or moved to activate the fragrant oils. Such a garden could be used as a border atop a retaining wall or terrace, where it would be easy to bury your nose in the plants without bending over.

A potpourri garden of scented herbs could have an old-fashioned June-blooming rosebush in the center, or a central bed could be circular and planted to look like a nosegay or tussy-mussy. Tufts of clove pink bordered in white-edged silver thyme will give the appearance of lace surrounding rosebuds. Sweet and spicy plants such as rosemary, lemon verbena, scented geraniums, mints, lemon grass, lemon balm, lavender, chamomile, and bay make fragrant additions to this garden.

Try to make room for a bench where you can pause for a moment to enjoy the aromas. Such a scented corner might be set against a banking, with fragrant flowers growing at nose level behind the bench or roses planted at each end of it. A sweet-smelling shrub, such as mock orange or an arbor behind or over the bench, could offer some shade.

In choosing plants, look for a variety of scents, not just the sweet heavy ones. Lemon verbena and lavender are invigorating, while lemon balm and chamomile are soothing. Plant chamomile and woolly thyme between the paving stones. Clove pinks add a spicy fragrance, and scented geraniums can be set in pots that can be brought indoors for winter.

© Jerry Pavia

Fragrant plants lining a walkway release their scent whenever someone brushes past them.

Although a scented garden, especially if it is planted atop a wall, can be a simple border, you can also use a more formal plan. If you have a bench at one end, you could use a very old design called a "goosefoot." Actually, it looks more like a fan, with a series of wedge-shaped beds radiating from a single point to form a semicircle. This same design is also good for a garden that lies with one side against a wall or arbor.

A circle within a square is an attractive arrangement. Beds are laid out much as in the simple square herb garden but the center is a circular bed with a path around it. This center bed gives you the luxury of a showy focal point. Tall plants such as beebalm could be grown there, or a large pot of bay or rosemary could be placed there and taken indoors in the winter. In kinder climates, where these plants winter over outdoors, they can be planted directly in the ground.

Another good place for an olitory is on either side of a front walk as a simple border. Guests are greeted with fragrance as they walk along the path to the front door.

# FRAGRANT PLANTS TO GROW

**CHAMOMILE** is hardy enough in a moist climate to be grown as a lawn. Once established, it can be mowed in paths in a fragrant garden or be used to cover a bench bordered in stones.

**CLOVE PINKS** are the gillyflowers of Elizabethan times. These pink blossoms are the ancestors of the carnation, but much more fragrant. While it is difficult to find these—they have been replaced by the less fragrant dianthus varieties—they are well worth looking for.

**CORSICAN MINT** grows so close to the ground that it can be planted between paving stones. Its strong peppermint aroma is released in the air whenever someone walks on the stones.

**HELIOTROPE** is a low-growing annual with a sweet scent that pervades the air whenever it blooms. Since many of the fragrant plants have no blossoms or bloom for only a short time, heliotrope adds a welcome touch of color with its pink blossoms.

**LAVENDER** is a stately plant with gray foliage and intensely perfumed spikes of purple blossoms. It is a fairly hardy perennial.

**LEMON BALM** is a low-growing perennial of the mint family. Although its leaves do not retain their fragrance when dried, lemon balm is well worth planting for the intense aroma of its leaves in the garden and its tidy growing habits.

**LEMON BASIL** has much smaller leaves than regular basil, and the plants are smaller as well. It has an invigorating scent that combines lemon with the tang of basil.

**LEMON THYME** is a variety of the common culinary herb, and it is also used in the kitchen. Less hardy than other thymes, it has the same compact growth and tiny leaves.

**LEMON VERBENA** has the only true lemon scent that remains when the leaves are dried. In a potpourri, it smells more like lemon than dried lemon peel. Although it will not survive a northern winter, it grows quickly and is worth replacing each year.

**MIGNONETTE** is a low-growing annual whose flowers are modest to look at, but extravagant in their fragrance. Its sweet, musky scent was popular in Victorian days.

**MINTS** of several varieties provide scent both in the garden and dried for potpourri and teas. Although spearmint is difficult to contain, it can be grown in a tub that is submerged to the rim in the ground. Or grow the intensely fragrant orange and eau de cologne varieties, both of which are slower to spread.

**SCENTED GERANIUM** plants come in a variety of fragrances, from a rich true rose to spicy cinnamon, ginger, and nutmeg varieties. Lemon is a particularly aromatic type that keeps its scent well when dried. These plants cannot be left outdoors for the winter, except in warm climates, but they make excellent houseplants.

## ROSES

Hybrid roses are larger than the old-fashioned June-blooming varieties and keep better in cut arrangements. But breeding to develop these qualities has taken its toll on their fragrance—or at least on its durability. While they are fresh, many hybrid roses are still strongly scented, and that sweet aroma will waft through your garden throughout the summer if you keep the faded blossoms clipped off.

You will, however, also want old-fashioned roses, the kind that grow wild along old stone walls on country roads.

It is for their fragrance when dried that the old rose varieties are most treasured. The aromas of *Rosa gallica, R. eglanteria, R. damascena,* and *R. canina* linger strongly when dried, and they are the preferred varieties as the base for potpourris. The colors remain, too, but will fade if the dried blossoms are exposed to sunlight.

Pick rosebuds to dry while they are still tightly closed and spread them on screens in a shady, airy place. For petals, pick when the rose is just fully opened, but before blossoms begin to shatter.

© Lynn Karlin

**Roses are everyone's favorite scented flower.**

If the roses are not picked, most varieties will "bloom" again in the fall with a crop of scarlet rose hips, full of vitamin C and tangy flavor. Rose hips can be snipped off as soon as they turn red and used fresh to make jelly or syrup. Dried and steeped, they make a favorite pick-me-up tea.

The fragrance of the old roses can lend an incomparable flavor to foods. Use fresh rose petals in fruit compotes, or sprinkle them in the bottom of a pan before pouring in white cake batter. Spread a layer of petals in an apple pie before adding the top crust for a flavor combination discovered by the Shakers. Rose sugar for tea and baking is easy to make by layering white sugar and rose petals in a jar and leaving it sealed for a few weeks. If the moisture of the petals makes the sugar lumpy, break it up in a blender.

Roses are easy to grow, and the better nurseries, such as Jackson and Perkins Co., send complete care instructions with each bush shipped. In the North, hybrid roses may need some winter protection, such as a cap to shield them from the alternate freezing and thawing that breaks tiny root ends.

## POTPOURRI

You will need to save and dry fragrant flowers, herbs, and leaves for your potpourri as they come into bloom. Nearly any flower or leaf can be a part of potpourri if it is attractive when dried. Along with those for fragrance, you will want colorful blossoms and larger blooms, whose main purpose is to create air spaces for the scents.

Plants with long stems can be tied into bundles and hung upside down in an airy, shady place. Hanging them inside a paper bag, as you would with herbs, will keep them clean and prevent losing little pieces. Since you won't need the stems in your potpourri, you can also dry single blossoms by laying them on a screen in a shady place until they are crisp. Store all dried flowers or herbs in bags or jars.

In some potpourris, you can add kitchen ingredients such as cinnamon sticks, whole cloves, and whole allspice. Be

**Rose hips may be used fresh or dried for a tangy tea.**

© Emily Johnson/Envision

sure to save all your orange, lemon, lime, and tangerine peels. Cut them into strips and dry to add a citrus touch to floral potpourris.

The scent of a potpourri blend is not the only consideration. Color is important in a blend that will be displayed in a glass or open container. Include plenty of bright blossoms just for their good looks. Bulk, as well as color, is provided by larger whole flowers, such as zinnias, marigolds, celosia, strawflowers, globe amaranth, delphinium, and statice. Some flowers, such as whole roses, provide color, bulk, *and* fragrance.

When the potpourri smells and looks right, its fragrance must be preserved and strengthened. Orris, the dried root of the *Iris florentina*, is the best fixative. It has no scent of its own but helps preserve others. Be sure to purchase orrisroot chips, not powder, which will give your potpourri a dusty look.

Drying evaporates some of the fragrant oils in flowers, but these can be replaced by essential oils. Rose is the most versatile of these oils and blends well with nearly any other scent. Lavender is the strongest and tends to predominate others. Bay, cedar, orange, lemon, gardenia, and carnation are also good additions, but since good oils are quite expensive, it is best to begin with one or two and add more if you find you enjoy the hobby. Be sure you are buying true oils, not artificial ones labeled "potpourri fragrance" or "refresher oil."

Mix your ingredients in whatever quantity you have or like, adding one or two tablespoons of orrisroot per pint. Mix the oil and orrisroot together first and then add to the flowers. Depending on the intended use for the potpourri, use four to eight drops of oil per pint of flowers. Stir or shake well and seal in a jar with plenty of air space. Shake or stir it daily for two weeks to allow it to blend and ripen.

Display potpourri in a jar or dish with a cover so it can be kept closed as many hours a day as it is open. Try to keep the blend out of the sun, which will fade both color and scent. If the fragrance does fade, simply treat it as you would a brand-new mix—add orrisroot and oil and let it blend in a large jar for two weeks.

While recipes aren't necessary—you can mix nearly any fragrant flowers and leaves for a potpourri—beginners may appreciate a few ideas to try. Add whatever else you have, leave out what you don't have, and keep experimenting to come up with blends that are entirely yours.

© Melabee Miller/Envision

**Even the tiniest sprigs pruned from fragrant plants may be dried for potpourri.**

Small fabric bags can be filled with potpourri and used to scent closets and bureau drawers.

### LAVENDER POTPOURRI

1 cup lavender flowers

½ cup roses

½ cup blue and white flowers

1 tablespoon lemon peel

2 tablespoons orrisroot chips

4 to 6 drops lavender oil

### SUMMER GARDEN POTPOURRI

1 cup rose petals or buds

½ cup lavender flowers

½ cup lemon verbena

½ cup mint

½ cup scented geranium leaves

½ cup pink or white globe amaranth blossoms

½ cup blue statice

3 tablespoons orrisroot chips

6 drops rose oil

2 drops lavender oil

### ROSE GARDEN POTPOURRI

1 cup fragrant roses

1 cup mixed pink flowers

¼ cup rosemary

¼ cup broken cinnamon stick

1 tablespoon whole cloves

½ cup broken bay leaves

3 tablespoons orrisroot chips

6 to 8 drops rose oil

© Lynn Karlin

# THE PERENNIAL BORDER

**B**order gardens are a favorite showcase for larger perennial flowers. They have several practical advantages as well: They are easy to reach and keep up, they change with the seasons, and they can often be used to hide a foundation or wall.

Flower borders can accent a building or diminish it, outline a vegetable garden or a terrace, border a walk or driveway. They are beautiful beside a stone wall or lend a graceful crown to a retaining wall. If they have a fence, wall, and building as a backdrop, they are planted tall in back and short in front. By staggering the plants, you can keep them from looking like soldiers lined up in formation. If they stand free, bordering a drive or walkway, they are planted like the letter "A"—tall along the center and tapering toward the edges. Those gardeners with a flair for design will enjoy placing plants to provide contrasting colors of foliage as well as bloom. Others will choose the English dooryard garden style of exuberant abandon.

By alternating perennials with annuals and biennials, you can plan a first-year garden that is full and attractive, even though most perennials take at least a year to begin blooming and to fill out into lush clumps. Even after the larger plants have become established, you may wish to add some annuals for bright splashes of color and because they bloom for a longer period.

Spreading or very bushy plants are not the best choice for borders. Tall delphinium, foxglove, hollyhocks, shasta daisies, and phlox are best in the background, while pinks, zinnias, cornflowers, and calendula fill the center. Nasturtiums, French marigolds, sweet William, and silver mound artemisia often line the front in compact mounds that hide the stems of plants behind them.

The ends of a border can present opportunities as well as challenges. They are the place for large bushy plants such as baby's breath, as well as spreading clumps of daylilies.

While balancing the size and growing habits of the flowers, you also need to remember the seasonal nature of perennials. Each has its own cycle and its own timetable. The first spring blossoms are bulbs—crocuses that can grow right in your lawn and be mowed over later; tulips, whose foliage dies back in time to be covered with annual beds; and daffodils, whose clumps of narrow leaves can be braided and tucked under the foliage of later perennials.

Along with the flowering bulbs come the dainty violets and pasqueflowers. These are followed by irises, thrift, primroses, mallows, and yellow globe flowers, then by poppies, delphinium, foxglove, and achillea. Careful gardeners will also want to include some that continue to bloom through the fall—coreopsis, golden marguerite, coralbells, and basket flower.

## GROWING PERENNIALS

Perennials develop more slowly than annuals, rarely flowering the first year. Once established, however, they bloom year after year, often expanding into showy clumps. They are usually started from plants, frequently taken from well-developed clumps by dividing the roots. It is important to know how quickly plants spread so you will know how much room to leave between them. Smaller plants set between newly planted larger ones can be moved to new locations as the larger plants spread.

Perennials usually bloom for a shorter period than annuals, so choose those which will flower at different times to keep a continuous succession of bloom. Don't forget to include flowering shrubs such as forsythia and azalea in your garden plan.

The soil should be free of weeds and grass and dug deeply for perennials, since their growth depends on a deep, sturdy

Hollyhocks are tall plants—a favorite choice in cottage gardens.

root system. If the soil is sandy, add some organic material to help it retain moisture. Perennials will last for many years, so the time you spend now will save you time in caring for them later.

## BORDER FLOWERS

**BABY'S BREATH** This perennial is white or pink with a cloud of tiny blossoms on a bushy mound. The plant usually grows to three feet and thrives in full sun. For drying, pick as soon as most blossoms are fully open and hang in a shaded place.

**BEARDED IRIS** This perennial is grown from rhizomes that should remain partially visible above the soil. The stately iris blooms in all shades from white to deep purple, including mauve and yellow. Blooms may continue for as long as four weeks in early summer.

**DAYLILY** This perennial is easily grown in sun or partial shade. It spreads quickly and is usually about three feet tall. It is very hardy and can be found beside old cellar holes where it has flourished without care for decades. Colors vary from yellow to orange.

© Jerry Pavia

**Iris blooms early in the summer, shortly after the last tulip blossoms have faded.**

**DELPHINIUM** This perennial comes in exquisite blue and purple shades, and grows from three to five feet tall in elegant spikes that may need staking for support. Its short blooming season in early summer can be extended by picking individual blossoms as they begin to fade. If none are allowed to form seeds, delphinium will usually bloom again in the autumn.

**FEVERFEW** A perennial of the chrysanthemum genus, feverfew will bloom the first year if seeds are started early. Clusters of small daisylike flowers on sturdy twelve- to eighteen-inch stems dry well for everlasting arrangements.

**FORGET-ME-NOT** This annual often self-sows in subsequent years. One of the earlier flowers, forget-me-nots will grow in sun or shade but prefer cool weather. They are very neat in the garden, where they are a favorite edging plant. Sow seeds directly in the garden in the fall in warmer climates.

**FORSYTHIA** A blossoming shrub, forsythia offers one of the earliest patches of color in the spring. Plants reproduce quickly from branches pushed into the soil and kept well watered until they take root. After its yellow blossoms have dropped, the forsythia is still an attractive though somewhat sprawling shrub.

**GLOBE FLOWER** This perennial grows in tidy clumps covered with bright yellow blooms. This old-fashioned plant blossoms early in the summer, long before most other yellow flowers. Its clumps may grow to two feet tall. It prefers rich, moist soil and thrives even in conditions of light shade.

**MARIGOLD** This annual is easily grown from seed or purchased plants. The compact mounds are usually about twelve inches tall; colors range from yellows to golden russets. Marigolds thrive in full sun, but they do not require rich soil.

**NASTURTIUM** This is an annual grown from seed planted directly in the garden. The flowers range from pale yellow to deep red, and they bloom best in full sun with sparse watering. Nasturtium does especially well in seaside gardens and grows well in window boxes, where it trails nicely. Dwarf varieties usually grow in twelve-inch mounds.

**ORIENTAL POPPY** This perennial is tall with little foliage. It is one of the showiest and most dramatic of all garden flowers, but its glory is short-lived. A blossom may last only a day or two, so plant in groups for a longer season of color. Difficult to transplant once established, the Oriental poppy is best bought from a nursery where it has been grown in pots.

**PASQUEFLOWER** This perennial is among the earliest to blossom in the spring. Low-growing lavender flowers thrive along rock walls where they get good drainage.

**PINKS** These annual and perennial varieties are related to carnations. Between twelve and eighteen inches tall, they have pale green foliage and bloom in shades of pink, white, and rose. Even the perennial varieties will bloom all summer long if you keep the spent flowers picked.

**SIBERIAN IRIS** This perennial grows in round clumps of tall, graceful leaves. Its bright purple blossoms last well and bloom in midsummer, after bearded irises have faded. About three feet tall, the clumps are best for beds, not borders.

**VIOLET** This perennial spreads by self-sowing. Clumps of violets bloom in white and purple at the same time as daffodils, a very attractive combination, especially along a rock wall.

**YARROW** This is a perennial in bright yellow, red, and deep pink, about three feet tall. Large flat clusters will bloom for several weeks in summer if the heads are kept picked. It is a favorite for dried arrangements if picked and dried just before it reaches its full bloom. Clumps increase to create a showy display in a very few years; it thrives in poor soil.

**YUCCA** This perennial thrives in hot, dry climates but will do well in the North in full sun. Its showy clump of white flowers may grow on a stalk as tall as six feet, but its palmlike foliage is only about two feet in height. A dramatic plant for beds, it's easy to grow and very hardy.

Violets are a welcome early bloom in the spring.

© Lynn Karlin

# A CUTTING GARDEN

**B**right bouquets on the dining room table are one of the great joys of flower gardening. Anyone who grows flowers can enjoy this luxury, of course, but flowers suitable for bouquets are not always in bloom in the perennial border. Low-growing annual flowers such as marigolds and petunias do not work well in large arrangements. And, unless the ornamental beds are in the fullest of their season's finery, many gardeners hesitate to strip them of their bright blossoms in order to decorate the inside of the house.

Some of the best flowers for cutting are not especially beautiful in the garden. This is especially true of the flowers usually classed as everlastings, which can be dried for winter bouquets. Strawflowers grow on tall, rangy plants. Statice blooms in a blaze of glory, but it must be cut at its peak if it is to be dried. The tall silver king artemisia's tendency to spread, while not uncontrollable, makes it a difficult neighbor in a bed of mixed flowers.

The perfect solution to these problems is to plant a garden specifically for cutting. Such gardens are often at one end of the family vegetable garden, adding a colorful accent to the backyard as well. Flowers here are planted in rows, just like vegetables, so they can be watered and cultivated in the same way. With an abundance of annuals and no concern for the aesthetics of their placement in the garden, you'll always have plenty of available blossoms to gather into vases.

Here is the best home for giant zinnias, asters, spikes of blue salvia, and larkspur. This array of blossoms can be mixed with a few stems of perennials from ornamental beds or used by themselves to create arrangements. Those that dry well can be picked at their peak or just before to provide bright color throughout the house all winter. These everlastings are also the perfect addition to herbal wreaths and can be used for a variety of crafts as well as in fragrant potpourri.

Since the cutting garden is planted in rows and is not intended purely for aesthetic enjoyment in the field, the position of the plants doesn't matter. Most of the plants are tall, but you should be aware of the direction of the sun so that the tallest of them (strawflowers and sweet Annie)

will not shade the shorter flowers. Fortunately, the spacing between rows usually solves that problem.

If the cutting garden can be seen from the house and there are no other considerations, plant the lowest-growing annuals, such as salvia, statice, and gomphrena, in the rows nearest the house, the middle-height ones, such as giant zinnia, next, and strawflowers and the towering sweet Annie as a backdrop. This arrangement gives a stunning wall of color at the height of the season, when everything is in bloom at the same time.

Strawflowers are not especially attractive and are sometimes grown in beds alternating with other flowers.

# FLOWERS TO GROW

**ANNUAL STATICE** Second only to the strawflower in popularity, this sturdy annual is available in beautiful shades of blue and purple, as well as pink, white, and yellow. Its stems are quite sturdy and hold their shape when dried upright. Be sure to cut statice just before it reaches full bloom to keep the colors vibrant. Although it can be hung in small bunches, statice crushes easily and is hard to separate when dry. Enjoy it as a cut flower by standing it in wide baskets and letting it dry upright. It will even dry mixed with other fresh flowers in vases of water.

**ARTEMISIA** Silver king and silver queen are tall branching perennials used for their gray-green foliage, which make beautiful bases for herb wreaths. They grow as tall as four feet and spread quickly from underground runners, so they are a good choice for a border along a fence. You can control their spread there and keep them in a perfect straight line by simply pulling up all the new sprouts early in the spring, which is the only time of year when they send out runners. Use these sprouted roots to extend the length of the bed or share them with friends. For wreath making, use artemisia while it is pliable.

**BLUE SALVIA** offers spikes of small blossoms that add variations in shape to flower arrangements. The color holds well when the plants are dried.

**GIANT ZINNIA** is the mainstay of summer bouquets. With plenty of room to branch out (room it seldom gets when used as a border plant), it will produce dozens of large flowers in a tremendous variety of colors. When buying seeds, look for mixed colors so you don't have a whole row of one shade. Smaller zinnias make good cutting flowers, too. Be sure to dry some of the beautiful heads for potpourri, since they keep their color well.

**Plume celosia's brilliant colors add interest to an annual border, or can be grown for cutting and drying.**

**GLOBE AMARANTH** is one of the lesser-known everlastings, with an abundance of blossoms that look like compact clover heads. They come in white, pink, orange, and rich reddish purples. If you pick off the first bloom of small flowers for potpourri, you will be rewarded with a hedge-like mound of large flowers that may be picked immediately or left on the plants for some weeks without deteriorating. Globe amaranth keeps its colors perfectly when dried, and takes up less hanging space if you strip most of the leaves from the long stems.

*LONUS ANNUA* has so many different names that it is best to check for the Latin name on the seed packet. It is quite small, but its heads of bright yellow flowers dry very well and can be wired to longer stems for use in taller dried arrangements. Seeds are not easy to find, but are well worth the search.

**PLUME CELOSIA** These feathery plumes come in a variety of vivid colors ranging from pale cream and yellow to deep russet orange and from pale pink to deep crimson. If the early annual flower plumes are cut off, the plants will produce subsequent crops of smaller heads on branching stems. While often used in borders, plume celosia intended for drying is better grown in the cutting garden.

© Anita Sabarese

© Joanne Pavia

Xeranthemum flowers provide delicate colors in dried arrangements.

## A WINDOWSILL BASKET ARRANGEMENT

Narrow windowsills are not wide enough to hold flower arrangements, but are too large a space for miniature bouquets. This basket of dried flowers is designed especially for a shallow space. It would be just as attractive displayed on a shelf or mantel. The choice of flowers can change with the seasons or the color of the room. In a sunny window, gold and yellow flowers will retain their colors better than pink, red, and blue ones.

The container is a long, narrow cracker basket, designed for serving saltines. Into this, set a brick of Oasis or other soft floral base, cut to fit the basket.

Begin with large strawflowers on wire stems, placing them so that the center ones stand slightly taller than the outer ones. Bend their heads forward slightly. Add smaller strawflowers, with at least one trailing over each end of the basket rim. Fill in with statice and other flowers, such as *Lonus annua* or yarrow, keeping the design slightly higher in the center and lower at the ends. Fill out the arrangement with grasses and sprigs of sweet Annie, adding a few in the back a little taller than the rest and some longer curving ones trailing at the ends. These provide a soft frame for the flowers.

If the arrangement is a little top-heavy, secure it to the windowsill with a small strip of florists' clay.

© Anita Sabarese

Although yarrow grows in a number of colors, it is the tall yellow variety that keeps its color best when dried.

**STRAWFLOWER** Probably the best known of all the everlastings, these annuals grow on rangy plants as tall as five feet. Colors range from white and yellow to orange and brown and all shades of pink and red. It is usually sold in mixed flats. Dwarf varieties are attractive in annual borders or mixed with marigolds or zinnias. Harvest by cutting each flower head individually just at its base. Place on wire stems and dry standing up. The plant will continue to produce until the first frost.

**SWEET ANNIE** is one of the few drying flowers that retains its sweet scent. Tall spikes of soft green flowers also stay green if picked early. Picked later in the season, they turn a rich brown color. Either way, they are a special fa-vorite of wreath makers where their abundant and fragrant foliage make a perfect foundation for arranging other decorative flowers.

**YARROW** The yellow varieties produce large flat heads of tiny blossoms on plants that may be three feet tall. Red and pink varieties have smaller flowers on shorter plants. All grow to mounds of fernlike foliage that spread moderately each year. Although yarrow is a perennial, it is so useful as a fresh or dried cut flower that you will want more than you can usually grow in an ornamental garden. Use it as a border to your cutting or vegetable garden, where it will create a "fence" of roots to help keep out invasive grasses.

# A WILDFLOWER GARDEN

No gardener who has lavished care and attention upon flower beds can fail to admire the independent attitude of wildflowers. What people do for garden plants, the wildflower does for itself. It grows, blooms, replants its seeds, hybridizes, adapts to new climates, and thrives on its own, with a little help from the birds and the bees.

Self-seeding is not the most efficient of systems: A single plant may produce thousands of seeds in a single season, just on the chance that the wind will carry a few to open ground where they will gain a foothold. Inefficient as it is, nature's seeding works, as any gardener who has pulled out unwanted wildling weeds can attest.

But one person's weed is another person's wildflower, and some of the rangiest roadside weeds can enhance a garden if used right. There is a tremendous satisfaction in creating a landscape of native plants and knowing that you are helping to re-establish the balanced ecosystem of your environment.

It is important not to dig the flowers for your native garden in the wild. Many plants are not plentiful, and most are difficult to transplant successfully. It is better to collect their seeds and raise new plants or purchase clumps of perennials from reputable wildflower nurseries.

Ecological safeguards are even more important in the case of rare and protected plants such as the lady's slipper and trillium. Nursery plants are grown in a confined space so that the roots are not in such danger of breaking when transplanted. Unless you are saving native plants from the bulldozer, leave them in the fields and forests where they have already found hospitable spots and start new wildflower plants for your garden.

The most easily grown are the meadow flowers, those sometimes rangy flowers growing by the roadsides and in fields and pastures. They include daisies, brown-eyed Susans, wild iris, asclepias, asters, phlox, vervain, steeplebush, debtford pinks, daylilies, Queen Anne's lace, evening primrose, bluets, violets, and even the tall and elegant Saint-John's-wort.

Especially if you enjoy making dried flower arrangements, look for wild grasses and grains with interesting seed heads. These are often annuals, but they will self-sow. To keep them in place, cut the heads just before the seeds begin to drop, and plant a few of them where you want them to grow the next year. Clumps of these give attractive cover to the lower stems of the late-blooming, tall perennials such as asters.

While the seed catalogs are fond of showing entire fields of mixed wildflowers to tout their seed mixes, common sense tells us that this is seldom possible. Even though some seed houses package blends for separate climates, it is virtually impossible for a field or meadow planted with such a mix to produce anything near the display shown. Every new wildflower plant is competing with grasses and weeds that have been on the site for years. Established plants have strong root systems and are in their own best habitat.

If you do use such a mixture, rather than scatter the seeds to be lost in a field, prepare a smaller bed, carefully dug to remove weeds and roots. Install an edging that goes at least a foot deep to keep grass roots from invading.

Sow the seeds and cover with one-quarter inch of soil; keep the bed moist. The annuals will sprout first, along with any weed seeds that survived in the ground. Unfortunately, when you plant an assortment, you will have very little idea of what plants to leave and what to pull out until the weeds have gotten so strong a foothold that removing them also risks damaging your wildflowers.

For better success, spend a little more on single seed varieties and plant them in clumps so you will recognize them.

For a massed effect, try using only two varieties, such as Queen Anne's lace and black-eyed Susans, in beds at least two feet square. When they come up, you will be able to distinguish them from the weeds because there are only two varieties.

The meadow is not the only place to show off your sun-loving wildflowers. Treat them just as you do cultivated perennials. Plant them, as the English do, along a fence or wall as a border or in freestanding flower gardens. Group them according to height, color, and blooming season.

Along the back (or in the center of a freestanding bed), use New England asters mixed with Saint-John's-wort and Queen Anne's lace. Just in front, use clumps of phlox alternating with brown-eyed Susans, asclepiad, or wild iris. Hide the lower stems of these with clumps of ornamental grasses, and among those plant evening primrose, columbine, and vervain. Front plants could include pinks, violets, or cranesbill geranium.

These will bloom at various times. As you watch them bloom and grow over two or three seasons, you will move some, replace others, and add new varieties.

*A Field Guide to Wildflowers* in the Peterson's guide series is invaluable in identifying flowers as well as giving information about habitats. Before purchasing seeds or plants, you can check to be sure they will be at home in your garden.

However you choose to plant your wildflowers in planned or come-what-may fashion, you are sure to enjoy their colorful beauty. They have made themselves at home in our pastures, fields, meadows, and woodlands for centuries, and they are part of our natural heritage. Besides, when a stray wild weed sends its seed on the wind and it sprouts right next to your violets, you can pass it off as a lovely wildflower!

**The delicate blossoms of Queen Anne's lace are lovely growing against a stone wall or fence.**

# WILDFLOWERS TO GROW

**BLACK-EYED SUSAN** is the state flower of Maryland, but it is common throughout most of the eastern United States. Its cheery clumps of bright yellow flowers can be grown from seeds planted in late summer or fall. The plant will usually bloom the next year.

**CONEFLOWER** is a very showy perennial with purple petals drooping below a cone-shaped center. The cones remain after the petals have fallen and are used in dried arrangements. It grows to four feet in height and blooms in the summer.

**LATE PURPLE ASTER** is a joy for the northern gardener whose flowers are ruined by frost in the early September. It will survive in poor soils, even in partial shade, and reward you with a full month of deep purple flowers on plants about two feet tall.

**PHLOX** is available in many varieties, most of which have pink or white blossoms. Phlox blooms throughout the summer and grows from one to three feet tall. It needs some afternoon shade to do well in extremely hot climates but thrives in full sun in the North.

**PINK COREOPSIS** is a warm-climate flower that quickly forms a neat, low mat that blooms all summer. It withstands drought conditions easily and needs full sun.

**PLUME GRASS** planted in clumps makes a dramatic background in a large garden or a striking bed of its own. As tall as nine feet, it is topped with feathery plumes that bloom throughout the summer.

**QUEEN ANNE'S LACE** is a delicate white flower with feathery foliage. It provides a subdued look between showier or more brightly colored flowers and is a perfect border plant along a fence.

**SUMMER-SWEET** is no shrinking violet in the garden. It is usually at least three feet tall and may grow as high as eight feet. But its pink flowers last well and will spread to attractive clumps even in low, moist areas. Unlike many plants, it thrives near the ocean.

© Lynn Karlin

Although you should not transplant from the wild under normal circumstances, do watch for woodland areas that are being cleared for development. Ask the owners or developers for permission to remove any rare plants that will be in the path of the bulldozer. Take along large boxes, a sturdy shovel, and newspapers. Dig so that as much soil as possible remains around the roots, wrap the roots and soil well in newspaper, and place in boxes. Replant immediately, watering well for the first few weeks until the plants have settled in. Observe their native surroundings and try to put them in a location as much like the one they left as you possibly can, bringing several neighboring plants with them as well.

As you obtain plants, consider their height, and place them in groups with the tallest toward the back or at least separated by low ground covers. Ground-hugging species such as goldenseal may be used between clumps, but be sure these don't choke out other plants. Most woodland flowers are not grown for their masses of bloom, and they will look better and survive best if given ample room.

# A WOODLAND PATH

Wildflowers are a particular favorite in shaded yards. So many of the common cultivated flowers require full sun that gardeners without it often give up. But some of our loveliest wildflowers are natives of the deep woodlands and their edges. Lady's slipper, trillium, mayapple, trout lily, bunchberry, Solomon's seal, and many others inhabit the deep woods natively, making them good choices for any shaded garden.

A woodland wildflower garden is easy to create in a deeply shaded yard or on the edge of a woodlot. Clear unwanted plants from the area beside the path, leaving as many species as possible. In most woodland settings you will want to leave most of the native plants, since they are the ones that fit into the local balance, but you can clear out patches here and there to make a place for rare plants.

It is a particular joy for the woodland gardener to be able to reestablish those flowers that were once plentiful in a locale. Trillium and lady's slipper once grew abundantly in the New England forests, along with trailing arbutus and others. But these have dwindled in number to the point where they are listed as protected species. By planting these, or other plants that have become endangered, in your own area, you can help bring them back to their place in the native landscape and ecosystem.

## PLANTS FOR A WOODLAND PATH

**BLUE PHLOX** is a good ground cover for woodland gardens, where it spreads quickly. Its flowers bloom in the spring and early summer and, unlike most woodland plants, make good cut flowers for bouquets. It may grow as tall as two feet.

**GOLDENSEAL** provides a lush carpet, only a few inches tall. Its tiny white flowers and red berries are a good choice for ground cover between larger or more showy varieties of plants.

**The centers of coneflowers are a nice addition to dried arrangements.**

© Lynn Karlin

**JACK-IN-THE-PULPIT** blooms in the spring with a unique green and dark purple "pulpit" on a single stem. While it is not showy, it is attractive and one of the easier plants to establish. You can grow these from seeds if you gather them in the fall and plant them in a well-marked place. They will sprout the following spring, but blooms will not appear until the second year.

**LADY FERN** has lacy light green fronds that are the perfect backdrop for a woodland path. They grow to two feet in height and adapt well to any environment as long as there is plenty of moisture in the soil.

Choosing plants for a wooded area can be the most difficult challenge in gardening.

**PARTRIDGEBERRY** is a trailing evergreen with tiny round leaves of lustrous dark green. Its white blossoms hug the stems and turn into bright red berries in the fall. The plant continues to thrive all winter, even under the snow. If you find a large patch of this trailing plant and have the landowner's permission, take a few lengths of the runner and transplant it to your own woodland garden. It likes the same soil as pine trees and often hides under their fallen needles. Be sure the little roots are gently pressed into the soil, then cover the plant lightly with pine needles until it takes root.

**SOLOMON'S SEAL** is large and showy and as attractive in single plants as it is in masses. Its white flowers grow in pairs along an arching stalk in the spring and early summer, and its foliage remains attractive throughout the fall.

**VIRGINIA BLUEBELLS** add their lovely blue flowers to the spring garden. The flowers emerge pink but turn blue within a short time. After the plant blooms, its foliage withers and disappears completely until the following spring, so be sure to mark its location and avoid planting other things over it.

**WHITE BEAR SEDGE,** a broad-leafed evergreen, is native in many parts of North America. It grows to about nine inches tall and will spread to form a good clump in the first season. Its white blossoms stand out in the spring and early summer against its blue-green foliage.

**WHITE WOOD ASTER** is one of the few woodland plants that blooms in the fall. Its heart-shaped leaves are attractive in the spring and summer as a background for the earlier flowers. Aster blossoms are about an inch in diameter. They do not require total shade, so you could plant these along the edge of the woods as well.

# A GARDEN FOR WINGED VISITORS

**W**hile most gardeners endeavor to keep critters, from crows to woodchucks, out of their cabbage, other gardeners are busy planting flowers that attract wildlife. Bees, butterflies, and birds—especially hummingbirds—are the chief quarry of these gardens, and the plants are chosen for their ability to attract and provide them with food and lodging.

Although bees, butterflies, and birds each have their own preferences and requirements, their needs blend quite well. You can plant a beautiful garden, your own little wildlife refuge, where these small winged creatures will feel welcome and safe.

You will achieve more than a pure aesthetic enjoyment watching the drifting butterfly and the hovering hummingbird in such a garden. By planting one, you are taking a positive step in preserving the natural environment and restoring the balance of its inhabitants. With increasing land clearing and development, such natural habitats are disappearing.

Even much of the land devoted to gardens might as well be a wasteland for all the support it gives native insect and butterfly species. So many popular garden flowers are exotics—plants that are not native to the place in which they are grown—that they are of little use to the native fauna. Some species are able to adapt to new food and nesting plants, but others are lost forever when their native "weed" habitat is replaced. The weed is some butterfly's nesting place or an important source of nectar to a bee.

**Butterflies are attracted by the color of flowers, as well as by their scent.**

One measure of a healthy ecosystem is the diversity, not simply the quantity, of its wildlife. The number of different species present indicates the ability of the environment to support its flora and fauna in good balance. Unfortunately, many plants that gardeners consider weeds and try to eradicate are important to this general balance, and the cultivated species chosen to replace them contribute nothing in return to the native fauna.

Your yard can become, or remain, a balanced habitat. By preserving as many native plants as possible, and adding those that are favorite food sources or nesting places for the bees and butterflies that help spread the pollen, you can make your yard into a haven—a rich, balanced part of the ecosystem.

For you, it will be filled with beautiful and colorful flowers. Butterflies and bees are attracted as much by color as by fragrance, both of which you can achieve through a steady succession of blossoming flowers. To choose the best ones, you must know a little bit about the habits of bees, butterflies, and birds.

© M. Long/Envision

Bees prefer yellow, blue, and purple flowers. They also need a quantity of the same flower, not just a single specimen. Massed plantings or large clumps of a single type of flower will provide them with more nectar than will a number of different flower species. While it is the color of the flower that initially attracts the bee, it is the scent carried back to the hive that tells other bees which flowers to look for.

Like the bee, the butterfly prefers purple and yellow flowers, or deep pink and mauve blossoms. The butterfly also needs a sunny spot, with no wind, for its perch. In addition to flowers that provide food for the butterfly, you need to consider plants that are favored places to lay eggs. Common milkweed, for example, is the favorite of the monarch butterfly.

Hummingbirds will feed on nearly any flower that provides a good supply of nectar, but they seem to favor those with a trumpet shape, such as trumpet vine. These flowers have such a deep tube that only the hummingbird bill can reach it, and they depend on this bird for fertilization. Orange and bright red blossoms rank highest in the hummingbird's preference.

A garden for bees, butterflies, and birds is not the place for extreme tidiness. What would be considered weeds in a formal flower bed are part of the garden plan here, and some of these creatures appreciate the cover provided by undergrowth that would seem untidy elsewhere. Save your energetic weeding for other beds. If anyone remarks on the resulting crabgrass that grows, just tell them it's a favorite resting place for butterflies!

© D. Long/Envision

**Bees help spread pollen from plant to plant—a vital link for plant reproduction.**

Butterfly weed got its name from its ability to attract the monarch butterfly.

While the form and design of the garden is not important to the creatures you hope to attract, its location is. All three need a sunny spot, and butterflies especially need protection from the wind. An unshaded spot facing south would be a perfect location, especially if a wall or fence faces the direction of the prevailing wind. Another windbreak possibility is an arbor. Plant trumpet vine or wisteria to cover it for a garden backdrop. A seat or bench underneath it can become the perfect spot from which to watch the activity in the garden.

Both birds and butterflies require water, so a small pool or birdbath would be a good centerpiece for this garden. This is not the place for fussy garden layouts; emphasize the wild nature of the garden. But do consider the height of the plants you use, keeping taller ones to the back and shorter ones to the front, so that you will be able to see and enjoy some of the wildlife you attract.

# FLOWERS FOR BUTTERFLIES, BEES, AND HUMMINGBIRDS

**BERGAMOT** is so popular with bees that in some places it is known as beebalm. Butterflies will also frequent its pink and red flowers. It spreads quickly, so leave it plenty of room by planting annuals around it the first year.

**BUTTERFLY WEED** AND **MILKWEED** are members of the same family, as you can tell from their distinctive pods of fluff-born seeds. The blossoms of butterfly weed are a showy red, but its growing habits are more modest. It rarely reaches three feet in height, whereas the common milkweed often reaches four or five feet. Both are home to the chrysalis of the monarch butterfly.

**DAYLILY** blooms afresh each day and continues for several weeks. Give daylilies room to spread, and divide the clumps every four or five years. For variety, plant some of the hybrids along with the lighter-colored native varieties. Both hummingbirds and bees frequent them.

© Sue Pastko/Envision

Small plants such as violets are likely to be overrun by the larger varieties in a wildlife garden.

**DELPHINIUM** is a stately plant with tall spires of blue or purple flowers. Bees and hummingbirds seek its nectar, and its tall stems make delphinium a good showplace for the gardener to spot the birds. Plant delphinium near a window or along a porch or patio for a better view of hummingbirds at work. The stems may need staking to keep them upright under the weight of the flowers.

**LUPINE** offers a good breeding place for butterflies, especially in the northwestern states, and is a favorite of hummingbirds. Give the plants plenty of room, since they spread. Hummingbirds will be more attracted to the red varieties, butterflies to the blue, so plant both.

**NASTURTIUM** is sought by butterflies, bees, and hummingbirds for its sweet nectar. For the gardener, it is a useful border, with rich foliage and a profusion of blossoms. It thrives in the sunny location required by this garden and blooms better if the soil is not too rich.

**RED SALVIA** OR **SCARLET SAGE** is an annual wildflower that blooms abundantly throughout the summer. About two feet tall, its spikes are covered with brilliant color and work well in a massed planting. Start these indoors for a longer blooming period in the North. Hummingbirds can't seem to get enough of it.

**VIOLETS** are modest little spring flowers, which probably account for the term "shrinking violet," but both butterflies and bees seem to find their purple and white blossoms. They self-sow with abandon, but you can transplant the new clumps easily. They are especially pretty between the stones of a wall.

© Mark E. Gibson

Nasturtium attracts hummingbirds as well as bees and butterflies.

# CHAPTER EIGHT

# A PATIO GARDEN

People without the space or time to grow a full garden have become so numerous that seed houses have developed strains especially for container growing. The availability of such tidy, compact plants has in turn encouraged more gardeners to grow vegetables in containers—even those gardeners with plenty of space for the conventional vegetable plot.

Container gardens have many advantages: no hoeing, little weeding, no strenuous labor, and easy mobility. But patio plants do need more attention than those planted in an open garden. Without deep soil in which their roots can seek water and nutrients, they must be fed and watered much more frequently. But for many, the convenience of having vegetables literally on the back porch, plus the attractive appearance of bush plants, outweighs the extra care required.

Choosing interesting and decorative containers is part of the fun of patio gardening. Clay pots, wine barrels, wooden planter boxes, window boxes, even large drain tiles make good planters. Porous material such as terra-cotta and untreated wood allow air and water to circulate easily, but they need more frequent watering. In hot, dry, or windy climates, nonporous materials such as glazed ceramic, plastic, or lined wood might be better choices.

Drainage is especially important; all containers must have holes or several inches of coarse gravel in the bottom. Setting pots on platforms helps air to circulate and protects patio floors from stains and puddles. Bases with wheels are easier to move if you need to follow the sun from one spot to another.

© Anita Sabarese

The second most important difference in growing patio plants is the soil. Potting any plant in garden soil is unwise, since its constricted roots need a richer soil with more moisture retention. Also, garden soil carries soil-born fungi, diseases, and insects that can quickly destroy plants in a limited environment.

There are excellent commercial potting soils available, or you can mix your own from equal parts perlite, vermiculite, and peat moss, adding one tablespoon of ground eggshells per quart of soil to counteract the natural acidity of the peat moss.

When digging plants from the garden to move indoors, you should first root prune them by running a spade down into the ground around the plant. Water the plant well and leave it in the garden for about a week so it can recover from the shock to its root systems.

Geranium plants stay compact and full if they are kept well pruned.

While it may seem like a drastic measure, one further precaution should be taken when potting plants that have been growing in the garden—complete repotting in sterile soil. After assembling all the supplies for repotting, wash the plant's roots completely in a bucket of tepid water. Work the soil loose from the root ball with one hand while supporting its stem and swishing the plant about in the water with the other. Wash the foliage in tepid water as well, checking under the leaves for any pests or eggs that might be clinging to the undersides.

Fill a newly scrubbed pot about one-third full of dry potting mix and tip it so the soil lies along one side. Lay the plant roots against this soil and fill the pot, shaking it slightly to firm the soil and being careful not to injure the tiny root ends. An easy way to pack the soil snugly is to run a spatula blade down the edge of the pot and push the soil away from the edge with a prying motion. Then add more soil along the edge. Soak the soil thoroughly and set the pot in a shallow dish full of gravel so it can drain. If there has been considerable root damage, or the plant is very straggly at this point, prune it to encourage the development of more root and base growth.

Repotting takes a little time but saves you a lot of possible trouble later. Set any newly potted plant from outdoors away from other plants for a week or so to give it time to acclimate and to be sure it is not harboring pests that could start an epidemic. While it is not as essential to repot greenhouse-grown plants from a nursery, it is still a good idea, since you could be bringing diseases or pests into your patio garden, where plants have less resistance to them.

Many herbs make excellent container plants. Scented geraniums are frequently grown in pots, even outdoors. Bay and rosemary are often brought in for the winter. In fact, northern gardeners often leave these herbs in large pots year-round, setting them in the center of an herb garden or along a stone wall. Marjoram, thyme, lemon verbena, pineapple sage, chives, lemon balm, winter savory, and miniature basils do well.

Potted herbs, like all container plants, require regular watering, but they should be allowed to drain well after-

The abundant bloom of geraniums makes them a favorite for container growing.

ward. Twice a week is usually about right. If they become too dry before that, perhaps they need a larger pot or soil with more humus content. Vegetables require more water, usually once a day, unless they get natural rainfall. Plants will need to be watered more frequently in hot or windy weather. Plants take both food and water through their roots, so a thirsty plant is also a hungry plant. Water each time until the excess runs freely out the drainage holes.

Unless they have full sun all day, patio plants tend to become "leggy" and may need to be pruned regularly to keep them full and tidy. Check the leaves carefully for any sign of disease or infestation, and treat plants to an occasional shower of soapy water if you find aphids or other insects crawling on them.

The location of the pots will depend on which plants you are growing. Conversely, the ones you will be able to grow successfully will depend on the location and exposure of your patio or terrace. With a sunny southern exposure, you can grow vegetables, herbs, and flowers. With afternoon sun in a western exposure, you can grow some vegetables, especially salad greens, and most herbs. If your patio is in the shade most of the day, you will be limited to shade-loving flowers, such as impatiens and begonias. If the pots are mobile, you can extend your sunshine by moving the pots from place to place, but that involves more work and, of course, being at home during the day.

Some seed catalogs have a separate page for varieties of vegetables, flowers, and herbs recommended for container growing. Look for these in the descriptions about each variety to see if the plant you like will thrive in that environment. Shepherd's Garden Seeds has developed a number of bush vegetable plants especially for this use. Tomatoes, peppers, lettuces, leafy salad greens, and even a bush cucumber are among the plants offered in the catalog.

## HANGING BASKETS

Hanging pots and baskets bring dimension to a terrace or patio garden and attractive decoration to a porch. They are especially effective planted with trailing or cascading plants. If carefully planned, the pots may contain several different compatible varieties. Wire baskets should first be lined with sphagnum moss, then with a layer of black plastic punched with holes for drainage. Fill halfway with potting mix and set the plants in place. If you are mixing varieties, put an upright plant in the center and cascading ones to the edges. Fill the basket with soil, pressing firmly around the roots of the plants. Water thoroughly. Since wire baskets are open to evaporation from all sides, they need watering more frequently than pots.

Because of the water, these plants can become quite heavy, so be sure the brackets or hooks that support them are strong and secure. Rotate the planter periodically so that each side gets adequate sun.

Thyme, winter savory, and prosrate rosemary are good herb choices. Nasturtium is lovely with its mound of cascading foliage filling a pot. Some scented geranium varieties cascade well, and large-blossomed geranium plants are traditional decorations for summer porches. Bleeding heart, begonia, and impatiens also cascade nicely.

© M. Long/Envision

**Clay pots must be kept well watered to protect plant roots from dehydration.**

# PART THREE

COUNTRY

## HERBS

TECHNIQUES, RECIPES, USES, AND MORE

KATHI KEVILLE

# CHAPTER ONE

# YOUR COUNTRY HERB GARDEN

**Y**ou don't have to live in the country to have a country-style herb garden. In fact, some of the most delightful herb gardens I have seen have been contained in an eight-foot square. Even a planter box or a series of large pots can provide enough space for herb gardening. My first garden held forty different herbs in an eighteen-square-foot plot.

An herb garden will give you pleasure throughout the year. Spring contains the excitement of plants emerging from the earth with bursts of energy. The summer garden is filled with beauty and fragrance. Autumn brings the bountiful harvest. Winter is a time for dreaming and planning and enjoying all of your dried and preserved herbal creations.

## HERB GARDEN DESIGN

An exciting facet of herb gardening is the design. This is your chance to be an artist, using nature as your canvas. Nature itself is your assistant, since herbs have a way of creating beauty no matter how they are combined. Still, certain techniques can make your garden especially attractive. The fun in planning is choosing and putting together different elements to create your own unique style.

Country herb gardens are versatile. They can be grown on a terraced slope, in a border wrapped around the side of a house or lawn, and even in pots on your porch or balcony. Basic design for a garden is like any art. You create a contrast in color, texture, and form. The most appealing herb gardens keep your eye moving from bed to bed in visual delight. The herbs themselves offer much to work with.

Design inspiration can come from many sources: a diagram of a traditional herb garden, gardens you visit, and nature. An excellent place to see garden design in action is in established herb gardens. Find them at historical homes, herb nurseries, botanical gardens, museums, herb shops, and private homes. Your visits will help you choose favorite varieties and get a feel for which herbs are best for your particular garden. Local herb and garden societies have a wealth of information about local growing conditions and sources of plants.

Sketch your designs on paper, where they can be easily changed. Once you choose a final plan, lay out the garden with strings tied to stakes so you can walk through and visualize your dream garden. Make sure that pathways are wide enough to allow herbs to trail and bush out into them. Check to see that the herb beds are a convenient size for harvesting.

Herb gardens are for enjoyment, so have fun with them from the beginning. While designing your herb garden, keep in mind that you can always make changes. Even well-established herbs can be moved after they are planted. If you think the tansy has become ungainly, as it tends to, or the pink yarrow might look better next to lavender than it does to sage, dig them up and move them. A small herb garden can always be enlarged and an area overgrown with weeds can be dug up and replanted.

# CHOOSING THE HERBS

A combination of tall- and low-growing herbs create depth and variety in your garden. Tall fennel and angelica, and small trees and bushes such as bay, juniper, and myrtle, add more dimension to your garden. Know how tall and wide your herbs will grow so you are not surprised one day to find the little pennyroyal and sweet woodruff hidden by an overbearing wormwood. The simplest designs place large herbs in a central location or in the back row, then work down in height to the smallest herbs.

Colors can contrast strongly, moving gradually from softer hues to a brighter crescendo, or they can follow the color wheel. Herbal leaf colors range from soft blue-grays to yellow-greens, and they exhibit a variety of textures. Though many herb flowers are small, they often are so numerous that they seem to cover the entire plant. A rambling thyme plant in full bloom looks like a floral carpet. Herbs like echinacea and calendula provide large, bright blooms. Don't hesitate to include the colorful accents of nonherbal flowers, such as daisies, cosmos, bachelor buttons, and zinnias, because they provide additional color for your herbal crafts projects. Even subtle color contrasts can work well if the herbs present a variety of textures. One of herb gardener Aldema Simmons's most famous gardens at Caprilands in Connecticut is filled with gray herbs and gray stone walkways.

# DESIGNING THE BEDS

Ideally, herb beds should be narrow enough so you can reach in and harvest what you want without disturbing the garden. If you prefer wider beds, stepping stones can give you easy access to the herbs. Traditionally, many herb gardens were planted in raised beds. The reason was both practical and decorative, since taller beds bring low-growing herbs up to an easy height to pick or smell. Creeping thymes and mints are very pretty growing over the edges of raised beds.

Increase the bed height by moving topsoil to it from path areas or other areas of the garden. Topsoil can also be purchased from nurseries or garden centers. Gently slope the dirt edges, or contain the beds within railroad ties, thick wooden boards (which last about six years, then need replacing), or even the spokes of an old wagon wheel. Brick, cement, or rock walls can also edge beds. In medieval monastic gardens, like the Cloisters Herb Garden of the New York Metropolitan Museum of Art, willow and other flexible branches were woven together to hold the beds. Traditional monastery herb gardens offered gardeners and visitors a raised chamomile bed or a bench to sit upon and enjoy the garden.

Banks overflowing with herbs, sunken areas, and small pools add interesting dimensions to an herb garden. An impressive bank of overgrown lavender and rosemary at the Los Angeles County Arboretum makes the herbs look eight feet tall. This arboretum and also the Stryburg Arboretum in Golden Gate Park, San Francisco, use banks held by rock walls to bring fragrant gardens close to the hands and noses of the blind.

European gardens of the sixteenth century favored herb beds surrounded by hedges of germander, thyme, hyssop, and santolina. These were pruned into square or cylindrical shapes. The most elaborate version was the knot garden, where contrasting herbs, carefully planted and trimmed, gave the impression that they were knotted together. In *The Art of Gardening* (1568), Thomas Hyall wrote that English Tudor knot gardens were made "with hyssop and thyme or with winter savory and thyme for these endure all the winter through green." If you have some spare time (or a hired gardener) to keep the hedges trimmed, you might want to create a knot garden.

Most perennial herb plants do not grow to full size until their third summer. So, when designing your herb garden, keep in mind that initially there will be empty spaces between the herbs. You can temporarily fill this space with other perennials that can later be moved, or with annual herbs or flowers. There are many free-sowing annual and biennial herbs that fill in every available gap year after year. Borage, evening primrose, marigolds, sesame, parsley, or poppies will all be happy to volunteer.

# POTTED GARDEN

Any size containers can be placed together to make an herb garden. Old crocks or hollow cinder blocks are interesting pots. Oak barrel halves, available at some nurseries, or planter boxes can hold a collection of many different herbs. Planter boxes can become window boxes, but be sure they are made strong enough to hold the weight of the dirt. Set wooden containers up on bricks or stones so they do not rot. Incidentally, small planters with three or four herbs make wonderful gifts. For instance, you can give a culinary garden of thyme, rosemary, sage, and basil.

Potted herbs also fit into the garden scheme. Traditional English herb gardens often included small potted bay trees and other herbs that are sensitive to the cold. They could be carried into the hot house for the winter. Hanging pots of herbs are always attractive. A number of herbs, including Persian catnip, trailing rosemary, and ground ivy hang very gracefully. Elizabethans were especially fond of hanging rosemary pots.

Be aware that peppermint, pennyroyal, and other members of the mint family are notorious for their ability to spread throughout the garden. And, they are not the only ones! Other roving herbs include white and pink yarrow, ground ivy, creeping thymes, and perennial clovers. These herbs can work to your advantage to fill in areas, but they need restriction in a small garden. Plant them in enclosures, such as clay pipes, cement bricks, or pots that go down at least six inches if you want to keep their roots contained.

I have seen herb gardens where all the plants are actually in pots buried in the soil. When fall comes, the pots are dug up and placed in a greenhouse. They sprout extra early in the spring and then the entire garden is tilled to eliminate weeds before the pots are again "planted."

# PATHWAYS

Traditional herb gardens were almost always designed in symmetrical squares or circles, accented by pathways. Paths not only look nice, but they are also practical, since they allow easy access into the garden for weeding, harvesting, and, of course, enjoying. Paths can radiate from the center, form concentric circles, or spiral through the garden. Since a country herb garden can also be informal, the path can ramble casually through the plants.

Paths can be constructed from flagstones, cement forms or bricks set into patterns. Gravel, small rocks, sand, and even sawdust can be set around stepping stones or can form the path itself. One simple garden design sets square cement steps, about two feet wide, in a checkerboard pattern and fills in the space between them with herbs. Level and pack the dirt under the path area to keep down the weeds. Consider laying heavy gauge plastic, tar paper, or even sawdust under the path as a weed barrier. Sand or sawdust between the plastic and the stones increases its life span.

Anyone who strolls down an herb garden path has the pleasure of brushing past a potpourri of scented herbs. You might even allow a few sprigs of these herbs to escape into the path, where they will scent the walk when they're stepped on. In his *Essay of Gardens*, Francis Bacon said the plants that "perfume the air most delightfully . . . when trodden upon are burnet, wild thyme and . . . mint."

Bacon suggested that "whole alleys" of such herbs be planted for pathways and that the entire path be a bed of herbal ground covers. It is a little more work to maintain, since herbs in the bed and path will always be trying to invade each other's territory, but the effect is very herbal. Some herbs tolerate being walked on quite well. For instance, Roman chamomile was one of the most popular plants for the scented lawns of sixteenth-century Europe. Shakespeare's character Falstaff comments that "the more it is trodden upon, the faster it grows or the better it wears."

© Maggie Oster

Herb gardens with pathways are not only attractive, they are also practical since they allow easy access into the garden.

© Maggie Oster

# CULTIVATING YOUR HERB GARDEN

E ven if your green thumb seems to be more of a brown shade, don't despair—growing herbs is easy if you know a few tricks. Herbs are naturally wild plants that are very forgiving to even the most inexperienced gardener. Since most herbs have not been hybridized, they are hardy survivors and are quite resistant to drought and insect invasions. In fact, many herbs contain natural pesticides.

Look to the country where the herb's ancestors originate. Duplicating that environment as much as possible will make your herbs feel right at home. Most of our classical cooking and fragrance herbs, such as lavender, rosemary, and thyme, come from the Mediterranean. Although you may not be able to duplicate a Grecian hillside overlooking the Aegean Sea, their native home and climate will provide guidelines for preparing garden soil and watering. These herbs prefer little rain, well-drained soil, and lots of sunshine.

Many of the most popular herbs from other parts of the world adapt well to a Mediterranean-type herb garden. The few exceptions include shade-loving plants, such as sweet woodruff, rosemary, and sage, which prefer to dig their roots into rich, loamy soil. A specially prepared section of your yard will make them completely happy.

# SOIL

Let's start with the basics. How is your soil? The old gardening cliché is "poor soil, little water makes strong herbs." Well, only to a point. It is true that over-pampered herbs become less hardy with fewer flowers and less fragrance. Yet, while herbs do not need the rich garden soil tomatoes and corn demand, they do require nourishment.

Mediterranean soil tends to be high in alkaline and well drained. If your garden soil is too acidic, add lime, hardwood ashes, and ground eggshells. How do you know if your soil is acid? Garden supply stores have inexpensive tests available and lots of advice. You can also send a sample of your soil to the local county cooperative extension office for analysis. Most herbs do not like to keep their "feet" wet. A well-drained soil lets water drain down, encouraging roots to search deeply for water and nutrients.

The best fertilizer I have found to improve any type of soil (and I have dealt with quite a few) is a simple organic compost. Even when my garden started out with heavy, red clay soil that seemed better suited for pottery than gardening, compost came to the rescue. Raised beds improved the poor drainage somewhat. Adding sand helped, but you can only dump so many truckloads of sand into a garden. Compost gave life to the soil and corrected the overacid PH. You can buy compost or make your own by layering garden dirt and kitchen waste into a heap.

Perennial herbs live for years (an average of ten). If the herbs spread, as many of them tend to, the plant will live forever. Since your herbs may be in one spot for a long time, they will be healthier and happier if you feed them at least once a year. A layer of compost "dresses" the soil around the roots in fall or early spring. A spray of diluted fish emulsion or seaweed on the leaves a few times a year gives them an extra boost.

Mulch—any soft, organic material like old grass clippings or straw—can be useful in the herb garden. During the summer, a layer on the ground around the plants preserves moisture in the soil and keeps weeds down. In areas where there are winter freezes, mulch protects the roots of less hardy herbs. Mulch is not always suitable for moist areas where pests, such as slugs, snails, pill bugs, or earwigs, like to make themselves at home.

# WATER

If you live in an area with regular summer rainfall, let nature do the work. Otherwise, herbs do fine watered by a drip system, by hand, or by overhead sprinklers. Avoid overhead watering during the sunniest part of the day; like most plants, herbs prefer to be watered when the sky is overcast or the sun is low in the sky.

The proper amount of water depends on where you live, but drooping leaves are your signal to grab the watering can. If leaves turn crisp on the edges or start falling off, your herbs are badly in need of water. My own garden receives almost no rain during the summer, and so I water it two times a week; more if the weather is extremely hot.

Overwatering, like overfertilizing, also creates a problem. Too much water dilutes an herb's essential oil concentration, making it less fragrant. The plants become weaker because they begin to depend upon more water and also become more susceptible to early freezing.

# HUMIDITY AND SUN

You have little control over humidity unless you grow your garden in a greenhouse. In humid regions, herbs should be planted in full sun to fight mold and mildew. In addition, give your plants plenty of room and keep them well trimmed, especially along the ground.

I had great success creating a more humid environment in a lath house with an automatic watering system that sprayed a few times each day. A lath house is similar to a greenhouse, but the structure is covered with thin wooden slats (laths) instead of glass or plastic. It provides partial shade for shade-loving plants and is ideal for raising seedlings and potted plants. Not only did my plants thrive, but I enjoyed working in the refreshing dampness.

Full sun is best for your herb garden. If your only garden spot is shady, emphasize shade-loving herbs. Herbs grown in shade have less flavor, but herb gardeners can use this to their advantage. If French sorrel is too sour or watercress too bitter for your taste, then more shade will result in a more delicate flavor.

# STARTING HERB PLANTS

Herb plants can be started a number of different ways. It is good to become familiar with all the propagation techniques so you can choose the most practical methods for your herb garden. You can plant seeds, sprout cuttings, or divisions from already established plants, divide plants at the roots to produce two or more plants, or encourage extra root growth to produce side shoots. It is easiest to transplant already established herb plants into your garden, but this can get expensive and the herbs you want may not be readily available.

## SEEDS

Herb seeds vary in the amount of time it takes to germinate. Annuals must flower and make seed in one season, so you should expect to see them popping up in a week or two. Perennials can take two to six weeks to germinate, so be patient; they are in no hurry because they have many years ahead of them. I have disheartedly put aside flats of perennial seeds that did not come up all summer, only to have them sprout in mad profusion the next spring!

Seeds for annual herbs should be planted as early as possible in the spring. Perennials and biennials can be started in the spring or throughout the summer. Perennial seedlings that have established a good root system will usually survive the winter.

Seeds from plants originating in very cold areas need to have germination stimulated by freezing temperatures. Called stratification, this can be done by placing the seeds in water and freezing them for a couple of days in the refrigerator. Plastic ice cube trays work great because you can use each section for a different variety of seed. If you live in an area where the ground freezes during the winter, you can sow the seeds in flats and place them outdoors to naturally freeze and thaw, so they sprout when they are ready.

Herb seeds are often very tiny. The result is that they easily shift in the soil or get washed away. I sow most herb seeds into flats so I can keep track of them. I move the flats into a warm place on chilly nights, then out into the sun the next day. My favorite flats are not the traditional cumbersome wooden boxes used by nurseries, but small plastic containers, such as the ones yogurt, cottage cheese, or tofu are packaged in. These miniflats are easy to manage and keep each seed variety separate.

One of the biggest problems new seedlings face is a fungus on the soil surface that is encouraged by dampness. Known as "damping off disease," it causes new stems to weaken and the little plants to fall over. Since the disease is carried in soil, buy sterilized potting soil from the nursery. If you want to sterilize potting soil yourself, cook dirt in the oven at 180°F (82°C) for one hour. (You had better warn your family ahead of time that you are not baking brownies!) Combine the cooked dirt with equal parts of vermiculite and sand. Use clean sand and not ocean sand, which contains salt residue. When I reuse containers for flats, I wash them, then dip them in a diluted bleach solution (20 percent bleach) to thoroughly clean them.

Fill the miniflats with about two inches of damp soil. It is best to use distilled or boiled water to avoid bacteria from well water or chlorine from treated water. Gently scatter the seeds on the surface, about twice as many as you want plants to come up, since all the seeds will not germinate. Cover the seeds with dry soil to a depth about twice as thick as one seed. Pat down gently, then use a fine spray to just dampen the surface soil. The soil should be wet, but not soaked, since too much moisture encourages fungus growth.

You can turn your miniflats into mini greenhouses by stretching plastic wrap over the top and securing it with a rubber band. The inside will remain moist as the water trapped inside keeps circulating. (Note that you do *not* need to punch holes in the container.) With this method, the seedlings probably will not need watering until they are ready for transplanting. You can even abandon them and go on vacation! An average temperature for germination is 70°F to 80°F (20°C to 25°C).

Always remove the plastic cover before the leaves touch it. Then, start watering the flat. When the second set of leaves emerge, the seedlings are ready for transplanting into the garden or into larger pots. Use a small trowel, or even a spoon, to dig out seedlings. If plants are growing tightly together, snip off extra ones at the ground instead of pulling them out and disturbing roots of other plants.

At this stage, your herbs are very tiny and vulnerable to insects, diseases, and sunstroke, and need to be "hardened off" before being exposed to the sun's full strength. They are less likely to dry out and wilt from the sun's heat in partial shade. If they go directly into the garden, cover them with upside down pots, cardboard boxes, or anything else suitable to give them a few days of protection from sun, heat, and wind. I prefer to transplant seedlings, especially slower-growing perennials, into pots or trays where they can grow sturdy before being introduced into the garden. In the early spring, most seedlings need to wait until danger of frost has passed.

**Transplanting is an easy way to start an herb garden. For best results, plants should be planted into already wet soil.**

© Robert Perron

## CUTTINGS AND DIVISIONS

Making cuttings is the "shortcut" for starting an herb garden. First, find some herb plants, perhaps in a friend's garden. You can take cuttings from most herbs that have firm stalks, but it is often best to start off with an easy volunteer from the mint or sage family.

Cut a healthy looking stalk about four inches long. The plant should not be budding or flowering. You may be hesitant to do it, but remove all but the top four to six leaves. The herb does not have any roots to support all those leaves so this gives the roots a chance to grow enough to catch up and support more leaves.

The end of the cutting can be dipped into rooting hormone available at nurseries. Rooting compounds are not necessary, but can be used with difficult stem cuttings. Dip the end of the stem into water and then into the rooting compound so it coats the cut area. Another alternative is to water the cuttings with a strong willow stalk tea to encourage rooting. To make this tea, chop one cup of tree twigs and pour two quarts of hot water over them. Let sit overnight. If you've seen willows sprouting in a vase of water, you can understand how much natural rooting hormone willows contain.

Place the cuttings upright in a container of clean sand or vermiculite drenched with water. Do not use soil or liquid fertilizers. You want the cuttings to send roots out in search of nutrients. In a couple of weeks, some of the cuttings should sprout roots. Pull them out very carefully to check their progress. When they start rooting, plant them in a pot of soil and let them grow large enough to move into the garden.

## ROOT DIVISION AND LAYERING

Many herbs spread by sending new roots out just under the soil's surface. The new roots sprout and can be cut away from the mother plant. You can also encourage herbs to sprout by layering. To layer a plant, first select a low-growing stem still attached to the mother plant and pile a mound of dirt over the stem. Tap the dirt down, leaving the leafy tip above ground. Eventually, the stem will root and can be left there to spread or it can be made into a division.

Old and woody herbs with inflexible lower stems can still be layered by covering the entire lower section of the herb with a dirt mound. Cut the top of the herb back to encourage new growth. Roots will sprout along the buried stems. You can also divide large plants when transplanting them.

The fastest method of starting new plants is root division. Mints and lemon grass are examples of plants that spread by sending roots out from their base to form new plants. Any section of the plant where there are stems coming out of the roots is a suitable candidate for a new plant. Use a shovel to make a clean cut into the root clump to remove the new plants. Or dig up the entire plant and divide it into sections. Many herbs will easily break into new plants. Cut back the top of the new plant so it can concentrate on root growth. Pot the divisions until they are strong enough to go back into the garden. Larger sections can go directly into the garden.

Herbs whose roots grow by "crowns" make little plants around their base. Gently cut or break off the small plants from the crowns, or mother plant. If you wish, the larger roots can be transplanted back into the garden.

The focal point of this raised bed is St. Fiacre, the patron saint of gardening.

# TRANSPLANTING

Any plant experiences some shock and setback when it is transplanted. Your job as an herb gardener is to make the transition as smooth as possible. Keep the roots undisturbed and away from air exposure. Have the new home ready with pots or holes already waiting. In either case, water the soil before transplanting so it is already damp.

To remove the herb plant from a pot, turn the pot upside down, holding your hand over the top, with the stems between your fingers. A few sharp taps with a trowel against the bottom of the pot will loosen the dirt, and the plant should slide out of the pot. If some soil does fall off of the roots, replace it with your free hand, then turn the plant upright and place it in its new home. Tap down the dirt around the roots and water the transplants right away in order to fill in air pockets around the roots.

It is possible to move even very large herbs around the garden. Dig straight down around the root's perimeter with a shovel. You can assume that the roots extend out at least as far as the stems. Once the circle is completed, push the shovel under the root ball and pick up the entire plant. If the root ball is large and heavy, you may need to dig under the roots to release it.

The best time to transplant into the garden is in the late afternoon or on overcast days. Cover the new transplants with inverted pots for a few days until they are well established. Garden pots work well since they have a vent hole in the top. Water clay pots to keep them extra cool during hot days. Large herbs that have just been transplanted can be covered with cardboard boxes or wet burlap bags supported on three sticks lashed together at the top into a "tepee." Your herbs will appreciate this transition time to become adjusted to their new home.

© Anita Sabarese

**Trim back the foliage on large herbs just before transplanting to avoid "transplant shock." Have tools and water handy, and bring a basket to collect the trimmings.**

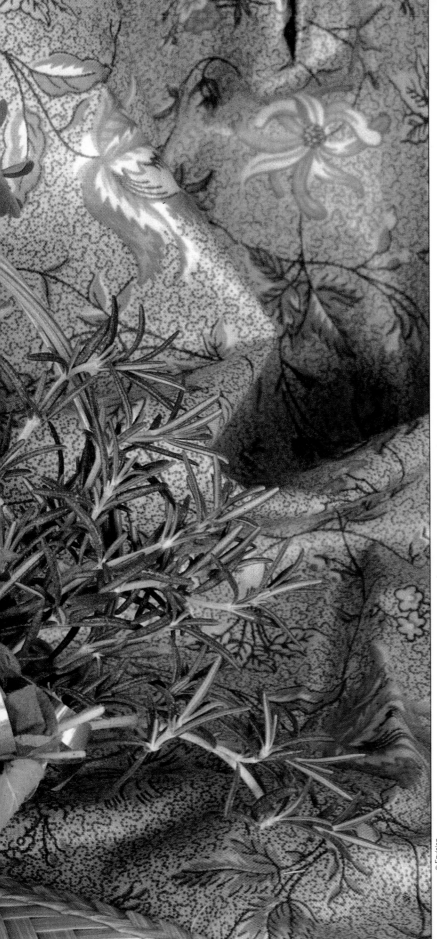

# HARVESTING HERBS

One of the greatest rewards the herb garden offers is a bountiful harvest. A typical summer morning finds me with basket in hand, a straw hat shading early morning rays from my eyes, strolling through my herb garden clipping and snipping. Soon my basket is filled with sprigs that will flavor food, scent potpourri, and fill my house with color for the next year.

Your garden will provide you with the best-quality herbs possible, as you grow, harvest, and dry them with care. Even average-quality herbs harvested from your own garden will be better than those from the store. You can enjoy and judge the quality of your herbs by how they look, smell, and taste.

Perennial herbs grown in beds should be harvested so that the plant retains its shape, and so there is ample foliage left to support the plant for years to come. Annuals can be harvested solely by frequently picking off the tops. This encourages the plants to grow bushier and send out side branches.

## WHEN TO HARVEST HERBS

A few general guidelines are all that you need to produce garden herbs with the best flavor, fragrance, and color. Ideally, each herb should be harvested at its peak potency. The time of year and the time of day are the most important considerations.

© Envision

## TIME OF DAY

Old herb books say to harvest herbs in the morning, just after the dew dries from the leaves, and for good reason. Plants concentrate their essential oils during the night, then release them as the sun begins to warm the morning. Walk through an herb garden on a hot day and notice that the air around you is filled with delicious herbal scents as these oils are released.

Whenever possible, harvest the garden when it has not been watered or rained on for a few days. Since the object is to dry the plants, the less water they contain when picked, the better. The exception would be a dusty environment. In this case, give the plants a light sprinkle to wash them off the day before harvesting.

## TIME OF YEAR

The best-quality herbs are harvested at their prime. There is no need for complicated charts and graphs to know when to pick each herb. Simply watch your garden grow. Plants change throughout the year as they respond to the seasons. In spring, warmer, longer days literally pull plants from their roots in bursts of energy. Leaves reach maximum potency just before the first flowers open. Most herbs will resume growth after they are cut back and can be harvested two to four times in the summer and into the fall.

Once they begin blooming, plants concentrate on their flowers. Lower leaves begin turning brown and lose potency. Most flowers should be harvested just before they are fully open; a few, however, are picked while still in their bud stage. Don't be shy about picking them—it encourages more blooms. Seeds are formed after the flowers die back. Harvest these just as they ripen, but before they fall from the plant.

Dig roots during the plant's winter dormant cycle, when they are most potent. During the cold months, roots serve as a storage system. Many references suggest harvesting roots only in the fall or early spring, but if the ground does not freeze where you live, roots can be gathered throughout the winter. Biennial roots, which live only two years, need to be harvested in their first fall or second spring. By the second fall, the plant is ready to die and the root loses potency. You might want to stake out their location in the fall so you can find them after they die down. By the way, useful roots are almost always perennials or biennials since the roots of annuals are not needed for winter storage.

It may not always be possible to harvest your herbs at the optimum time of their cycle or hour of day. If you miss their peak, you can still harvest them. Judge an herb's quality by smelling and tasting it. If the flavor and taste are strong, they are good. When culinary herbs like oregano and basil have already gone to flower, harvest the topmost leaves and the flowers, too. Most flowers carry the same scent and flavor as the leaves.

**Most herbs, including oregano, should be harvested before they bloom.**

## HOW TO HARVEST

A sharp knife, pruning clippers, or scissors will make clean cuts on the stems for harvesting leaves or flowers. Avoid tearing the stem or making jagged cuts. You will find that many flowers and some leaves are easier to pick by hand. When harvesting, be sure to leave a substantial part for the plant's health. Either cut a few stems back all the way or cut many stems halfway down. Cut plants with hard stems, such as rosemary, back to last year's growth; if you want to shape the bush, then prune it back even farther.

When I first began herb gardening, it always seemed that herbs such as dill dropped their seeds the day before I was ready to harvest them. I finally learned to beat them

to it! Wait until the seeds begin to come off easily into your hand. Place a paper bag, upside down, over the top of the plant and tie the top of the bag tightly around the stem. Any seeds that haven't already fallen off will fall into the bag. When it is time to harvest, cut off the stem and turn the "plant bag" upside down and hang it up until the seeds are completely dry. By then, most seeds will have fallen off, but if any still remain on the stem, gently brush them off into the bag.

Dig roots with the shovel pointing straight down to avoid slicing them. Or, if the soil is loose enough, pull them up with a garden fork. Once you have uncovered the root and knocked off any loose dirt, give it a short soak in

© Rogers Associates

cold water to rinse off any remaining dirt. (Hot water or long soaks can leach out the root's properties.) Scrub the root right away, before dirt becomes permanently embedded in crevices and pockets on its surface.

Keep herbs out of direct sun after harvesting them. The sun will blacken them and quickly evaporate their essential oils. There is nothing so discouraging for gardeners as putting all their love, care, and work into their herb gardens and then have their beautiful harvest turn to compost.

## DRYING HERBS

Country gardeners used to dry their herbs by tying them into bunches and hanging them from attic rafters. All summer and fall, the attic in my old house was filled with picturesque drying herbs. It was very warm and dark and the side windows provided air circulation. You may not have the perfect herb-drying attic, but any dark, warm place will do.

Notice how quickly clothes dry on hot, breezy days. The same is true for herbs. It is fine if the drying area cools at night, though the drying time will be extended. Herb growers living in humid climates use forced air dryers to circulate hot air around the herbs. Total darkness is not necessary, but keep drying herbs away from direct sunlight to retain their color and essential oils.

Choose a drying method that is most practical for your

space and for the herb's eventual purpose. The advantage of hanging herbs upside down is that they dry with straight stems and upright flowers then can be used in dried flower arrangements. To make bunches, cut the stems long enough to tie with string or rubber bands. The size of the bunches depends on the air's humidity. In my dry climate, I tie nice, big herb bundles with about fifteen stems to a bunch. On the other hand, if you live in a more humid climate, tie only a few stems together to prevent mold. When in doubt, keep an eye out for mold growing where the stems are tightly tied together.

There are many ingenious drying racks for hanging herbs. A folding clothes-drying rack, the kind made with long dowels, holds about fifty bunches. It is portable, can be set up almost anywhere, and folds for easy storage. Another type of clothes dryer suitable for herbs is the wooden wall racks that lie flat against the wall, then fan out for hanging. A hanging umbrella-style clothes rack will also work for a few herbs. Your kitchen walls can be decorated with bunches of herbs that are light enough to hang from push pins. Wooden wall racks with pegs, such as Shaker-styled hat racks, can also accommodate drying herbs.

A paper bag makes a handy, portable dryer that keeps sun and dust off the herbs. Put a bunch into the bag with the stems protruding from the top. Tie a string tightly around the top of the bag and stems. In humid areas, cut little "U"-shaped windows in the bag to increase air flow.

This is a great method if you harvest in the countryside. Hang the bags anywhere, even outside in the shade. Yes, your neighbors will probably ask you if this is some new way to keep crows out of the trees, but you can't beat the method for ease and practicality.

Herbs can also be dried by laying them on screens. This is especially useful for flowers or herbs too small to tie in bundles. A well-washed window screen will work, or you can custom-make your own by stretching stainless steel screening (from a hardware store) over a wooden frame. Individual flowers can be carefully pushed through the holes in a large mesh screen. Screens can be stacked about eight inches apart using bricks or wood-block supports or you can construct a wooden frame they slide into. When I was drying herbs commercially, I set six-by-four-foot screens into tall frames that held eight screens each. For smaller jobs, eighteen-inch frames are a good size. Small screens can also be suspended in tiers from string and hung in warm areas of the house.

When you lay out the herbs on screens, layer them thinly so air can circulate freely around them. Stiff herbs will provide enough air space around them, but limp herbs need to be stirred or tossed every day to dry them evenly and prevent molding. In humid areas, you may have to lay the herbs so there is no overlap.

© Robert Perron

## STORING HERBS

You will know when your herbs are dry when they are crispy and break easily. Unless you want to keep the leaves on the stem, remove them by gently running your hand from the top down. Leaves tend to grow upward at an angle, so a downward motion pulls them off quickly.

Herbs are best stored in airtight jars or plastic bags, away from light, heat, and moisture. Personally, I find culinary herbs so attractive I can not resist putting some in clear spice jars out in the kitchen. I do keep most herbs in a dark cupboard and keep refilling my small, clear jars from these larger storage jars. Herbs stored in jars tend to stay a little fresher then those kept in plastic bags.

Label herbs when you first put them in containers so you will be sure to know what they are and when they were harvested. If any droplets collect on the inside of the container, act fast to rescue the herbs. Such moisture tells you they were not completely dry and are destined to mold unless you take them out and finish drying them.

It is often said the flowers keep for a year and roots and bark keep for two years, but there is no exact cutoff date. The better they are stored the longer they will last. Store your herbs whole or cut instead of ground if you are keeping them for longer than a couple of months. Ground herbs quickly lose their essential oils, flavor, and scent. Judge the quality of dried herbs the same way you determine the quality of fresh ones. If they look and smell the way they did when you first dried them, the herbs are still good.

I have little trouble with bugs infesting my dried herbs. Many herbs, such as santolina and wormwood, are bug repellents. Roots are the most susceptible to bug invasion. The ones to watch out for are brown mealy moths and grain weevils (the same bugs that eat grains in the kitchen). If you discover webs, little holes in the herbs, or if you find the bugs themselves, you have an infestation. If the herbs are salvageable, placing them in a freezer for two days kills the bugs.

# DRYING TECHNIQUES

Special drying techniques preserve flowers or other delicate plants for dried floral and herbal arrangements. These techniques are more work, but are great for herbs that are difficult to dry by simply hanging bunches or laying them on screens. Reserve these techniques for delicate flowers like rosebuds, lilacs, or other plants that tend to shrivel or lose their color when air-dried. Sturdy herbs like yarrow, tansy, marjoram, and oregano do not need these special techniques.

## DESICCANTS

Materials called desiccants absorb water from plants quickly, so that when they dry they retain most of their original shape and color. One old-fashioned method used ground flour. I find medium-ground cornmeal works best. A less-favored method, popular in the seventeenth century, uses sand; however, sand is less absorbent and too heavy for delicate flowers. Hobby stores sell a modern version called silica gel, which is known to chemists as a xerogel of silicic acid. It has increased absorbency (40 percent of its own weight) and a quicker drying time.

Put about one-half inch of either cornmeal or silica gel in a plastic box, which prevents moisture from being drawn in from the surrounding air. A cardboard box will work if it is kept in a dry place. Lay the flowers or other plant material on top of the absorbent material and care-

© Derek Fell

fully sprinkle more material in and around them until they are completely covered. Make sure the material has contact with all the petals. Be careful not to bend the plants when covering them, unless you want a special effect.

The flowers take about two weeks to dry with cornmeal and one week with silica gel. When dry, they should feel like paper and have no flexibility left. They are very delicate and break easily at this stage. If left too long, the flowers become too brittle and fall apart. Flowers removed too soon can droop or loose color. Scoop or pour out the silica gel or cornmeal, then carefully lift the plants out with a fork. Remove the flowers, then carefully brush off excess material will a soft watercolor or makeup brush.

Both cornmeal and silica gel are reusable. Most types of silica gel contain blue crystals that turn pink when they have reached maximum absorbency. To dry these crystals for reuse, place them in an oven set at 300°F (148°C). Store either material in an airtight container so it won't absorb moisture.

## MICROWAVE DRYING

Using a microwave is the newest and fastest way to dry herbs and flowers that will be used for herbal wreaths and other crafts projects. Plants can be microwaved by placing them between two paper plates. A microwave oven will also shorten the time it takes to dry plants in silica gel (as described above). Dry the plants buried in silica gel in a microwave oven container without a lid or in a cardboard box.

The cooking and setting times vary with different types of microwave ovens and the number and type of plants, so some experimentation is needed. It takes about two minutes to dry plants buried in one-half pound of silica gel. The setting is low, between 200 and 350 watts. Afterwards, the flowers will need about 10 to 30 minutes of standing time before removing them from the silica gel.

Not all plants dry well in a microwave oven. Very delicate plants, those that lose their color easily, and ones with thick leaves or petals, often look better dried in silica gel or cornmeal.

## GLYCERINE

Herbs and flowers for wreath making and other decorative purposes can be preserved with glycerine, a nontoxic by-product of soap making. The preserved plants stay flexible, which is important if you are making head wreaths, flowered hats, or any dried flower craft that may occasionally be touched or bumped.

Not all flowers lend themselves to glycerine preservation but those that do provide herbal crafts with more variety. The colorful flowers of annual statice are most commonly preserved with glycerine, since they are very brittle when air-dried. It is fun to experiment with different types of flowers and leaves to see what effect glycerine gives them. Glycerine does darken colors, although the slight darkening is often attractive, giving floral crafts a nice accent. For example, white flowers turn ivory and many leaves become dark and leathery.

Glycerine is sold in drug stores and some craft shops. Stir one part glycerine into two parts warm water. Set the flowers you wish to preserve in at least four inches of the mixture in a jar or vase. The plants must be freshly cut to be able to absorb the glycerine and water mix. Pick them from your herb and flower garden, or buy them at a flower or farmer's market.

It takes about two weeks to treat the flowers. If they drink up all of the mixture, add more. When they are done, they will be flexible and soft to the touch, even though they are no longer fresh. If left in the glycerine solution too long, they become sticky. The lower stem that was in the glycerine solution will be too sticky to work with, so cut it off. Store the plants in cardboard boxes in a dry place until you are ready to use them.

© AGE Fotostock/FPG International

# HERBS IN THE COUNTRY KITCHEN

**A** well-known expression calls something exciting the spice of life. The word *spice* also describes the zesty effect some herbs have on foods. Herbs play many roles in making meals a memorable experience. Since oils, vinegars, mustards, and spice combinations are so often incorporated into cooking, herbs offer a quick and easy way to spice up your life. In this chapter I am going to describe some of their many uses.

Herbs can turn an ordinary bottle of vinegar into a gourmet delight. The most popular herbal vinegars are sage, rosemary, thyme, tarragon, and basil. But do not stop there. Put your imagination in gear to create all kinds of vinegars. Try parsley, oregano, or peppermint, for example. Those who like a little bite can even mince fresh onions or garlic and leave them in the vinegar.

Your herb garden is filled with many herbs just waiting for experimentation. Some of the most unique varieties can be found only in your garden. Chive flowers make an excellent vinegar. Far more interesting than the chives themselves, the flowers turn the vinegar a lovely purple and add a definite chive flavor. Another unusual but tasty vinegar is made from salad burnet. As its name implies, it was once a popular salad herb, but its strong flavor makes it best suited for herbal vinegar.

© Robert Lima/Envision

### HERBAL SALT SUBSTITUTE

*1 tablespoon each, ground*
    *basil*
    *coriander*
    *thyme*

*2 teaspoons each, ground*
    *cumin*
    *onion*
    *parsley*

*1 teaspoon each, ground*
    *garlic (minced)*
    *mustard*
    *paprika*
    *cayenne (optional)*
    *kelp (optional)*

This all-around handy blend gives herbal zest to any meal. Put it on the table in a salt shaker and use it as a salt replacement.

### ITALIAN SPICE

*1 tablespoon basil, ground*

*2 teaspoons marjoram, ground*

*1 teaspoon oregano, ground*

*½ teaspoon each, minced*
    *garlic*
    *onion*

These herbs are famous for what they do for pizza, spaghetti, and almost any tomato dish. If you are a garlic or an onion fan, you can double those quantities, but be careful not to overpower the basil. Its sweet taste is part of the secret of Italian cooking.

### MIDDLE EASTERN SPICE

*1 tablespoon cumin*

*2 teaspoons parsley*

*1 teaspoon each*
    *black pepper*
    *garlic*
    *onion*

This spice blend flavors beans or any other dish you think is worthy of an exotic Middle Eastern flavor.

**The spicy dishes of Mexico, India, Thailand, and China all use mustard and peppers with a liberal hand.**

## MEXICAN CHILI SPICE

*1 tablespoon paprika*

*2 teaspoons each*
   *cinnamon*
   *coriander*
   *oregano*

*1 teaspoon each*
   *black pepper*
   *cayenne (or other chili pepper)*
   *garlic*
   *mustard seed, yellow*

There are many types of chili peppers, each with a slightly different taste and pungency. This recipe makes a hot chili, so if your taste buds prefer life a bit more mellow, use ½ teaspoon instead of 1 teaspoon of the last four ingredients. For a sweeter chili, double the cinnamon. Kidney beans are the most common to put in chili, but try it out on other types of legumes, like lentils and peas.

## EAST INDIAN SPICE

*1 tablespoon each, ground*
   *coriander*
   *cumin*
   *turmeric*

*1 teaspoon each*
   *allspice*
   *black mustard seed, whole*
   *cayenne*
   *cinnamon*

Black or white peppers, chili peppers, garlic, and yellow or black mustard heat up a curry. If cooling down is more your style, use paprika instead of cayenne. You might have an herb called curry plant in your garden. Although it is not an ingredient in East Indian cooking, its smell and taste resemble curry, thus giving it its name. When curry became the rage, but spices from the East were too expensive for most Europeans to afford, they substituted this native plant.

© Derek Fell

## FRENCH LOUISIANA SPICE

*1 tablespoon allspice*

*2 teaspoons thyme*

*1 teaspoon each*
   *bay*
   *black pepper*

*½ teaspoon each*
   *cayenne*
   *cloves*

This traditional cuisine combines herbs from many cultures. Cayenne and bay from the New World blend with spices of the Far East. Turn this recipe into a gumbo by adding 2 teaspoons ground sassafras leaves to thicken and flavor the dish.

## CHINESE FIVE-SPICE

*1 tablespoon each*
   *cinnamon*
   *fennel*

*1 teaspoon each*
   *star anise*
   *black pepper*
   *cloves*

All of these herbs are easily obtained, except for star anise, which is sold in the Oriental food section. If you can not find it, regular anise has a very similar taste. While looking for Oriental foods, buy Szechuan pepper instead of regular black pepper, if you can.

# HERB SALT AND SEASONINGS

There is often not enough time to do the selecting, grinding, and preparation involved in making herbal blends from fresh herbs, especially if you are preparing a meal at the last minute. One alternative is to make herb salts and spice blends ahead of time. Most standard recipes can be adapted by replacing the total amount of all herbs required with your spice blend. Spice blends can season soups, stews, breads, muffins, bread sticks, eggs, beans, pasta, potatoes, cakes, pies, cookies, and specialty dishes. The following recipes offer an assortment of flavors to brighten any table.

If you make a number of blends, you can choose whether tonight's meal will be Italian, Oriental, or Mexican—all with just a few shakes of the spice jar. It may be common to match spices with the appropriate food, but why not be daring? Why not try some Chinese refried beans, an Italian stir fry, or Mexican pizza for a change of pace?

Start with good-quality dried herbs from your garden or buy whole or cut herbs. Avoid purchasing ground herbs since they will have lost much of their flavor. Grind the herbs in a coffee grinder, blender, flour mill, with a mortar and pestle, or whatever is convenient in your kitchen. If pieces of stems remain in the blend, strain them out with a colander, kitchen strainer, or flour sifter. The herbs can be finely ground or left a little chunky, depending on your preference. Small chunks of herbs give a variety in texture to a ground mixture. The following recipes all call for ground herbs, unless otherwise indicated.

© Burke/Triolo

## THAI SPICE

*1 tablespoon lemon grass
    leaves (can be fresh,
    chopped instead of dried)*

*1 teaspoon each
    black pepper
    coriander (or fresh
        cilantro, if available)
    ginger*

Thai food is gaining in popularity. Noted for its hot and sweet combination, it often contains lemon grass, an herb used more commonly for tea than as a flavoring.

Spice Blend Variations: Have fun coming up with your own ideas for other spice blends. If you want a salty taste, but are trying to cut down on your salt intake, add a small amount of kelp powder, available in the herb section of health food stores.

Chopped, dehydrated vegetables give your spice blend a new taste and look. Tomatoes and red or green peppers make it especially colorful in clear spice bottles. Dry your own vegetables in a dehydrator or buy them already dried at health food or grocery stores.

© Steven Mark Needham/Envision

**Ground coriander gives a distinctly different taste than either coriander seeds or cilantro leaves.**

## HERBAL MUSTARD

2 tablespoons ground mustard

2 tablespoons flour

½ teaspoon each
    turmeric
    ginger

1 cup apple cider vinegar

½ cup water

1 tablespoon honey (optional)

a jar

Mix mustard, flour, and spices together. Mix vinegar, warm water, and honey together. Combine dry and wet ingredients in a saucepan. Bring mixture to a boil, turn down the heat, and let simmer for two minutes. Pack into very clean jars while warm. Push out any air pockets. Store in a cool place.

This mustard will last for many months, although its flavor does change as it ages. Mustard connoisseurs say it is best when not more than a few weeks old. One way to keep it fresh is to add a slice of fresh lemon to the jar, on top of the mustard. Replace the lemon with a fresh slice every few days.

Variations: The consistency may be thinned with more water or thickened with more flour, but watch out. Water will make the mustard hotter. In fact, for a very hot mustard, replace ¼ cup vinegar with water (vinegar counteracts the "heat"). If you prefer a mellow version, use oil or mayonnaise instead of water.

To give mustard a French flair, use red wine vinegar, or even wine instead of vinegar. The true French Dijon mustard replaces vinegar with champagne! Duplicate Chinese mustard by using flat beer instead of vinegar.

Different herbs added to mustard create distinct flavors. Make an extra-hot mustard by adding ½ teaspoon of grated horseradish. Horseradish's flavor is produced while you grate it, so add it fresh, if possible. One teaspoon of whole mustard seeds provides an interesting texture. Whole black mustard seeds give mustard color contrast. A dash (⅛ teaspoon) of powdered cloves or dill or both is often added to mustard. A teaspoon of any herb or spice blend from this chapter creates even more mustard varieties.

## PICKLED HERBS

Pickled herbs provide a tasty highlight to meals. They can be served as a side dish or incorporated into other foods. Use them to spice up stir-fried food, soups, and stews.

Herbs that are especially appropriate for pickles include chopped basil, French sorrel, chive leaves, whole nasturtium flowers or pods, and whole, peeled garlic cloves. Pickling makes a lot of wild herbs, such as wild sorrel, young dock, and dandelion leaves (ones most people would never invite to their dinner table), quite palatable. If you have a flair for the unusual, give one of these a try. They are sure to be a showstopper at your next dinner party!

1 cup fresh herbs, whole

1 pint vinegar, your choice

1 tablespoon spices, ground
    (optional)

a jar

I like to use old canning jars to show off the pickled herbs on my shelf, but any jar or crock will do. Take herb leaves off their stems and place in a clean jar. Completely cover the herbs with vinegar, stirring to make sure there are no air bubbles. For a variation, add pickling spices or another herb blend to the vinegar to give it added flavor. Let sit for at least four weeks. Store them in a cool place, but as long as the herbs remain submerged, there is no need to refrigerate.

Variations: Mint Sauce: Pickled mint leaves, either chopped or whole, can easily be made into mint sauce by mixing 2 tablespoons of warmed honey with ½ cup of mint vinegar.

Pickled Nettles: An interesting condiment combining vinegar and oil in the same preparation. Fresh stinging nettles, for example, make a very different, yet delicious, pickle. I learned this one from an Oregon herbalist, Svevo Brooks. Cook them first to remove the stingers, then prepare the whole leaves in either a vinegar or an oil according to the instructions above. When they are ready, drain off extra liquid and submerge the pickled nettles in olive oil, or the oil nettles in vinegar. If you wish, add a few cloves of whole garlic or sprigs of dill to enhance the flavor.

# HERBAL DINING COUNTRY STYLE

Country dining is known for its simplicity, yet it is also famous for its fine taste. Every gourmet cook knows that herbs have the ability to turn a good meal into a delicious feast. The finest cooks prefer using fresh herbs, such as the ones you can harvest from your own herb garden.

Country dining encompasses everything from a picnic to a clambake to a seven-course Thanksgiving or Christmas dinner, and everything from jams and preserves to cider and apple pie.

Fresh and dried herbs can be the stars of any country meal, and the recipes included here are sure to please every family member and friend.

*All recipes serve four, unless otherwise noted.

## FRENCH SORREL SOUP

French sorrel is easily grown in your herb garden. Its pleasingly sour, lemony flavor gives this soup a delicious tang.

*2 cups French sorrel leaves, chopped*

*1 tablespoon vegetable oil or butter*

*4 cups water*

*¼ cup milk*

*¼ cup cream*

*1 bouquet garni (see below)*

*chervil and parsley, chopped*

Sauté leaves in oil or butter. Stir in water, milk, cream, and bouquet garni, and bring to a simmer. Turn off heat and let sit ten minutes. Garnish with chervil and parsley (or fines herbes) and serve.

Variations: You can make a mild version with chard or, if you are adventuresome, make a "wild" soup with any edible wild green, including chicory, dock, and wild sorrel. (Just be sure it is properly identified!) While in Greece, I enjoyed a similar dish called *horta* (or "plant"), which was prepared with fresh, young dandelion leaves.

© Burke/Triolo

## BOUQUET GARNI

These small bouquets are used to garnish (*garni*) soups and stew. For the best flavor, use fresh herbs whenever possible. Both bouquet garni and fines herbes are French seasonings that vary depending on the cook's preferences and what is handy in the garden at the time.

*4 sprigs parsley*

*2 sprigs thyme*

*1 bay leaf*

*1 sprig chervil*

*1 sprig marjoram*

Tie the herbs' stems into a bundle with string. Add one bouquet for every 2 quarts of soup about twenty minutes before the soup is done. Before serving, pull out the bouquet and discard.

Variations: A dried bouquet garni can be made with chopped herbs tied in four-inch squares of cheesecloth. Store them for future use in a tightly covered container.

## FINES HERBES

Fines Herbes is a blend of fresh herbs used in sauces and cheese and egg dishes. In a pinch, you can replace them with dried herbs, prepared the same way as a bouquet garni. To retain their fresh flavor, they are added to a dish just before serving.

*1 sprig each*
    *parsley*
    *tarragon*
    *chervil*
    *chives*

Finely mince herbs, add to dish, and serve.

## PESTO

Pesto is a popular condiment that goes with many dishes. It is delicious with pasta, potatoes, bread, or muffins. Pesto is an excellent way to keep herbs fresh for months after they are harvested. I like to freeze it in ice-cube trays, then store the cubes in a plastic bag in the freezer to keep them handy throughout the year.

⅛ cup pine nuts

¼ cup olive oil

1 cup fresh basil

Parmesan cheese, grated (optional)

Chop the nuts in the blender. Blend in olive oil, basil, garlic, and cheese. To store, press into a container and freeze, or cover with a thin layer of olive oil and keep refrigerated.

Variations: Pesto is usually made from fresh basil, but don't limit yourself, especially if you have a garden full of herbs. Other fresh soft-leaved herbs like parsley can replace the basil or be combined with it. Pine nuts can be replaced by walnuts, or for some really unique flavors, try cashews or pistachios! Traditional it is not, but it makes a new and exciting herbal condiment. For yet another variation, add 1 teaspoon of one of Chapter Four's herbal seasonings.

© Burke/Triolo

EIGHTEEN HERBS TO GROW FOR COOKING

Basil (*Ocimum basilicum*): annual
Bay (*Laurus nobilis*): perennial, not hardy
Chervil (*Anthriscus cerefolium*): annual
*Chives (*Allium schoenoprasum*): annual
*Coriander (*Coriandrum sativum*): annual
*Dill (*Anethum graveolens*): annual
*Garlic (*Allium sativum*): annual
Horseradish (*Armoracia rusticana*): perennial
Marjoram (*Origanum vulgare*): perennial
Oregano (*Origanum vulgare*): perennial
Parsley (*Petroselinum crispum*): biennial
Rosemary (*Rosemarinus officinalis*): perennial
Sage (*Salvia officinalis*): perennial
*Salad Burnet (*Poterium sanguisorba*): perennial
Savory, summer (*Saturia hortensis*): annual
Sorrel, French (*Rumex scutatus*): perennial
Tarragon, French (*Artemisia dracunculus sativa*): perennial
Thyme (*Thymus vulgaris*): perennial

*Edible flowers. Some other edible flowers include: clove pinks, elder, lemon, mallow, pansy, and roses.

## HERB MUFFINS

Muffins from my kitchen are never boring because of the selection of herbs from which I can choose. It doesn't take much time to make muffins from scratch, but you can also add herbs to a plain muffin mix.

*2 cups flour*

*2 tablespoons baking powder*

*½ teaspoon salt*

*2 eggs*

*2 tablespoons vegetable oil*

*¼ cup honey*

*1 cup milk*

*2 tablespoons herbs (your choice)*

Sift flour, baking powder, and salt together. Beat eggs, add oil, honey, and milk. Combine dry and liquid ingredients and mix. Preheat oven to 400°F. Pour dough into a well-oiled muffin tin and bake for twenty-five minutes, or until done. Remove from the oven and let cool a few minutes before popping muffins from the pan. This makes about one dozen muffins. Try a warm, spicy muffin with herbal honey, herb butter, or pesto.

Variations: Suggestions for seasonings to include: allspice, anise, basil, cinnamon, cloves, ginger, orange peel, sage, or thyme, or an herbal blend from Chapter Four. You can even make different-flavored muffins in the same batch. Mix the ingredients, without the spice, so the batter is still slightly lumpy. Pour a few muffins' worth of batter into an extra bowl. Add about ¼ teaspoon herb per muffin, finish stirring, and pour into the muffin pan. Pour a little more batter into the extra bowl, add another herb, and continue until you have a selection of flavored muffins.

# COUNTRY TEA BLENDS

Herbal teas are a healthy alternative to black tea or coffee. Create your own blends by mixing equal parts of your tastiest garden herbs, or buy bulk herbs from a natural food store. If one flavor predominates, reduce the amount until you get the recipe just right. Teas can be made from fresh or dried herbs. Use 1 teaspoon per cup either way. Fewer fresh herbs fit into a teaspoon, but they are stronger tasting.

Steep flowers and leaves in a teapot or cup by covering with boiling water and letting sit for five minutes. Ground herbs in tea bags steep even faster, taking only two or three minutes. Roots and barks take longer to extract, so heat at a very low simmer for five to ten minutes. Keep a lid on the teapot or pan to keep in the flavor. Strain the herbs, add sweetener if you like, and enjoy the tea! In any season you can keep a jar of prepared tea in the refrigerator for a couple of days, handy whenever you want it.

After working in your herb garden on a hot summer day, enjoy a glass of iced herbal tea. Prepare a tea, let it cool, then add ice cubes. Jazz up iced tea with carbonation by making a concentrated tea, using 2 teaspoons of herb per cup instead of 1. When the tea cools, add an equal amount of carbonated water and serve. A slice of lemon or lime make a beautiful decoration for your iced tea.

© Burke/Triolo

| EIGHTEEN HERBS TO GROW FOR TEA |
| --- |

\*Borage (*Borago officinalis*): annual
\*Calendula (*Calendula officinalis*): annual
　Catnip (*Nepeta cataria*): perennial
　Chamomile, German (*Matricaria recutita*): annual
\*Geranium (*Pelargonium* species): perennial, not hardy
　Lemon balm (*Melissa officinalis*): perennial
\*Peppermint (*Mentha piperita*): perennial
　Spearmint (*Mentha spicata*): perennial
\*Sweet woodruff (*Galium odorata*): perennial
\*Violet (*Viola odorata*): perennial

\*Edible flowers. Some other edible flowers include: clove pinks, elder, lemon, mallow, pansy, and roses.

© Robert Perron

# FRAGRANCE IN YOUR LIFE

**M**ost people are intrigued with fragrance. It affects their moods, recalls memories, and, in general, enriches their lives. No wonder country homes have used aromatic herbs for centuries. Your home, too, can come alive with inviting aromas from potpourri jars, pillows, pomanders, and incense of special-smelling blends.

## POTPOURRI

Potpourri is a blend of fragrant and attractive dried plants. There are many recipes available, but I encourage you to learn the true art of potpourri making by creating your own blends. Potpourri is translated from the French as a "combination of diverse elements," and it is diversity that gives the blend character.

Like perfume, individual scents are slightly elusive because they become a harmonious blend—a true potpourri of fragrance. Many plants lose their scent and color no matter how carefully they are dried, so try a few samples first. Some delicate flowers that will not keep their color or fragrance if air dried can be successfully dried in silica gel, as explained in Chapter Three.

Not all potpourri ingredients need to be fragrant. Similar to herb garden or herbal wreath design, a good potpourri is visually appealing because it incorporates contrasting colors and textures. Color can be subtle—pale shades of pink roses with lavender, or bright, with red roses, green cedar leaves, and yellow calendula petals.

Plants from your herb garden and from the wild provide the choicest potpourri materials. Most potpourri ingredients are herbal or floral, but any plant material that dries with an interesting fragrance, color, or texture is suitable. Mosses and lichens, small cones, or evergreen leaves are a few of the materials you may find beyond your garden fence. Materials can also be purchased if you need more variety. Visit a store that sells bulk herbs and let your eyes and nose choose for you.

## ESSENTIAL OILS

Potpourri may be enhanced with fragrant essential oils. The fragrance of old-fashioned potpourri depended exclusively on aromatic herbs and flowers, but modern potpourri makers almost always use essential oils. When using essential oils, remember that you are only trying to bring out the herb's true fragrance, not overpower it. Start with small batches, adding essential oils drop by drop, until you get the smell of it. Keep a record of how many drops you use so you can duplicate your best creations later. Formulas may still need some adjustments, since essential oils vary greatly in quality and strength. Quality may be difficult to judge at first, but your skill will develop with practice.

## FIXATIVES

Fixative herbs make a potpourri's fragrance last longer. Unlike most herbs, whose fragrance declines with time, fixatives improve their scent, and the scent of the entire potpourri, as they age.

Orris root (an iris you can grow in your herb garden) is the most popular fixative because its light, violetlike scent is not overpowering. It comes powdered, in chunks, and sometimes whole. Small, white chunks are preferred, since potpourri ingredients lose their luster when coated with orris powder.

Other fixatives include patchouli, sandalwood, vetiver, balsam of Peru, and gum benzoin, all available as dried herbs or essential oils. Another fixative, tonka bean, is sold whole or chopped. The mild scent of sandalwood and the vanilla-like benzoin, balsam of Peru, or tonka bean easily blend into potpourri, while patchouli and vetiver must be added carefully. The heavy, earthy smell of these last two herbs is one that people either love or hate. Cleveland sage, a fragrant cousin of culinary sage, is another fixative. Although not usually commercially available, it will readily grow in your herb garden.

### TEN HERBS TO GROW FOR FRAGRANCE

Chamomile, Roman (*Chamaemelum nobile*): perennial
Clove pinks (*Dianthus carophyllus*): perennial
Geraniums (*Pelargonium* species): perennial, not hardy
Lavender (*Lavandula angustifolia*): perennial
Lemon verbena (*Aloysia triphylla*): perennial, not hardy
Orris (*Iris florentina*): perennial
Rose (*Rosa* species): perennial
Sage, clary (*Salvia sclarea*): biennial
Sage, Cleveland (*Salvia clevelandia*): perennial
Violets (*Viola odorata*): perennial

© Derek Fell

## BASIC POTPOURRI

*2 cups dried herbs*

*2 tablespoons orris root (or other fixative), chopped (for powdered orris root, or other fixature, use 1 tablespoon)*

*½ teaspoon essential oil blend*

Combine the ingredients and let them sit one week in a closed container to develop the fragrance, which grows richer as it ages. Potpourri keeps fragrant for a few years closed in a container and lasts for months when used as a room freshener. When it finally begins to lose its scent, recharge it with essential oils. Sprinkling brandy on a potpourri is an old technique used to bring out its hidden fragrance.

Variation: Instead of blending the ingredients, layer in a clear glass jar.

## FLORAL BOUQUET POTPOURRI

*1½ cups pink rose buds*

*½ cup lavender flowers, whole*

*½ cup rosemary leaves, whole*

*½ cup pink globe amaranth flowers, whole*

*¼ cup pearly everlasting flowers, whole*

*¼ cup clove pinks, petals*

*2 tablespoons orris root, chunks*

*¼ teaspoon bergamot essential oil*

*⅛ teaspoon rose geranium essential oil*

*¼ teaspoon lavender essential oil*

## WINTER SPICE POTPOURRI

*½ cup red rose buds*

*½ cup uva ursi leaves, whole*

*¼ cup cedar leaves, cut*

*¼ cup cinnamon sticks, broken*

*⅛ cup juniper berries, whole*

*⅛ cup orange peel, pieces*

*⅛ cup star anise, whole*

*⅛ cup red rose hips, whole*

*2 tablespoons orris root*

*¼ teaspoon orange essential oil*

*⅛ teaspoon cinnamon essential oil*

*⅛ teaspoon clove essential oil*

## COUNTRY GARDEN POTPOURRI

*1 cup lemon verbena leaves, cut*

*1 cup calendula flower petals*

*½ cup Cleveland sage leaves, whole*

*¼ cup peppermint leaves, cut*

*¼ cup ammobium flowers, whole*

*¼ cup coriander seeds, whole*

*2 tablespoons orris root, chunks*

*½ teaspoon sandalwood essential oil*

*⅛ teaspoon clary sage essential oil*

# SACHETS

Grind a potpourri into powder and it becomes a sachet. Sewn or tied into cloth bags, sachets often find a home in the linen or lingerie drawer, where they lightly scent sheets and clothes. Sachets enclosed in envelopes can be tucked into letters and packages. Your cat will apppreciate a catnip sachet ball on a string. Moth-repellent sachets are ecological replacements for toxic, smelly mothballs. For the best-quality sachets, grind the potpourri yourself; herbs that are already ground will have lost much of their scent.

### MOTH-REPELLING SACHET

*2 tablespoons each*
    *cedar chips*
    *lavender flowers*
    *rosemary leaves*
    *wormwood leaves*

*½ teaspoon cedar essential oil*

Combine ingredients, grind or blend, and tie into sachet balls. Each one-inch sachet ball replaces one mothball. Lightly crush the bags to release more scent. Recharge them with essential oils every year or two.

Variations: The leaves of bay, patchouli, costmary, peppermint, rosemary, rue, southernwood, and sassafras are also used to repel clothes moths, so use whatever your herb garden provides. For extra-strength balls, add ⅛ teaspoon camphor essential oil (nonsynthetic).

### BASIC SACHET

*2 cups potpourri*

Grind the potpourri in a coffee grinder or blender. Store in a sealed jar or bag for one week to allow the fragrance to completely permeate the ground herbs.

### SACHET BALLS

*1 tablespoon powdered sachet*

*6-inch square of fabric*

*8 inches ribbon or string*

To make sachet balls, cut the fabric with pinking shears. (Choose thin fabric with a tight weave to contain the powder.) Place a heaping tablespoon of the sachet powder in the center, bring the corners together, and tie them with ribbon or string.

# STOVE-TOP POTPOURRI

A tablespoon of stove-top potpourri (also known as simmering potpourri) fills the house with wafting herbal fragrances when simmered in water. You can buy ceramic potpourri cookers that have bowls heated by a candle or electricity. Stove-top potpourri can also be simmered in a pan of water placed on a wood stove or other heat source. These potpourri rely mostly on essential oils for their lasting power. It is easy to turn any potpourri into a stove-top version simply by increasing the quantity of essential oils.

### BASIC STOVE-TOP POTPOURRI

*2 cups potpourri*

*2 teaspoons essential oil blend
(your choice)*

© Steven Mark Needham/Envision

# POTPOURRI PILLOWS

Potpourri-filled pillows can be simple gingham squares or fancy satin and velvet pillows with ribbons and lace edgings. It was once common to stuff bed pillows with herbs to enhance sleeping. "Dilly" pillows, filled with dill seeds and other herbs, were put in cradles to lull babies to sleep. Victorian women used to land on lavender-filled "swooning" pillows to help revive them when they fainted.

Fill pillows with herbs instead of stuffing them. Throw pillows are too heavy and lumpy when stuffed completely with herbs; instead insert a thin, herb pillow of muslin next to the regular batting. (Sew baffles in the inner pillow—as on a comforter—to keep the herbs from shifting.) A potpourri-filled hot pad produces wonderful fragrances every time a hot pan is laid on it.

## DREAM PILLOWS

A sleep pillow, to be placed under your bed pillow, can be small. I make mine five by four inches. Hops encourage sleep. Turn sleep into dreams by adding mugwort, which has a reputation for instilling dreams. Lavender is said to make dreams pleasant and thyme to prevent nightmares. To recall dreams, Shakespeare suggested, "Rosemary, that is for remembrance." Include roses for dreams of love and everlasting flowers to ensure that love lasts forever.

Your friends will appreciate receiving dream (or love) pillows, especially if you enclose a card explaining the old traditions. Refer to old herbals for more ideas. When giving someone a dream pillow, you might enclose a blank journal so they can record their wonderful herbal dreams.

## LAVENDER WANDS

Lavender buds keep their scent for years when kept in these wands. When they do begin to lose their scent, you can gently crush them to release the fragrance and memories of a summer herb garden. People love these wands, but they always ask me what to do with them. Popular in the Victorian era, they were used like sachets.

If you are like me, you may be too busy in the summer garden to complete this project right away. The stalks can be secured with a rubber band while they dry, then put away to wait for a lazy winter day.

© Anita Sabarese

**Europeans have slept on pillows stuffed with hops since medieval days to encourage restful sleep.**

## BASIC PILLOW INGREDIENTS

*½ cup hops*

*¼ cup lavender flowers*

*⅛ cup rosemary leaves*

*⅛ cup thyme leaves*

*2 tablespoons mugwort leaves*

Blend ingredients and sew into small pillows.

## LAVENDER WANDS

*fresh lavender stalks*

*rubber bands*

*1 yard satin ribbon, ⅛-inch thick*

Cut thirteen fresh lavender bud stalks from your garden just before the buds open. This is generally in July or August, when lavender is most fragrant. Carefully bend the stems over, just below the flowering heads. Insert the end of a ⅛-inch satin ribbon into the buds. Weave the ribbon through the stalks, going under one, over the next, and under again, keeping it tight enough to enclose the buds. Continue weaving down the stalk. Tie off with a knot and make a pretty bow. The lavender wand will bulge over the buds and the stalks will form a handle.

© Anita Sabarese

C H A P T E R  S E V E N

# PRESSED HERBS AND FLOWERS

**P**ressing herbs and flowers preserves nature's colors and forms and provides another way to bring your garden and the countryside into your home. Pressed plants can decorate wall hangings, book covers, boxes, furniture, or any other flat surface. They make very special greeting or note cards from your garden. Use them when you give any of the gift ideas in this book and for any special occasions. They can also decorate name tags and stationery.

I press flowers not only for their beauty, but to keep a record of herbs that grow in different places. These flower journals bring back wonderful memories of Grecian hillsides blanketed with flowers, the highlands of Guatemala, and backpacking in the High Sierra.

Once you start pressing flowers, you will see plants to collect everywhere you go. Although the technique is commonly called flower pressing, any interesting part of the plant can be used. Part of the fun of plant drying is to see how each plant is transformed when pressed. Be prepared for some colors to fade either during pressing or after they are dried, but even then, most dried plants keep their charm. The only plants to avoid are those that are poisonous.

# PRESSING FLOWERS

Any book will press flowers but, even when protected with newspaper, pages may become stained and warped. The absorbent pages of an old phone book make a quick press, although dried flowers easily break if the book is bent. A spiral notepad is a handy press on nature walks since notes can be jotted down right next to plants taped on its pages. Children enjoy making their own flower books during family outings and vacations. When you get home, place the notepad under a stack of books for pressing.

Plants must be pressed fresh. Collect them when they are as dry as possible and dust off any pollen, bugs, or dirt. If you gather flowers while strolling along a country lane and your bouquet wilts on the way home, set it in a vase of water to perk it up before drying.

Manicure scissors, X–Acto™ knives, and tweezers are helpful tools of the flower-pressing trade. Pick flowers very carefully, by their stem whenever possible, since delicate ones can bruise just from handling. Fat plant parts, such as thick buds, stems, and leaf ribs need to be sliced in half so the plant can lie flat. Take off a back section, since it won't be seen.

Carefully lay out the flowers so they do not overlap another plant or themselves, unless you purposely want this special effect. Small pieces of nonpermanent, clear tape (available at office-supply stores) will help hold down sturdy stems and leaves. Some flower parts are easier to press separately, then reconstruct later. Flower clusters also need to be pressed individually. For variety, press some flowers with a "profile" instead of open faced and bend some stems into graceful curves. Be sure to press more plants than you need so you have a good selection from which to choose.

# MOUNTING PRESSED PLANTS

Once dry, pressed plants are very delicate and feather light. Transport them with tweezers or on small slips of paper, being careful that they don't fly around the room.

© Christopher Bain

They can be stored on sheets of cardboard in a box. Keep a list of the flowers it contains so you can quickly locate the ones you want.

A storage method I learned from Milaika Edwards, a creative fourteen-year-old who has been drying flowers for years, is a "magnetic" photo album with self-stick pages. The stiff pages are covered with clear plastic to protect the flowers and make it easy to flip through the book to select them. You do need to carefully peel the clear pages back so the flowers don't break. Avoid putting very thin, delicate flowers in the album, since they tend to adhere to the sticky pages and break.

Small drops of rubber cement will secure dried flowers to their permanent surface. (White glue wrinkles the plants and paper as it dries.) Make sure the cement doesn't get on the plant's surface. When the completed "flower picture" is dry, you can cover it with clear contact paper or shellac, or place in a glass-covered picture frame. If you have access to a laminating machine, it can be used to protect the plants.

You can protect your flowers by either spraying on a clear-drying fixative or painting a clear-drying preservative over them. (Both are available at craft, hobby, and art stores.) Use a very soft bristled brush when painting on a preservative and work carefully to avoid breaking the plants. This technique is particularly handy when making a project where you don't want to cover the entire sheet with plastic, but do need to protect the flowers. In a pinch, if you can't find the right materials or you want an inexpensive protection of children's projects, you can brush on a thin layer of white glue.

One way to display and protect your floral pictures is to frame and hang them on the wall. Buy a wooden or plastic frame with a plate glass insert designed for framing photographs. Select a heavy paper that does not bend too easily and cut it to fit in the frame. Follow the instructions for mounting pressed flowers on paper. When the flowers are dry, place the picture in the frame and fasten on the back of the frame to secure it. Your floral picture is ready to hang and enjoy for years to come. The color of some of the flowers may fade with time, but they will keep their delicate form and beauty. The colors will last longer if kept out of direct sunlight.

# PRESSED FLOWER CARDS

Quality paper for making your own cards is available from craft, stationery, or gift stores, or from a printer. Matching envelopes are often available. Before folding the card, "score" it by running the scissor blade lightly along a ruler to slightly indent (not cut) the paper where you want the fold. Fold the paper away from the dent to make a nice even crease that doesn't buckle. Pressed flowers can be glued with rubber cement directly onto the card or onto another piece of paper that is then glued onto the card.

Once the dried flowers are on the card, they are still very delicate and can easily be damaged. To protect them, let the glue dry, then cover them with a piece of clear contact paper. (Contact paper is sold at variety stores and at some grocery and hobby stores). Cut the contact paper exactly the size of the front of the card. Peel the backing off the sticky side and lay one edge along the matching edge of the flower picture. Allow the contact paper to roll down inch by inch until the picture is completely covered. Gently press down any air pockets that are left around the flowers. Applying contact paper smoothly may take some practice, so try it on a few samples until you get the hang of it.

| FOURTEEN FLOWERS TO GROW FOR PRESSING |
|---|
| Bleeding hearts (*Dicentra* species): perennial |
| Clematis (*Clematis* species): perennial |
| Coreopsis (*Coreopsis* species): annual; perennial |
| Echinacea (*Echinacea* species): perennial |
| Geraniums (*Pelargonium* species): perennial |
| Hellebore (*Heleborus* species): perennial |
| Hydranga (*Hydranga* species): perennial |
| Hypericum (*Hypericum* species): perennial |
| Larkspur (*Delphinium* species): annual; perennial |
| Lilys (*Lilium* species): perennial |
| Lobelia (*Lobelia* species): annual; perennial |
| Pansy (*Viola* species): perennial |
| Poppies (*Papaver* species): annual; perennial |
| Sage (*Salvia* species): annual; biennial; perennial |

## FLOWER MOBILES

A unique way to display dried flowers is to make a double-sided card and hang them individually or as a mobile. Children seem to be especially fond of flower mobiles. They also provide a visual decoration for people who are bedridden. Small dried flower cards can be hung almost anywhere, including the Christmas tree.

Cut a stiff card in the shape or shapes you prefer (but don't fold it in half). Glue flowers on the one side, let dry, then cover with clear contact paper. Glue flowers on the opposite side, let dry, and cover them with contact paper. You will have a double-sided card that can twirl and display the flowers. Another version, but one that takes a steady hand, places the pressed flowers directly on a piece of clear contact paper and covers them with another sheet of contact paper. This way both the front and back of the flowers are visible. Since these are flexible, be careful not to bend them and break the flowers.

A more elaborate mobile can be made from glass. Purchase small, clear glass pieces from a craft store or a stained-glass supply store. Microscope slides (from a science-supply or hobby store) will also work. Cut the card the same size as the piece of glass. Glue pressed flowers to both sides and let dry. Lay the card on one piece of glass and cover with another piece exactly the same size, placing tiny dabs of glue around the inner edge of the glass to adhere it. The flower card will then be contained between two pieces of glass. To cover the rough edges and to provide a hanger, glue a cord (from the fabric store) all around the edge and make a loop at the top. If you prefer, the flowers can be glued directly onto one piece of glass; then glue the two pieces of glass together so both the front and back of the flowers are displayed and you can see through the glass. Very small glass can even be hung from earring wires or worn as a necklace.

Either of these techniques can be adapted to making pressed-flower kitchen magnets. Glue the flowers on a card and glue a piece of glass over them. Cut a stiff piece of cardboard into the same size and glue it to the back. Glue a magnet to the middle of the cardboard. (Small magnets and magnetic strips that can be cut to size are sold in craft and hardware stores.)

## FLOWER PRESS

If you plan to do much plant pressing, buy a press or make your own. A homemade press uses blotting paper to absorb the plants' moisture, corrugated cardboard to increase air circulation for quick drying, and plywood ends bolted down to press the plants flat. You can make a flower press any size. A small press is convenient for children or to carry on hikes.

*2 pieces plywood, 10 inches square*

*4½-inch bolts with wing nuts*

*8 pieces corrugated cardboard, 10 inches square*

*16 pieces blotter paper (or 32 pieces of newspaper), 10 inches square*

*paint or lacquer (optional)*

*mat knife or razor blade*

*drill*

Drill a ¼-inch hole in each corner of the plywood, about three-quarters of an inch from each edge. The wood can be sanded, then painted or varnished if you wish. (Later, you might want to decorate the top with dried flowers.) Cut the corners off the cardboard sheets and blotting paper 1½ inches from each corner. Stack the cardboard pieces with two sheets of blotting paper between each one. (The flowers you want to dry will go in between the sheets of blotting paper.) Place the stack between the two sheets of plywood like a sandwich and bolt it together, with the bolts going through the holes in the plywood. The bolts should miss the cardboard and blotting paper where their corners have been cut off. The bolts need to be just tight enough to keep the layers of cardboard very flat. Keep the press in a warm place with good air circulation while the flowers are drying. The cardboard will keep air circulating in the rack.

## MINI FLOWER PRESS

When you are out in the country, or any time carrying a press is impractical, use a mini press so you don't have to pass by a beautiful flower. Fasten a small stack of corrugated cardboard squares and blotting paper together with a heavy rubber band. When you get home, place it under a stack of books to finish pressing the flowers.

© Christopher Bain

© Derek Fell

# HERBAL WREATHS

**H**erbal wreaths give any home a country feeling. They not only look nice, but they also carry light aromas of the herbs they contain. Make wreaths for the wall, small candle wreaths, or large wreaths to enclose a festive punch bowl or to use as a centerpiece. They can be draped in swags over windows and doors and even be worn on the head. Wreaths dress up weddings and birthdays and lend themselves to many other occasions.

Head wreaths are appropriate for any festive day. They also look lovely as hatbands on straw hats. When not being worn, head wreaths can be used to decorate the wall. For weddings, they can be attached to the bride's veil. You can also make head wreaths for bridesmaids and flower girls (and matching corsages and boutonnieres and even dried flower bouquets).

Creating a wreath is one of the most rewarding of herbal crafts. Even those who describe themselves as "all thumbs" make absolutely beautiful wreaths. All you need are the right materials, a little time, and a few step-by-step instructions.

The plants for your wreath can be harvested from your herb garden, collected in the wild, or purchased from nurseries. Cones, barks, nuts, mosses, and twigs that might otherwise be overlooked can accent your wreath. Even objects you might not think of as wreath materials, such as shells, dried chili peppers, small gourds, miniature corn on the cob, and various leaves can create fascinating wreaths. Always keep your eye out for interesting materials. Ribbons, small feathered birds (sold in craft stores), or other additions can be used.

Good sources for dried materials are craft and hobby stores (find them in the phone book). Farmer's markets, where local gardeners sell their produce, grocery stores, and shops at herb farms often sell fresh herbs and flowers that you can dry yourself, following the instructions in Chapter Three. Dried or fresh plants can be used and even combined in the same wreath. A wreath made with fresh materials should be laid flat until it is dry, to prevent it from sagging as it dries.

The biggest problem for beginning wreath makers is using more material than is needed. The first wreath I made must have contained a quarter of my garden. It still hangs on my parents' wall and when I see it now, I realize it contains enough material to make a dozen wreaths.

**Dried peppers provide intense color and intriguing shapes in this wreath.**

## WREATH TECHNIQUE #1 STRAW-BASED WREATHS

The most common wreath-making technique uses a straw wreath base, purchased from a craft store. This technique is especially useful if you want a thick wreath that stands out from the wall or plan to cover it with heavy materials, such as cones. If you've seen straw bases and wondered how they manage to stay together, a Styrofoam core supports the flexible straw. The straw looks more natural, but a plain Styrofoam base works just as well. If you want to make sure a white Styrofoam base doesn't show through the herbs, buy a green one or spray-paint it before using.

*10-inch straw or Styrofoam base*

*dried plants*

*wired sticks (from craft store)*

*spray fixative (optional)*

Divide the plant materials you choose into thirty-six miniature bouquets, about 2 inches in diameter and 5 inches long, with about 2 inches of stems. The easiest design is to make twelve each of three different bouquets. Each style can be composed of all one plant or of different plants. Lay out the bouquets, but don't bother to tie them.

Most plant stems are too flimsy to directly stick into the base. Craft stores sell small wooden sticks with thin wires attached for winding the bouquet stems on the stick. You can then poke the stick into the base. There are also wreath-making machines that automatically attach the bouquet to a pointed metal stick. If you're making many wreaths at once, you can rent one of these machines from some craft stores. Another method uses metal pins (about the same length, but wider than bobby pins) that pin each bouquet on the base. Materials can also be glued on, although it takes a lot of glue, so most wreath makers reserve glue for final touch-ups.

### Making the Wreath

Insert the bouquets into the wreath at an angle so they lie against the wreath base. They should all slant the same direction and overlap like feathers on a bird's back. Space the bundles evenly, just far enough apart so the base doesn't show through. You can work your way around the base in any direction, starting with the inside, outside, or top row first.

When the wreath is covered with flowers and herbs, stand back and admire your creation. Glue on any minor corrections and extra materials. Choose the best direction to hang the finished wreath. Then, make a hanger by twisting a short piece of florist wire into a loop around your finger. Turn the twisted wire ends into a J and insert it securely into the base and your wreath is ready to hang.

# WREATH TECHNIQUE #2 WIRE-BASED WREATHS

This is my favorite wreath technique because you make your own base, allowing more flexibility of size and shape. This technique uses about one-third of the amount of the materials as a straw-based wreath, so it ends up saving time and money.

Make a wreath base out of a heavy-gauge wire macrame ring sold in craft and hobby stores. These rings come in all sizes, so your wreath can be as large or as small as you wish. Specially made heart wires are also available. (You can make rings by bending heavy wire, from the hardware store, into a circle and soldering or wrapping the ends together.) I suggest not using coat hangers or other flexible wire because they are too flimsy. To wrap your wreath, use florist wire on a "paddle" or "spool" that is held in one hand, with the wire through your fingers. (Twenty-eight-gauge wire is flexible, but strong enough so it won't easily break.)

A possible disadvantage to the wire-based wreath is that you are limited to using plants that have flexible stems that won't snap off when wrapped with wire and tops that are full enough to give it width. German statice, sea lavender, airy baby's breath, fluffy pearly everlasting flowers, and gray wormwoods are a few excellent choices. Sweet Annie is popular, but has a notorious reputation for an allergic reaction. Moss works well, especially Spanish moss, which looks like lace. I also like grey santolina and the colorful annual statice, but use both of these fresh since they become too brittle when dried.

*8-inch wire ring*

*dried plants*

*florist wire (28-gauge)*

*glue (optional)*

*spray fixative (optional)*

The wreath base can be made from almost any flexible odds and ends from the garden that are not attractive enough for the wreath itself. Don't worry about its appearance, only the wall will see it! You can also use long pine needles, moss, or thin, flexible twigs. One of my favorite base materials is a stiff, long rush grass that grows wild in marshy areas where I live.

Fasten a bundle of the base plants (about ¾ to 1 inch thick) to the wire base by wrapping florist wire a couple of times around it. Twist the wire ends together to "knot" it and to tighten the plants on the ring. Continue wrapping the wire around the wreath with about a ½-inch space between each wrap, giving each a small tug to tighten it. At the end, overlap the plant material a little, then cut off any excess.

When the entire base is wrapped, cut the wire, leaving a few inches at the end. Wrap this end under some wire that is already wrapped and twist the two together. Tuck this twisted wire away, down into the wreath.

## Making the Wreath

Make each bouquet about 4 inches across and 5 inches long. An 8-inch ring takes twelve bouquets. Imagine a clock with twelve numbers and space them so each is on a number. Don't bunch them too tightly as many overzealous beginners, who discover they have used only eight of their twelve bouquets before they are halfway around the base do!

Wrap the bouquets onto the wreath base with florist wire, with the same technique used to wrap the base. Each bouquet requires about three wraps as you work down its stalk. Place the next bundle on top of the stems of the first bundle and wrap another three times. When the base is covered, cut the wire and twist it to "knot" it. At this stage, your wreath will look beautiful, but you can still glue on more material, even plants that are brittle or have no stems. This wreath can be hung on a push pin or small nail. Catch the inside of the ring on the nail or make a wire hanging loop (see Technique #1).

© Robert Hoebermann

## WREATH TECHNIQUE #3 HEAD WREATHS

The head-wreath technique is similar to that for a wire-based wreath, but it uses a flexible wire that adjusts to different head sizes. You can make a "headlet" to tie under the hair or partially encircle the head, with ribbons hanging on the side, or one that encircles the head, with ribbons hanging down the back.

Choose flexible plants that withstand an occasional bump without shattering, such as pearly everlasting, German statice, and sea lavender. Annual statice and baby's breath look beautiful on head wreaths but must be made flexible by being preserved with glycerine (described in Chapter Three). Since this wreath is designed to be worn, use florist tape, which is much more comfortable than wire.

*flexible wire (from hardware store)*

> *for a half wreath—16 inches long*

> *for a full wreath—26 inches long*

*dried plants*

*florist tape, ¼-inch thick*

*white glue (optional)*

*spray fixative (optional)*

*ribbons*

Wrap the entire length of the wire with florist tape to create a nonslippery surface. With pliers, twist the wire's ends into ¼-inch loops (for the ribbons). Make eight plant bouquets, about 2 inches across, for a half head wreath (or twelve for a full head wreath). Starting on one end, wrap the first bundle onto the wire with florist tape about three times. Place the next bundle facing the same direction so that it overlaps the stem of the first and wrap it. Continue along the wire until it is covered. Bend the wire carefully into a U. Tie matching ribbons through the loops and the wreath is ready to wear.

Opposite page: Dried swags offer a whole new dimension to interior design. Drape them over an arched entry, around a window, or to frame a baby crib. Above: A beautiful dried grass wreath with cones, gourds, and pods.

© Robert Hoebermann

# FINISHING THE WREATHS
## GLUING ACCESSORIES

As a last step, different materials can be glued onto any of your wreath projects. When making your first wreaths, you will have the best success by limiting the number of extra materials glued on. Choose perhaps four items; you can always add more later. Arrange them, then glue them on the wreath. When finished, hang your wreath and step back to check for places that need to be filled out.

You have your choice of white or hot glue. White glue takes a while to dry, but gives you plenty of time to change your mind. Hot glue dries instantly and is great as long as you work fast and are sure of placement. (If you do make a mistake, carefully cut pieces off instead of pulling them, and a quarter of the wreath, off the base.) One problem with hot glue is it leaves trails resembling spiderwebs.

Hot glue comes in two forms. Glue sticks are used in a glue gun that is very mobile, but leaves you with only one hand free. Hot melt glue chips are melted (use an old electric pan) and plant materials are dipped into it, which can be awkward, but leaves both hands free. In either case, be careful with the hot glue.

## SPRAYING THE WREATHS

If you wish, wreaths can be sprayed with a fixative to extend their life and help keep tiny pieces intact. (Unless, of course, you make an edible herbal wreath for use in the kitchen!) Lacquer and shellac produce a slight sheen on pods and cones but don't change the appearance or fragrance of most herbs and flowers. Air out for twelve hours to get rid of the fumes. The most ecological method is to use ordinary hairspray, which is available in nonaerosol spray bottles.

Your wreath will keep for many years if it is hung away from direct sunlight and moisture. If you cannot resist hanging a wreath on your front door, bring it in for the winter. Or, since you know how to make them, replace your outdoor wreath with a new one every year.

# HERBAL GIFTS FOR A COUNTRY CHRISTMAS

**W**inter in the country is a special time. The chores of harvesting herbs, preserving the garden's harvest, and cutting firewood are done. The time has come to enjoy the warmth of the wood stove and friends and to bring some cheer into winter's cold, short days. It also brings time to make gifts. When the holiday season arrives, they will only need the addition of a ribbon, then they can be sent on their way or placed under the tree.

If you want to have the most charming old-world Christmas imaginable, make your own herbal ornaments and gifts, for which recipes and projects abound in this chapter. The country Christmas tree is an old-fashioned tree, filled with handmade ornaments, candies, and little gifts hidden among the boughs. It may have small bunches of dried flowers and even candles. This is a tree of wonder and imagination that represents a lifestyle that takes time to create fantasies and gifts to share with friends.

# ORNAMENTS

## POMANDER BALLS

A pomander ball is a spicy, hanging potpourri made from an orange or other fruit studded with cloves. The cloves act as a wick to draw out the fruit juice and as natural preservatives to keep the fruit from spoiling as it dries. A spicy pomander powder covers the ball and preserves its aroma for years to come.

Oranges are the most popular fruit to use for pomander balls, but apples, lemons, limes, and even grapefruits, will work. Pomanders always make a nice gift, reminiscent of old-world charm. Hang them on the Christmas tree, use them in centerpieces, and tie them on packages. Pomanders take weeks to dry, so start this holiday project ahead of time.

*Oranges or other fruit*

*Whole cloves*

*⅛-inch-thick ribbon*

*Cinnamon, powdered*

*Orris root, powdered*

*⅛-inch-thick strips of masking tape*

*Nail*

Placing cloves in an orange can be very time-consuming, so I space the cloves far apart and leave room for plenty of ribbon. It makes for a more attractive pomander with less work—a perfect combination!

Ribbons looks best lying flat against the fruit rather than over bumpy cloves, so reserve a space for them with the masking tape. Fill the space between the masking tape with cloves by first piercing the orange's skin with a nail (or other pointed object). Leave the space of one clove between each one. You can place the cloves closer, but not touching, or they will pop each other out when the orange shrinks from drying. While it is difficult to keep the little bud on the end of the clove, try not to break the star at the clove's base.

When the fruit is covered, peel off the masking tape and roll the clove-studded ball in the powdered herbs. Keep the pomander in a cardboard box or paper bag where there is warmth and good air circulation, such as on a high kitchen cabinet. Every day for the first week, roll it again in the powdered herbs. After a few weeks, it will be dry and very lightweight. Glue the ribbon in the space reserved for it. To dress up your pomander, glue on extra bows, ribbon streamers, and tiny dried flowers or spices.

Variations: Add ⅛ teaspoon essential oils to the pomander powder before you roll the ball. You can also use other powdered herbs, like nutmeg and ginger, with or in place of the cinnamon. To hang, pomanders can be strung like beads if a hole is pierced all the way through before they are dry.

## MINIATURE WREATHS

Miniature wreaths, only a few inches wide, can be made on a wooden ring—the kind used to hang draperies. Find them at craft and hardware stores. I save tiny flowers left-over from wreath and pot-pourri making for this project.

Miniature wreaths are ideal to tie on gifts, hang on the tree, or display on the wall. A small magnet (available at craft and hardware stores) glued on the back makes your wreath into a refrigerator magnet. These wreaths are also the perfect size for taper-candle wreaths. Make a pair and give them as a gift with a set of candles color coordinated to the wreaths. When the taper is placed in a candle holder, the wreath slides down over the top and is supported on the holder.

*1 wood ring, 2 to 4 inches
    wide*

*dried flowers*

*glue*

Glue the flowers on one side of the wooden ring. Let the glue dry and the wreath is finished. It's as simple as that.

## MULLING MIX

Mulled cider and wine were once the rage in England's country homes. The seventeenth century poet, John Gay, said, "Drink new cider, mulled with ginger, warm." Mulling herbs fill the house with holiday aromas, managing to make even the simplest occasion festive. At a party, you will notice people taking deep breaths as they comment, "Mmmm, that smells like Christmas!"

Serve mulled drinks to company and your family not only during the holiday season, but throughout the winter. Use sweet, red wine, apple cider, or any fruit juice or juice blend. The spices used were traditionally varied in view of what was available, so change the proportions to suit your taste. A bag or jar of mulling spices, decorated with a bow and a few cinnamon sticks, along with a bottle of wine, makes a special hostess gift.

4 sticks of cinnamon, 3 inches
    long*

2 heaping tablespoons dried
    orange peel, chopped

2 heaping tablespoons star
    anise, whole

1 tablespoon allspice, whole*

2 teaspoons cloves, whole*

1 teaspoon ginger powder

1 teaspoon nutmeg powder*

Combine ingredients and use one tablespoon of the mixture for every quart of wine or juice. Sweeten with two tablespoons of sugar or honey, if you wish. Gently simmer for about fifteen minutes. Heating removes wine's alcohol so if you want your drink to keep its punch, make a double batch of mulled wine (one teaspoon spices per pint), then dilute it with unheated wine before serving. Strain and serve warm.

Mulling herbs look great floating around in the pot, but to avoid having to strain the herbs before serving, put them in a cloth "mulling" bag during cooking. Buy a muslin bag with a drawstring top or tie the herbs in a cheesecloth sac. By the way, dry fresh orange peel by chopping the fresh (unsprayed) peel into ½-inch squares, and placing it in a warm place until it is dry.

Variations: For a simple mulling mix, use only the starred (*) items.

© Derek Fell

# BATH GIFTS

Body-care products make wonderful, personal gifts that people can pamper themselves with again and again. Most of these are amazingly easy to make, but your friends and family won't believe it. Don't tell them it only took you ten minutes to make the elegant bath oil; we will keep it a secret.

Taking a fragrant herbal bath is a totally luxurious experience. It warms up cold winter days and drives away holidays pressures. This is a perfect gift if you are someone who has decided to make all your gifts, and it is already Christmas Eve. As long as you have the supplies on hand, you can have your gifts done in thirty minutes. Then, wrap them up and enjoy the evening, giving yourself a pat on the back for your creativity.

---

### TWENTY USEFUL ESSENTIAL OILS

| | |
|---|---|
| Benzoin | Lime |
| Bergamot | Orange |
| Cedarwood | Patchouli |
| Cinnamon | Peppermint |
| Clary sage | Petrigrain |
| Clove | Pine |
| Ginger | Rose geranium |
| Grapefruit | Rosemary |
| Lavender | Sandalwood |
| Lemon | Wintergreen |

---

### BATH OIL

*2 ounces vegetable oil (your choice)*

*¼ teaspoon of lavender oil*

Mix the oils and stir. It's done—really. If you are mailing it, don't even bother to stir it, the postal service will do that for you. Make fancy bath oil by adding a small dried flower sprig to each bottle. Either tie the sprig on the outside with ribbon or submerge it in the bath oil.

## BATH HERBS

In this formula, the salt softens the water while the oatmeal turns it into a skin-softening, milky cream. Essential oils and herbs provide fragrance. The combination creates a creamy, herbal-scented, skin-softening solution every time you squeeze the bath bag. These bath bags can be used in place of soap, so they are good for those with sensitive skin, or for anyone who enjoys bathing.

For a gift, fill a fancy bottle with the bath herbs. A bag tied with a string or ribbon or with a drawstring is handy to fill and refill. Make the bag out of cotton or terry cloth, or get one of the muslin, drawstring bags (available at many natural food stores).

*¼ cup each*
    *calendula flowers*
    *chamomile flowers*
    *lavender flowers*

*½ cup quick-cooking oatmeal*

*½ cup table salt*

*2 teaspoons lavender oil*

*a small bag*

Combine ingredients and put ¼ cup in a small, cloth bag, about four inches square. Use for two to three baths, then refill the bag.

Variations: Use different herbs (almost any potpourri combination will work) or another oil or an oil blend instead of lavender.

## SCENTED BODY POWDER

*½ cup arrowroot powder*

*½ cup cornstarch*

*2 tablespoons orris root, powdered*

*¼ teaspoon each carnation and violet essential oils*

Combine the powders in a plastic bag, tie the bag well and mix by turning the bag over a few times. Add the essential oils to the powder, drop by drop. Break up any clumps that form. Let sit for at least five days while the scent spreads throughout the powder. Use as body, bath, or baby powder.

Place the finished body powder in a wide powder container and apply with a puff. For a shaker container, use a spice jar with a perforated lid insert or the shaker containers sold for salt, pepper, and sugar. (Containers are available in import and housewares stores or look for ceramic containers at craft fairs and handicraft stores.)

# PART FOUR

TIMOTHY W. FREW

# INTRODUCTION

**T**here is an immediate and rewarding satisfaction in working with stencils. The process is easy, and the results appear right before your eyes.

Stenciling began as an affordable alternative to wallpaper, rugs, and printed fabrics. Many people brightened their homes by stenciling colored patterns and designs on walls, floors, furniture, bedclothes, window coverings, and any other surface that seemed appropriate. In addition to floors and walls, stencils were used for decorating furniture, picture and mirror frames, wood and tin boxes, chests, cupboards, tablecloths, draperies, and more.

The art of stenciling has deep traditions and roots in virtually every country of the world. In 2000 B.C., the Egyptians used stencils to decorate the vaults of their dead. Even before that the Chinese used stencils to produce repeated designs on everything from pottery to clothing.

With the opening of trade routes between China and the rest of the world, the art of stenciling quickly spread. In the Middle Ages, the French decorated everything from playing cards and games to textiles and wallpaper with colorful stencils. In England, stenciling was used to decorate the walls and furniture of medieval churches.

If you're not experienced with stenciling, then start small; stencil a welcome plaque for your door; your name or house number on your mailbox; or stencil a few flowers and a heart on a wooden birdhouse. It really doesn't matter how much you do or on what, for it is in the act of actually stenciling that the real pleasure comes. When the project is finished and you see the results, your satisfaction and sense of achievement will inspire you to try larger and more complicated projects.

This book is designed to inspire as well as instruct. As you leaf through these pages, look at the beautiful designs created by other artisans. Borrow from these ideas and incorporate them into your own designs. Once you have mastered the few basic design skills and application techniques, you will see that a whole new world of decorative ideas is yours for the taking.

# TOOLS AND MATERIALS

**T**he basic techniques involved in stenciling are simple. It takes very little artistic ability to perform all of the tasks necessary to complete a stencil project. There are, however, a few skills that must be mastered in order to attain the most beautiful results. As with most artistic endeavors, having the proper tools and equipment at hand is half the battle.

You will need to purchase a few inexpensive items in order to get started on your new hobby. The following chapter provides a guide to the different tools and materials you will need. Many of these items can be used for other crafts projects besides stenciling. The number and variety of materials you buy will, to a certain extent, depend on how involved you plan on getting in the craft of stenciling. There is one thing to keep in mind, however, when purchasing tools and materials for any craft: Do not skimp on quality. Inadequate brushes, cheap paints, and poor quality materials will lead to nothing but frustration for any would-be artisan.

# BRUSHES

A complete set of high-quality brushes is probably the most important component of a stenciler's kit. Never skimp when it comes to buying stencil brushes. Poor quality brushes will lead to nothing but headaches in the long run. The bristles will quickly fall out, and paint will not go on evenly.

A stencil brush is vastly different from an ordinary paint brush. Designed to be held like a pencil, the traditional stencil brush is short and stubby and has stiff hog's hair bristles that are cut flat at the end. Instead of using a stroking motion as in most types of painting, the stenciler holds the brush perpendicular to the surface and applies the paint with a tapping motion. By varying the speed and intensity of this tapping, or pouncing motion, the stenciler can control the depth of color and shading of the design.

Stencil brushes vary in size from 1/5 of an inch to 2 inches (.5 cm to 5 cm). The size of the brush you use depends on the size of the opening on the stencil you are applying—the larger the opening, the larger the brush. It is best to have several different brush sizes on hand so that you are ready for anything. In addition, you should have a separate brush for each different color of paint you are using on your stencil design. This way you will not have to stop and clean your brushes every time you want to switch to a different color. If you do use the same brush for two or more colors, make sure it is thoroughly cleaned and dried to avoid any unwanted mixing of colors. To clean oil-based paints from a brush use either turpentine or mineral spirits. To clean water-based paints, use a mild soap and warm water.

Stencil brushes also come in a variety of different handle lengths and widths. The type of handle you use is largely a matter of personal preference, although short-handled brushes are generally easier to use when stenciling in and around tight areas. Before purchasing your brushes, pick each one up and hold it. Test its balance and how it feels in your hand. If you are a beginner, you may want to try a variety of handle lengths until you find the brush style that best suits your technique. Before using a new brush, twirl its head between your fingers to remove any loose bristles. Wash it thoroughly, using one of the two methods described in the previous paragraph. Make sure it is completely dry before using it.

# THE STENCILS

Beginning on page 375 are more than fifteen different pre-printed stencil motifs. There are designs suitable for children, French country motifs, a beautiful selection of floral and nature-inspired designs, as well as stencils that echo the traditional qualities of Early America. In addition to the main stencil designs, there are a few matching stencil borders that can be used in combination with the main stencils, as part of an overall design, or they may just as easily be used separately. Whatever your specific needs, there are myriad creative possibilities with this collection of stencils. To use these designs, cut the pages directly from the book and use them as actual stencil templates, or preferably, transfer them to heavy-duty stencil paper, a stencil card, acetate, or Mylar® by using either tracing paper or a photocopier.

If you do use these pages as stencil templates, or if you transfer them to a stencil card or some other sort of un-coated heavy paper, it will be necessary to treat the paper with a combination of turpentine and linseed oil to help protect the stencils (see page 220).

In addition to using the motifs provided here, I encourage you to design your own stencil patterns. You can find inspiration for these stencil designs all around you. Just keep in mind that you will be dealing only with silhouettes. Look around the room at the objects you have collected and imagine how they would look in silhouette and as a repeated pattern. Also, look at magazines, at printed or woven fabrics, and at china and earthenware. Any of these can provide inspiration for a stencil design.

## WHAT TYPE OF STENCIL PAPER SHOULD I USE

The complexity and involvement of your project—whether it is a small box or an entire room—will, for the most part, dictate what type of material you use for your stencil template. For small projects, such as a box, an article of clothing, or even a small piece of furniture, you can use **stencil paper**. This semi-transparent waxed paper is inexpensive and easy to use. Because you can see through it, stencil paper allows you to cut a stencil from a design placed directly beneath it, eliminating the need to transfer a design to the template. The problem with stencil paper is that it is not very durable and, therefore, not good for large projects or repeated uses.

One step up from stencil paper, is **stencil card** or **oaktag**. This is a thick piece of flexible paper that in most cases has been treated with linseed oil to give it a smooth, impermeable surface. Untreated stencil card is also widely available; however, it should be treated with a combination of turpentine and linseed oil before it is used. This is the material that most widely resembles the stencils used in the past. Designs can be drawn or photocopied directly onto it, it is easy to cut, and it is strong enough to handle extremely intricate designs. Stencil card is not transparent, however, so registration marks must be used to line up the templates precisely when applying the stencils. Beginners may find it difficult to work with stencil card because the surface below the stencil cannot be seen.

One of the best materials for making stencils is **acetate**. These thin, transparent plastic sheets come in a variety of sizes and gauges. For most stenciling projects, I recommend using a sheet of acetate between .0075 and .010 gauge. When using strips of acetate to make long straight lines, it is best to use thicker, stronger gauges. Acetate is extremely durable and can withstand repeated uses. In fact, with proper care, acetate stencils should last for years.

Stencil outlines are drawn directly onto the acetate with a technical marking pen filled with permanent ink. Any mistakes, however, must be immediately removed with damp cloth before the ink dries. Acetate stencils are great for applying multicolor designs where a different stencil must be used for each color. Because it is transparent, acetate enables you to easily line up the various colors of a single design. The trickiest thing about these plastic stencils is that they are somewhat difficult to cut. If your razor knife becomes at all dull, or if you are cutting intricate curved shapes, the acetate has a tendency to split. To avoid this, always use a very sharp knife and change the blade frequently.

**Mylar®** is perhaps the most versatile, durable, and easy to use of all the stencil template materials. Mylar® is a trade name for a frosted plastic film that is very similar to acetate. Its main advantage over acetate is that its slightly frosted surface can be drawn on with a pencil, making it easy to correct mistakes. In addition, Mylar® is less rigid than acetate and does not have as great a tendency to split while it is being cut. Available in virtually all art supply stores, Mylar® comes in a range of grades, .004 or .005 being the best for stenciling.

## CUTTING UTENSILS

A craft knife with replaceable blades, such as an X-acto® knife, is the ideal cutting tool for any type of stencil material. A sharp knife is essential to successful stenciling. Using a dull knife will result in ragged cuts and may cause you to slip and damage the stencil. These ragged edges and unwanted cuts will then show up on the stenciled surface. You can avoid wasted hours of work and sloppy results by changing the blade in your knife often. A blade can never be too sharp, so always have plenty on hand. Blades can be purchased at any hardware, hobby, stationery, or art supply store.

In addition to a razor knife, you should have a heavier utility knife and a good pair of strong scissors for cutting and trimming sheets of acetate or stencil card to the proper size. Craft-style hole-punchers, which come in many sizes, are also valuable cutting tools for tapping out neat circles from intricate stencil designs.

# PAINT

Virtually every type of paint can and has been used in the art of stenciling. In the old days of professional country stencilers, the artisans mixed natural pigments, such as brick dust or clay, with skim milk to make a usable paint. As a result, the colors used in stenciling were often determined by the materials at hand in a particular region. If the area was rich in brown or yellow clay, then these would be the prevailing colors in most stencil designs. In spite of this, the artisans could achieve at least a limited variety of color by mixing the paints. Working from three or four basic colors, the stencilers of old could work and rework the color combinations until they found something they liked.

Today, premixed paints are available in any color, shade, or hue; however, a good working knowledge of color and paint mixing is essential for best results.

In addition to the many colors of paint available, there are also several types of paint that you will need to consider before you begin your stenciling project. Different types of paint have different characteristics and advantages. Your choice of paint depends on what surface you are stenciling and what type of results you are looking for.

## ACRYLIC PAINT

Acrylic paints are probably the most versatile and easy to use of all stenciling mediums. They are inexpensive, fast-drying, and are available in an extremely wide variety of premixed colors. Because they are water soluble, acrylics can be cleaned and thinned using ordinary tap water. Once dry, they form a tough skin that will last for years.

These easy-to-use paints are suitable for most dull surfaces that will not receive a lot of wear and tear. If the surface you are stenciling has a high gloss or will receive a lot of traffic you will be better off using japan or some other oil-based paint. Acrylics, however, will adhere to most surfaces. They are suitable for wood, concrete, plaster—virtually any paintable surface. On fabrics, acrylic paint stays pliable and survives repeated washing.

## JAPAN PAINTS

Most professional stencilers prefer to use japan paints for large projects such as walls, floors, ceilings, and large pieces of furniture. Japan paints dry quickly to a matte finish and, like acrylics, are available in a wide range of colors. These paints, however, are oil-based, making mixing and clean-up a bit more involved than with acrylic paints. Japan paints must be cleaned and thinned using either turpentine or mineral spirits. When using these paints you must be very careful to clean up any mistakes or spills immediately. Japan paints are as permanent as they are fast-drying.

Japan paints are ideal for glossy, nonporous surfaces such as glazed ceramics, metal, glass, and plastics. They are also a bit more durable than acrylics, so if you are stenciling a floor, or some other area that will receive a lot of wear and tear, japan paints may be your best choice.

## SPRAY PAINTS

In recent years, many artisans have experimented with the use of spray paints in stenciling. The effect that these enamel paints produce can be very lovely and is somewhat different from the stippled effect created by a brush. Proper use of these paints, however, requires a steady and practiced hand. If the paint is applied too quickly it has a tendency to run under the stencil. The stencils must be firmly in place, and the paint must be applied in short, quick bursts to avoid this problem.

# SETTING UP A WORK SPACE

Prior to beginning any creative project it is essential to establish a good work space. This may be a temporary space that you set up before you work and then return to its original use when you finish, or a space that you permanently establish that will only be used for craft projects.

## THE SURFACE

No matter where you do your stenciling, begin with ample room and an uncluttered working space. The required elements are few. A firm, steady work surface such as a kitchen table, a work table, or a table you construct out of a heavy surface on solid sawhorses is essential. This work surface can be in the garage, in the basement, or in the kitchen; the location is not as important as the sturdiness of the surface. Stenciling requires consistent pressure and a gentle pouncing of the stencil brush onto the stenciling surface. A card table or any similar light-framed table may wiggle and impede your working rhythm, and the results could be disastrous.

The table should be high enough so that you don't have to bend over too far to do your work. A good guideline is to have a table that is level with, or just above your belly button when you are seated at a chair. Of course, if you work standing up the table should be higher. Nothing takes the fun out of a craft project quicker than a sore back and a stiff neck.

Stenciling projects require a great deal of cutting. To protect your work table lay down one or two layers of cardboard. It is best to tape down the cardboard with masking tape to prevent it from slipping. In the process of cutting away the printed pattern you will be cutting through the stencil paper and into the layer of cardboard underneath. Be sure to change the undersurface when needed to eliminate a build-up of ruts, which may throw the knife blade off course and damage the stencil.

The best surface for cutting stencils is a glass cutting mat. Simply purchase a sheet of ¼-inch (.6 cm) thick glass cut to approximately 12 inches by 12 inches (30 cm by 30 cm). Either have the edges filed down or cover them with masking tape. Also, it is a good idea to paint the underside of the glass white so that if you are using acetate stencils, the outlines will show up. The blade will move along smoothly without creating ruts or gouges. You will also find that this type of cutting board doubles nicely as a palette for mixing paints.

Another cutting surface option is a self-healing cutting mat, which can be purchased at an art supply store. These rubberized mats have a surface that will close up immediately after cutting. The main drawback of self-healing mats is that the knife blade tends to drag more than on a glass cutting mat.

## THE LIGHT SOURCE

Ample light is essential to a proper work space. If possible, set up your space near a window. Natural light is always pleasant, and tends not to distort color as much as artificial fluorescent light. It is important, however, to supplement natural light with an incandescent light source. Clip-on lamps provide mobility and are handy for directing light to specific areas. These lamps are inexpensive and readily available at most hardware stores. When situating your lamps, try to prevent casting unwanted shadows on your work area. Experiment by adding or moving lights until the work area is as bright and evenly lit as possible.

## THE WATER SOURCE

Because you are working with paint, it is necessary to have a source of water nearby. This can be a sink or a plastic bucket or bowl that you keep within reach. Acrylic paint cleans up so well with tap water and a mild soap that even the kitchen sink is an acceptable source. As long as you carefully rinse all surfaces, you will not damage the sink. If you are working with oil-based paints and turpentine you will want to use a utility sink rather than your kitchen sink for cleanup. Also, you should have an ample supply of paper towels or newsprint on hand to clean up spills and reduce unwanted mess.

## HELPFUL TOOLS

Additional materials that will help you with measuring and cutting include: a T-square, a clear plastic triangle (being able to see through your triangle is a great advantage), a tape measure, a plumb line, masking tape, a metal ruler for use as a cutting edge, an S-curve, a palette knife, a sturdy pair of scissors, a sharp pencil, and, as stated earlier, plenty of paper, cardboard, and extra razor blades. Paper of all kinds and sizes seems to always come in handy for masking out an area of the stencil, for testing out a possible design, for sketching out a completely new design, or simply for use as scrap paper. I find drawing paper, tracing paper, and graph paper all essential components of my studio inventory.

## MAINTAINING YOUR WORK SPACE

Almost as important as having a comfortable well-lit work space is keeping that work space clean and organized once you begin your work. Keep your materials in order. Always have plenty of rags or paper towels on hand to wipe up any spills. Paints should always be stored tightly covered. Periodically clean your hands to avoid smudging paint on your finished project. It is also very important to avoid a build-up of dried paint on the stencil card. Too much paint build-up will produce a fuzzy and distorted edge.

A gummed-up stencil brush can also lead to mistakes or accidents. Check the brush periodically and clean it with warm water and a mild soap. If you do clean your stencil brush in the middle of a project, be sure to dry it completely so that the excess water does not dilute the quality of the colors. Always do a test blot before going back to the stencil.

By keeping an orderly work space as well as clean hands and tools you will avoid countless mishaps. However, no matter how careful you are, the occasional accident is bound to happen. Don't panic; acrylic paint is easily cleaned from most surfaces with a damp cloth while it is still wet and oil-based paints can be cleaned with a quick application of turpentine or mineral spirits.

# BASIC TECHNIQUES

O nce your design plan is finalized, it is time to actually begin stenciling. While the entire process is fairly simple, it does require several basic steps that must be carefully followed for optimum success. These include transferring the designs to stencil card, acetate, or Mylar®; cutting out the stencil; measuring the project; preparing the surface; mixing the paint; applying the paint; and, finally, sealing the project.

None of these techniques is extremely difficult, but, all will require a certain amount of practice before they can be mastered. This chapter provides a basic outline for the various techniques involved in this craft. Through practice and repetition you will be able to expand upon these basic techniques and begin creating a working style of your own.

If you are not accustomed to using a razor knife, practice cutting out several working designs. Learn which cutting angles are easiest for you and develop your techniques for cutting out difficult curves and circles. Mixing paints and developing a personalized palette is a challenge that can perplex the most experienced of artists. The more you work with your paints, the more comfortable you will feel with color. If you are new at stenciling start off with a few small, simple projects consisting of only two or three basic colors. After you successfully complete these, you will be more at ease with the stenciling process, and then be able to go on to more involved projects.

# TRANSFERRING THE DESIGNS

When transferring a stencil design to stencil board or an acetate or Mylar® sheet be sure to allow a margin of at least one or two inches (2.5 to 5 cm) around the pattern to help keep the stencil strong.

While there are several methods for transferring designs, the simplest is to use a photocopier. Most modern photocopiers are capable of copying onto fairly heavy stencil board and even acetate. In a matter of seconds you can make enough copies of a single motif for a many-colored design.

If you don't have access to a photocopier and are using stencil board or paper, use carbon paper instead. Simply sandwich the carbon paper—carbon side down—between your design and the stencil board and secure it with masking tape. Next, trace around the outline of the design using either a hard pencil or a fine-tipped burnisher. Once the carbon design is transferred to the paper go over it again with a dark, fibre-tipped pen.

Another method is to trace your design onto tracing paper using a soft pencil, leaving as thick a layer of graphite as possible on the paper. Then place the tracing paper—graphite side down—on top of the stencil paper and secure with masking tape. Trace over the outline again using a hard pencil. The process should leave an outline on the stencil paper. Darken the outline with a fibre-tipped pen.

If you are using acetate or Mylar®, simply lay the sheet directly over the top of the stencil design, secure it with masking tape, and transfer the motif by using a technical drawing pen. Note: Water-based inks, such as in most fibre-tipped pens, will not hold on acetate. You must use permanent ink on acetate.

# CUTTING THE STENCIL

The most important thing to remember when cutting out your stencils is to make sure you know what gets cut out and what remains on the stencil. This sounds simple, but be careful; your eyes can play tricks on you, and, before you know it, you've made an incorrect cut. Do not cut the small bridges that separate one part of the design from another, as they hold the entire design together. If you do cut one of these bridges, carefully repair it with a small piece of masking tape.

The most successful way to cut stencils is to always use a sharp blade, a smooth undersurface, and even pressure that allows the knife blade to glide smoothly along the printed pattern. Again, remember to always have extra blades for your razor knife on hand; when the blade feels dull, put in a new one. A sharp blade is half the cutting battle so don't be stingy.

The most efficient way to cut a stencil is to maintain a downward cutting motion, rotating the stencil as need be. Use a light, constant pressure and try to lift the blade as little as possible. A few long cuts are much smoother than a lot of short cuts. A straight-edge ruler or an S-curve can be a great help when confronting long lines in a design. Many stencilers recommend securely taping the stencil down to the cutting surface before making a cut. This will prevent the stencil from slipping during the cutting process. I find, however, that keeping the stencil mobile makes cutting much easier. This way, you can turn and shift the stencil to achieve the best cutting angle possible. The best of both worlds can be achieved by using a glass cutting mat. Then you can secure the stencil to the cutting surface and still have the freedom to rotate stencil and cutting mat together.

The stencils included in this book are printed on thin paper. As stated earlier, I recommend transferring the designs to stencil card or acetate to provide sturdier stencils. If you choose to use the actual pages as your stencil, or if you transfer the designs to uncoated paper, you must treat these stencils with a protectant prior to use. This will aid in cleaning the templates as well as prevent them from soaking up too much excess paint. A thin coat of wax, acrylic spray, or linseed oil works well in protecting the stencil for repeated use. When using thick stencil card, rub a thin layer of turpentine on the stencil before treating it with linseed oil. This will help compress the paper and make it easier to cut.

© Christopher C Bain

# MEASURING A PROJECT

## SINGLE MOTIF

If you are stenciling a single shape onto an object, first find the center of the surface that is going to be stenciled. Even if you don't want the stencil perfectly centered, this will give a good reference point from which you can make adjustments if necessary. Make short vertical and horizontal lines across the surface, forming a cross or plus mark at its center. Then, using this mark as a reference point, hold the stencil in various places until you have found the position you want and mark it with a light pencil line. When you decide on the best placement, fasten the stencil down with masking tape.

Another method of finding the correct positioning for the stencil is to make a cut-out copy or actual proof of your stencil motif and use it as a template for finding a position. When it looks right, replace the proof with the real stencil and begin the process.

## REGISTER MARKS

Register marks are used for lining up a stencil if you intend to duplicate the design horizontally, vertically, or diagonally, or if you want to make multiple color stencils (see below). They determine the location or placement of the cut stencil design in relation to the overall surface. They ensure the proper alignment and even spacing of the stencil by remaining a fixed constant. If you use a border pattern, the register marks will allow you to keep the spacing of the repeated image even, while eliminating a great deal of measuring.

## MULTIPLE MOTIFS AND BORDERS

Stencil borders and multiple motifs can be placed in various ways on any surface. The trick is to keep these repeating patterns running straight and spaced evenly. This is where register marks come in handy (see above). The use of a cardboard template will also help. For example, let's assume you want to stencil a simple border running along the top of a wall. The first step is to determine exactly how far from the ceiling the border should be. Eyeball it, measure it, adjust and readjust it until you have the perfect distance. Then measure a piece of cardboard to use as a template to fit between the stencil and the ceiling. The dimension of the template should be adjusted to the border you have chosen. Fit the top edge of the template against the ceiling, and the bottom edge against the top of the stencil. This will place the border at a consistent distance from the ceiling. Tape down the stencil and apply the paint. Then move the stencil over and line it up using the template and register marks. Simply repeat this process across the room, being sure to carefully line up and tape down the stencil before applying any paint. When you apply tape to your original stencil always be very careful that you don't rip the bridges.

Another method for stenciling a border is simply to measure the distance you want the border to be from the ceiling, and draw a line the length of the wall, being very careful that it is as straight as possible. Then use that line as a guide for the register marks on the stencil.

If you are working out a placement for a large focal design in the center of a wall with a border leading up to it, you must start from the main design and work out from it. Mark a guide line along the length of the wall as described above. Then mark where you want the main design to fall. If the actual design is too large or too small, you can adjust it with a photocopier (see page 220). Then tape down the main design and apply it first. Next apply the border, working out from the main design.

To stencil a vertical border, use a plum line to mark a straight vertical guide line. Then check this guide line with the architectural line of the wall by using a right angle. Not all walls and ceilings are architecturally pure, especially in older houses. You may have to do some adjusting in order to get a usable guide line.

Ultimately, what is most important is the visual balance on the surface. Scale and proportion are the key elements in making the overall design work. Rely on your eye, and ask others to look at it before applying any paint. It is better to take the extra time to carefully lay out a project than to apply paint hastily and regret it later on.

The technique for stenciling borders is explained in greater detail in Chapter Four.

## PREPARING THE SURFACE

What kinds of surfaces can you stencil on? Well, just about anything. The best and most receptive surfaces are smooth ones, but you may apply a stencil on barn siding or cement, it is entirely up to you. Again, acrylic paints work well on most surfaces, except for high-gloss finishes, glass, and shiny metals. In these cases, japan paints are a better choice. Always read the information on the tube or can before using any type of paint. Some surface preparation is always necessary before the stenciling process can begin.

Courtesy Stencil-Ease

## PAINTED WALLS AND WAXED OR TREATED WOOD

Wash painted walls with mild soap and warm water and clean wood of any wax build up. Using a little #0 or #00 gauge steel wool on the surface will give the paint a greater holding quality. Try to avoid stenciling raw wood, at least at first, since it will absorb your paint into the untreated fibers, making it very difficult to hide any mistakes. It is best to treat the raw wood with a thin coat of sealer before stenciling on it.

## PAPER

Most papers will provide you with a base for stenciling. However, smooth papers work better than coarse ones, since the paint will not bleed as easily. You can create your own birthday or holiday cards as well as develop pictures you might later frame. You might want to try stenciling signs for school or community work.

## FABRIC

There is a multitude of possibilities when stenciling on fabric. You can decorate T-shirts or sweat shirts, ornament sheets, or adorn table cloths and napkins with beautiful patterns. Your home is an endless source of possibilities. Try stenciling some curtains or pillows for your porch. Use a stencil design along with a printed fabric or a checked pattern to create your own unique patterns. Fabrics are a versatile foundation for building creative projects.

Acrylic paint takes well to fabric and is machine washable, but you may also wish to explore some of the specific fabric paints available. Be sure to follow the directions on the paint container before mixing fabric paints, then follow the general printing instructions in this book. The technique is always the same.

Stenciling fabric is easy; however, there are a few rules you should follow to achieve the best results. If you intend to wash the fabric often, wash and iron it before applying the stencil. This will remove the sizing from the cloth and make it more receptive to the paint. If you are preparing fabric for drapes, you may work directly on the unwashed material.

Natural fibers take fabric paints better, but acrylic and textile paints will work well on all materials and fibers. Again, if you use specific fabric paint always follow the printed information provided on the package.

Fabric is porous and paint will penetrate through the fibers onto the undersurface. Change the undersurface often to avoid making a mess. When printing on fabric, it is usually better to use a cloth undersurface. Also, be sure the undersurface is directly under the layer of cloth you are stenciling. For example, if you are stenciling a T-shirt, put a piece of cloth inside the T-shirt to prevent the paint from bleeding through to the back of the fabric. Mistakes cannot be removed from fabric. Take the fabric off of the undersurface once you have stenciled it so that it doesn't stick to it. Placing a piece of cardboard under a garment will help it to hold its shape and prevent the paint from seeping through the garment.

When working with fabrics, the work table should be covered with cloth. I usually secure a soft but firm underpadding to the work table with duct tape. This provides a solid bed to stencil on and allows the necessary "give" for the pouncing of the stencil brush.

## OTHER SURFACES

Baskets, tables, chests, porch furniture, and other wood projects are all good materials for stencil designs. As your skill develops, larger and more complicated projects will be possible. Again, always check the surface you intend to stencil. If it seems very smooth, rub it with a little steel wool or some very fine sandpaper.

# MIXING THE PAINTS

No matter how complex, well-planned, or beautifully conceived a stencil project is, its success or failure is ultimately determined by the use of color. The degree of refinement and complexity you wish to give your finished stencil project depends on how well you choose and mix your colors.

Art supply stores offer a wide selection of premixed colors. Depending on how involved you wish the project to be, it may not be necessary to mix your own colors. Your options, however, can be further enhanced by mixing paints to achieve a nearly endless array of hues, tints, and tones. I suggest purchasing up to twelve different premixed colors. This will provide you with a good base from which to work. Here is a selection of paints which can be used as is or mixed to attain virtually any color needed: magenta, lavender, royal blue, green, both light and dark brown, orange, red, gold, yellow, white, and black.

Always use a separate dish for each color. Open the jar of paint and take out a small amount with a palette knife or an old kitchen knife and immediately return the lid to the jar. If you are mixing paints, use the palette knife to thoroughly blend the colors together until there is no trace of either original color left. Do not use the stencil brush for mixing paints. It is important to keep that brush as clean as possible.

Be sure to mix enough paint for your project, but remember that both acrylic and japan paints dry rapidly. If you notice your paints drying out as you are working, add a small drop of water to acrylic paint or mineral spirits to japan paint to keep the pigment workable.

Once you have arrived at the palette of colors you like, practice stenciling on some scrap paper that has a similar background color to the object you are intending to stencil. This testing process helps prevent mistakes and is well worth your time. Make adjustments to your color until you have found just what you are looking for. Once you have the paint on the walls it will be too late to make drastic color changes.

Always have plenty of water or mineral spirits on hand when working with paint. An old jar or a coffee can works well for this purpose. The water or mineral spirits will come in handy for thinning paint, correcting mistakes, and for cleaning the stencil brush. Never leave a paint-covered stencil brush sitting for very long. If it dries, you will have a pretty, but useless, brush. Mild soap and water will clean the brush easily if the acrylic is still wet, and turpentine or mineral spirits will do the job on japan paint. If you are leaving your work for a few hours and don't want to go through the trouble of thoroughly cleaning your brushes, wrap them securely in aluminum foil to keep them from drying out.

Stencils can be found on everything from seat cushions to floor cloths to carrying bags.

# APPLYING THE PAINT

Once the stencil has been secured to the surface with masking tape, take the stencil brush in hand and lightly dab the brush into the paint a few times until only the tip of the brush is thoroughly coated. Then blot the brush on some paper towels to remove the excess paint, being sure to leave enough for the painting process. Getting the proper amount of paint on your brush is a simple process that is critical to success; it does take some practice.

Using short, stabbing strokes, dab the color into the cut areas of the stencil. Only work with one color at a time. In most cases you should cut out a separate stencil for each color. However, if the area you are coloring is small, you may simply block out the part of the stencil design that does not receive that particular color. Use waxed paper, typing paper, or additional pieces of stencil paper to cover the areas you do not wish the paint to go through. A small piece of masking tape will work equally well. (Take care not to lift off the small bridges.) Blocking out these areas provides greater freedom.

The density or fullness of a particular color depends on the degree of pressure you apply when dabbing. Color saturation is determined through mixing, but if you apply the pigment lightly, the image or painted shape will appear faint. The tricky balance is to know how much paint to leave on the stencil brush and how much pressure to apply when dabbing. Practice is the best teacher. You may consider testing your technique on a surface similar to the one you intend to use for your final surface. Newsprint is also a good testing ground for working out technical control and color combinations. This will give you a chance to master the process before actually beginning. It is also possible to add shading or vary the tone of a specific area of the design by shifting the pressure on the brush. The more you experiment, the greater your control over the medium.

Allow yourself the time and flexibility to play with the materials. This book provides you with a great potential for understanding the foundations and techniques of the art of stenciling.

Use a smooth, constant stroke when cutting out the stencil design. The fewer times you lift the razor knife of the stencil, the fewer jagged edges you will have. If you do get ragged edges, use a piece of fine sandpaper to smooth them down. A straight edge and an S-curve are extremely helpful tools when cutting out a stencil.

Once the stencil is cut out, tape it securely to the surface you wish to paint. Adjust, readjust, measure, and eyeball it until you have the exact position you want.

Put a small amount of paint on a plate or palette and lightly dab the end of the stencil brush into it, being careful to only cover the tip of the brush with paint. Remove excess paint from the brush by dabbing it on a paper towel.

© Ralph Bogertmann

© Ralph Bogertmann

Apply the paint to the open areas of the stencil using a light pouncing motion. Never use a stroking motion. The pouncing motion will apply a smooth, even layer of paint.

Add more paint to the brush as needed, making sure not to saturate the bristles. An overloaded brush will cause the paint to run. When applying more than one color to a stencil, complete one entire color before moving on to the next.

Once the stencil is applied, carefully lift the template off of the surface, being careful not to smudge the paint.

# PROTECTING THE PROJECT

Even though acrylic and oil-based japan paints are very durable, it may be necessary to protect your project with a sealant. This will depend on how much wear and tear the painted stencils will receive. How you seal your project largely depends on the type of surface you are stenciling. Fabrics stenciled with acrylics or fabric paints need only be sealed with a hot iron and then gently washed. In most cases, wall stencils do not need to be sealed at all, unless they are lower down on the wall and in an area that receives a lot of traffic, such as a hallway.

Most projects, however, require some sort of protection so that the paints will last through the years. Polyurethane varnish is the most commonly used sealant available today. It is easy to use and provides a durable water-resistant film on any painted surface. Polyurethane is available in gloss, semigloss, and matte finishes. Gloss produces a clear, highly lacquered look; semigloss gives a naturally polished silky sheen; and matte has no shine at all.

Before applying any varnish to your project, make sure the stencil paints are completely dry. For oil-based paint wait at least twenty-four hours. Acrylic paints dry much faster, but you should wait for at least six hours before applying varnish. Apply two or three coats of varnish to the project, making sure that each coat is completely dry before applying the next. For large projects, apply the varnish with a flat, one- to two-inch (2.5-to 5-cm) paintbrush, being careful to avoid brush marks. Spray varnish is great for small projects. Follow the instructions on the can.

There is the possibility that the varnish you use will cause the paint to bleed slightly. This is especially true with red pigments. Always read the labels of both the varnish and the paint cans to be sure you are using the correct combinations. In addition, test a small area of the stencil before applying varnish to the whole project.

Once your project is sealed it should last for years under normal wear and tear. At times it may be necessary to touch up both the paint and the varnish. There is more information on protecting your projects in the chapters that follow.

© Nancy Hill

# SMALL OBJECTS

The stencil is the perfect medium for decorating a wide array of small objects, from toys, wooden boxes, and picture frames to wrapping paper, stationery, greeting cards, and placemats. Virtually everything that can be painted can be stenciled. Objects with smooth surfaces will take a stencil much better than those with uneven surfaces.

While many people think of stenciling chiefly as a means for embellishing walls, floors, or furniture, artisans throughout history have been using the medium as an inexpensive way to put personal decorative touches on otherwise mundane items. In fact, if you are a novice stenciler I strongly recommend that you direct your first endeavor toward a small object, such as a Shaker box, a picture frame, or a greeting card. This will give you an opportunity to become comfortable with the medium and the basic elements of design and color before you tackle a larger, more permanent project. The basic concepts of design, placement, measurement, and application are essentially the same for smaller objects; however, because you will be working within a limited space with fewer variables, it will be much easier to achieve success.

Look around you. Practically every object you see could be enhanced by the addition of a well-placed stencil. A wastepaper basket, a tissue box, a bread basket, a planter—all of these objects offer possibilities to the creative stenciler. An old cookie sheet can be transformed into a colorful serving tray; a hat box can be turned into a lovely container for cosmetics, letters, or bric-a-brac; even an old mayonnaise jar can be transformed into a bank for a child with the application of a few stencils.

# DESIGNING SMALL-SCALE STENCILS

If there is one thing to keep in mind when developing a stencil design for a small object, it is not to get too carried away with it and over-stencil the object. Because you will be working within a tight, confined area, a little bit of stenciling goes a long way. If you let loose with your brush, stencils, and paint, the result will look jumbled at best. Subtlety is a wonderful aspect of any stenciling project, large or small. When working with a box or a picture frame, it is easy to get carried away in the process. A bit of refined, intricate stenciling can be much more effective than an overwhelming mishmash of flowers, borders, and cross-hatching.

The use of a stencil key can be very helpful when designing a pattern or a series of motifs for a small object. This entails making a template, or a tracing, of the various surfaces of the object you will be stenciling (a box or a jar, for instance). By converting your three-dimensional object into several two-dimensional surfaces, you will be able to get a good overall idea of how the pattern will ultimately fit on each surface.

First, trace each of the surfaces of the object onto a separate piece of tracing paper. Next, tape each of the templates you have just made to a separate piece of graph paper, lining it up with the grid on the paper. This will help you to center your design, as well as to line up and space each of the motifs.

Sketch the main motifs you will be using in your project on separate pieces of graph paper, making several copies if you will be using repeated motifs (this is where a photocopier comes in handy), and cut each of them out. Now you have a graph paper record of each surface, as well as loose motif templates that you can rearrange to come up with your design. As you move the various elements around try to achieve a balance and spacing that is pleasing to the eye and appropriate for the size of the surface you are working with. As you develop your design, you may realize that the

Courtesy Yield House, N. Conway, NH

motifs you are using are either too large or too small. Once again, a photocopier is great for making fine adjustments in size. If you don't have that luxury, make sketches by hand, using graph paper as a reference.

When you are happy with the design, carefully attach each element to the template with rubber cement or transparent tape. Next, either photocopy the final design onto a piece of stencil paper or carefully trace it onto tracing paper and transfer it to stenciling paper using one of the methods outlined in Chapter Two. Once you have repeated this process for each of the surfaces of your project, you will have a complete set of premeasured stencils ready to cut and apply.

Courtesy Stencil-Ease

# TINWARE

Painted tinware, or toleware, was once a staple of the colonial household. Brightly colored pitchers, cups, candlesticks, trays, coffeepots, and other tin pieces were sold by "tinmen" who traveled from town to town. These light, decorative items offered an inexpensive way for colonial families to brighten up their otherwise rather drab interiors.

The tinware was both hand-painted and stenciled, usually on a thickly lacquered or painted surface. The colorful designs consisted of motifs taken directly from rural life. Intricate borders would frame lavish decorations of fruits, flowers, animals, even highly detailed barnyard scenes.

The favorite objects for this type of tinware decoration were serving trays, which came in a wide range of sizes and shapes; hinged document boxes, the colonial version of the safety deposit box; buckets, used primarily as planters or spittoons; and coffeepots and pitchers.

With today's growing interest in the rural lifestyle of eighteenth century colonial America, decorative tinware is again becoming popular. Craft stores, flea markets, and county fairs often offer an array of stenciled and hand-painted tinware. It is much more satisfying, however, to purchase plain tinware from the hardware store and decorate it yourself using stencils. Tin watering cans, buckets, pitchers, mugs, trays, and boxes can all be transformed into beautiful decorative items.

The process for decorating a piece of tinware in the traditional way is simple; however, there are several steps you must follow for optimum results. If you are stenciling a piece of old tinware with traces of paint or varnish on it, first remove all of the paint with a commercial paint stripper. Next, use a coarse piece of steel wool to smooth the surface of the tin. The smoother you get the surface, the better your final results will be. If the metal is rusted or pitted, go over it with rust remover and sand it smooth with a fine sandpaper, then wash the piece thoroughly with soap and water and wipe it clean with a tack cloth to remove any stubborn dirt.

Next, apply two coats of metal primer to prevent the tin from rusting in the future as well as to give the background paint a good surface on which to adhere. Allow at least twenty-four hours for the primer to dry after each coat. After the final coat is completely dry, rub it down with a piece of fine steel wool to roughen the surface a bit for the background paint and to eliminate any brush marks. Then use a tack cloth to remove any dust from the surface.

Now apply at least two coats of background paint to the tinware. Use a flat, oil-based paint in any color you choose. The traditional tinware artists primarily use black, red, or yellow for the background. The color you use will largely depend on the colors you have chosen for the stencil design. Again, allow the paint to dry thoroughly between coats and gently rub the surface with steel wool before you begin stenciling.

The most difficult aspect to stenciling tin is getting the paint to the proper consistency because the metal is very hard and smooth. It is best to use japan paints on this type of surface. Water-based paints have a difficult time adhering to tin. When stenciling on tin, it is best to pay less attention to shading and more to producing sharp outlines.

After the stenciling is complete, allow it to dry for about three days and apply a coat or two of varnish to protect the final work. Many artisans also like to give the tinware a final coat of clear paste wax for a soft sheen.

# BORDERS

The border is the most traditional of all stencil forms. Throughout the history of the art form, this simple framing device has been an integral part of more elaborate stenciling projects. Walls are rarely stenciled without some sort of border treatment to the frieze, floorboard, chair rail, or all three. Similarly, floors are frequently marked off with some sort of border. either elaborate or simple, before the main stencil design is completed in the middle. Floor borders are also used to highlight rugs, tile work, or the plain wood.

The versatility of the stenciled border and its ability to improve proportions, delineate boundaries, compliment ornamentation, and highlight architectural details have made it an extremely effective tool in interior design. Aside from its role within more elaborate projects, the border can be used as a distinct form of decoration on its own. Essentially nothing more than a series of repeated motifs spread out in a straight line, the border is used in every type of traditional stenciling project. Walls, windows, door frames, floors, staircases, floors, floorcloths, furniture, boxes, shelves, curtains, bedspreads, virtually everything that is stenciled receives some sort of border treatment.

The border is a great device for visually altering and improving the proportions of a room. You can compensate for a ceiling which is too high by placing a narrow border at picture-rail height. Such a border will break up the large expanse of space between the floor and ceiling and focus the eye lower on the wall. Another well-placed border at chair-rail height will further serve to alter the visual dimensions of a room. If, on the other hand, you wish to visually increase the height of the ceiling, use borders to form vertical panels on the walls. This will carry the eye upward and make the ceiling appear higher. Take care, however,

Courtesy Stencil-Ease

not to create too much of a separation of wall areas with borders. This can create a jumbled and confused effect that will overpower the eye. A heightening effect can also be achieved by adding a border either directly above or in place of the baseboard, thereby adding visual weight to the lower part of the room.

The stenciled border has the subtle ability to pull together several aspects of an overall interior design. It can pick up a few elements of a pattern from a curtain, a piece of furniture, or even a set of china that is on display and then integrate it into the design scheme of the room. Use borders to accentuate doorways or archways. Enhance a sloping ceiling by adding a border along the wall just below ceiling height. Run a border around a window and then repeat the design on the bottom edge of the window shade.

Staircases offer a wealth of opportunity for border treatments. Run a thin border just above or below the banister or the baseboard on either side of the stairwell. A vine border running down the stairs themselves can also be quite effective. Add a floral border across each of the stair risers.

The border is most effective when it is not obtrusive; when it compliments a design rather than dominates it. This does not mean that a border has to be uncomplicated. Many of the most effective border designs are quite elaborate, requiring hours of careful planning and artistry. In general, however, executing a stenciled border is a fairly simple process that often looks much more complex than it actually is.

Borders can also be used to give a flat surface a three-dimensional effect. This *trompe l'oeil*, or "trick of the eye" effect has been employed by stencilers for years. By using foreshortening techniques, the stenciler can simulate a plaster relief frieze between a picture rail and the ceiling. Similar relief and three-dimensional effects can be stenciled onto furniture to imitate moldings and carvings.

## CHOOSING A PATTERN

The first step in creating a border is determining the pattern or motif you wish to use. Ideas for border patterns can come from a number of sources. Usually a border pattern is a much simpler motif than those used in large scale stencil designs. Look around the room you wish to stencil. What motif possibilities does it contain? Look at the carved wood borders on furniture and door frames. Architectural pediments and friezes may offer ideas for border outlines that can help to integrate the whole room. Other great ideas can be found in old tiles, plates, cups, ceramics, quilts, and draperies. You may also find inspiration from art and design movements of the past. Art deco, art nouveau, Victorian, early Egyptian and Greek art, Chinese etchings and prints, or French country motifs may offer the perfect design element for your stenciled border. The stencil designs in the back of this book contain motifs that will suit any taste or decor, from country to geometric to modern.

## TECHNIQUES FOR APPLYING BORDERS

The border is a simple device to stencil. The basic techniques for applying these stencils were touched upon in Chapter Two. Depending on how involved and complicated the stencil design is, the exact methods of application may vary. There are several techniques that are specific to borders alone.

Essentially there are two types of borders: those that run in a continuous straight line with a simple repeat, and those that have a larger, more complicated repeat. If the repeat is small and essentially continuous, such as a dentil border, geometric border, or a simple vine, very little measuring and preplanning is needed. You can simply start at one end of the wall and continue on until you reach the other end.

If, however, the border contains larger, more spread out repeating motifs, a little more planning is necessary. You must determine how many times the element will repeat in the given space, and exactly where each element will fall. Ideally you will want the repeating pattern situated in such a way that it avoids ending the border in a partial pattern. Also, you must consider the size of the motif and create a spacing that fits within the proportions of the design. The amount of space between repeats and the final size of the motifs will determine the final effect of the border design. If the stencil pattern will not fit into the space an equal number of times, and if a partial pattern at the end of the border will look awkward, then the size of the pattern may be too large or small for the room or the object you are stenciling. Do a few test proofs of your border on strips of paper. By holding or taping this paper to the wall you can get a pretty good idea of how the final border design will appear and exactly where each element will fall.

## MARKING YOUR BORDER

Once you have determined the sizing and spacing of your border design you must carefully mark it out on the surface. Lightly draw a line across the wall where the center of each stencil will line up. Use a soft lead pencil and straight edge to make sure the line is level. If the border is to go around a wall, measure down from the ceiling or up from the floor and mark it off every ten inches (25 cm) or so. If the border is running up the wall, measure from the corner where the two walls meet, or use a plumb bob and chalk box to achieve a straight line. Next, connect the dots with your straight edge. When marking off your project, you may find that the walls, ceilings, and floors of the room are not completely straight. As a result your line may curve in places. It is best to straighten out this line as much as possible. If your final border curves along with the wall or ceiling you will end up with an inaccurate design.

## TURNING CORNERS

There are two basic methods for making a right angle (from horizontal to vertical or vice versa) with a stenciled border. The first and simplest way is by "blocking." In this method you stencil out to the end of the horizontal border and then turn the stencil at a right angle and pick up the vertical section flush with the end of the last section you stenciled, basically forming the letter "L" with your border. Mask the end of the first border to prevent any overlapping.

The second method, known as "mitering," is a bit more complicated. This method provides a gentle, continuous

© Richard S. Mandelkorn

joint. To achieve a mitered corner, draw a diagonal line at a forty-five degree angle from the corner where the two sides of the border will meet. Place a piece of masking tape or some other type of mask along the line on the opposite side from which you are stenciling. Then, stencil up to and over the masking tape. Once that section has dried, move the masking tape to the other side of the line to mask the area just stenciled. Continue to stencil in the other direction so that the two sides meet at an angle.

If the border design is made up of free-form florals or small, simple geometric patterns, then no real planning is needed. The design will be easy to pick up when going in another direction. Turn the stencil plate around the corner and pick up the pattern halfway through.

## APPLYING A STRIPE

A plain stripe or band is perhaps the simplest type of border to apply. It is also one of the most common borders. Stripes are frequently used around a floor, a piece of furniture, or along a wall. Quite often they are used in conjunction with a more elaborate stencil design; however, they can also be effectively used on their own. As with a more elaborate stenciled border, it is important to carefully mark off the stripe with two parallel lines. It is important that the line is straight and that any curvature of the wall surface is compensated for. For making a striped border, all you need is two long pieces of acetate or stencil board. It is best to use a precut edge rather than an edge you cut yourself, which will not be as straight. Tape one of the sheets of acetate or stencil board to the surface so that the precut edge lines up with one of the lines. Then tape the other piece along the other line. Block each end of the stripe with a piece of masking tape. Apply the paint and move both pieces of acetate down to the next section of the striped border and continue until the stripe is complete.

Turning a corner with a stripe is simple. Stencil up to one edge and then turn at a right angle. Be sure to mask the end of the stripes you have already stenciled to avoid an unwanted buildup of paint.

# CHAPTER FIVE

# FLOORS AND FLOORCLOTHS

Just as the American colonialists used stencils as the chief means for decorating their drab walls, they also used stencils to provide colorful and inexpensive decoration for their floors. At the time, carpets and rugs were scarce and expensive so people used paint to adorn their plain wooden floors. The very first stencil and hand-painted floor designs in colonial America were primitive imitations of the rug patterns that were popular in Europe and in the growing cities of Philadelphia and Boston. These designs consisted mostly of simple geometric shapes—a central pattern of checks or diamonds surrounded by a plain striped border.

Today, stenciled floor designs have become more and more elaborate. Some designers lay out intricate floral or woodland scenes—all done with stencils—on their bleached oak floors. Three-dimensional checkerboard patterns and meandering basketweave or grapevine borders are all quite common. Yet, even though modern stenciling techniques and the continual interest in stenciling design have enabled artisans to stretch the boundaries of the medium, more and more people are opting for the simple stenciled floor designs of America's colonial past. Whereas thirty years ago, wall-to-wall shag carpeting was all the rage, today people are tearing up that carpeting to uncover beautiful bare wood floors that hold myriad possibilities for subtle design treatments and schemes.

There are three basic approaches to the stencil design of a wood floor. First, the floor can work as the dominant element in the overall interior design scheme. It can be a colorfully ornate design that serves as the focal point of the rest of the design scheme. This is usually only possible if you are starting the entire interior design of the room from scratch. It is often difficult to create a dominant presence in a room containing already established elements.

The second approach is to equally balance the impact of the floor design with the other dominant elements of the room. This can be accomplished by picking up a motif from the walls or the fabrics (i.e. draperies, upholstered furniture, etc.) in the room and incorporating them into the design of the floor stencils. You can also use the stencil as a unifying device by bringing together colors or motifs from two seemingly disparate elements already present in the room.

The third approach is to create a minimal effect with the stenciled floor, putting the design emphasis on the walls, furniture, or draperies in the room. Use a delicate pattern on the floor and perhaps just two shades of the same color. A subtle, yet beautiful effect can be achieved by outlining the floor with a simple border pattern and leaving an open expanse of finished wood in the center of the floor. Or, use a border to outline a plain area rug in the center of the room.

Floor stencils provide a very economical and easy way to put a final personalized touch to any interior design scheme. Floor stencils are especially well suited to rooms which receive a lot of wear and tear such as a kitchen, hallway, or child's room. Stenciling is a lot cheaper than carpeting and, if properly applied, will last much longer.

The possibilities for effective floor designs are only limited by your imagination and the degree of effort you wish to put into the project. In the dining room you can stencil a border around the area where the table will be placed. In the bedroom you can pick up a motif from a bedspread and continue it onto the floor. The floor in a child's room can be transformed into a play with stencils of farm animals or a circus train. Use stencils to cover an entire floor surface, or only parts of the surface, leaving a large area of wood. Many subtle effects can be achieved by using stains and varnishes instead of paint. There are a great variety of

Stenciled floor designs can be approached in many different ways. A sparse floral pattern works well on a plain, varnished wood floor. If you would rather not put a permanent design on the floor, then a stenciled floor cloth may be the answer (*above*).

paints and stains available that are suitable for floor stencils. Be sure, however, to always use oil-based stains and varnishes, because they can withstand the heavy traffic the floor will receive. Japan paint is the best choice for floor stenciling because it is both durable and quick drying. This is especially important because very often you will be kneeling or walking over areas that have just been stenciled when working on a project.

Some wonderful effects can be achieved by bleaching, staining, and painting the floor before applying the stencil.

# PREPARATION

Floor stenciling requires much more preparation than any other type of stenciling. For the best results, a wood floor should be new or completely redone before stenciling on it. Even the best paints will not hold on floors that are ingrained with wax, grease, and dirt. In addition, uneven floorboards, splinters, and indentations will result in an uneven print and will damage your stencils and brushes. On the other hand, some people like the rustic look that can be achieved by stenciling on an uneven or rough floor. If you want to attempt this, be sure to use acetate or Mylar® stencils and have a good supply of brushes on hand before beginning the project.

If you wish to achieve a sharp, well-defined stencil design it is best to have the floors sanded. You can do this yourself with a sanding machine; however, it is a very difficult and time-consuming task. I highly recommend having the floor sanded professionally. Be sure that the sanders do not use too fine a sandpaper when working on the floors. If the surface is too smooth the paint will not adhere to it very well. Once the sanding is complete, vacuum the floor thoroughly, mop it with a mild solution of soap and warm water, and then go over it with a tack cloth once it is completely dry. Dust and grime are the enemies of any stenciling project.

At this point, there are several ways to approach a stenciling job. You can paint the entire floor with a flat oil-based paint to provide a background base color. Use two coats for an even base and make sure the paint is completely dry before you begin stenciling. Oil-based paints take a long time to dry, so I recommend waiting at least two days. You can use latex paint, but it will be less durable and the water in the paint may raise the grain of the wood in places. Lightly sand the painted surface with a fine grain sandpaper in the areas where the grain has raised.

Bleaching is another very effective means for preparing a floor for stenciling. Oak is the best wood for bleaching as it results in a mild cream color. Pine will have a more yellowish tinge. It is best to have the floor bleached professionally.

Courtesy Adele Bishop

The process uses very caustic chemicals that can be dangerous if you don't know what you are doing. Once the bleaching is complete, lightly sand the floor to create a slight grain for the paint to grab hold of.

A similar effect can be achieved by a process known as simulated bleaching. This is a way of lightly staining the floor so it appears as if it has been bleached. It is a simple process that you can do yourself. Apply a thin coat of pale-cream, flat, oil-based paint to the floor and then immediately wipe it off with a rag. You should do small sections of the floor at a time so that the stain doesn't dry before you have a chance to wipe it up. Take care, however, to keep the paint as uniform as possible as you progress.

If a darker, wood-grained effect is desired, take advantage of the many colored stains available on the market. These stains can be used to color a wood floor or to simulate a certain type of wood you don't have. These oil-based stains will quickly absorb into a newly sanded surface and will not adversely affect any paint that is subsequently stenciled onto the floor. Be sure to always test a stain on a small patch of your floor before undertaking the entire job so that you can see exactly how the floor will look when the stain is dry. Wood swatches provided by paint and hardware stores will not give you an accurate picture of what your particular floor will look like. As always, allow the stain to dry for two or three days before you begin stenciling the floor.

While the basic techniques for planning, measuring, and applying the stencils to a floor are the same as with other large stenciling projects, stenciling a floor is probably the most physically exhausting project you can attempt. Be prepared to spend long hours stooped over on your knees applying the paint. In addition, you will be constantly stepping over and around areas you have just stenciled. Wear pads to protect your knees and a pair of white cotton socks (they are less likely to smudge freshly applied stencils). If at all possible, enlist the help of a friend.

## PROTECTING THE FLOOR

After you are finished applying the stencil to the floor, it must be sealed if your work is to last. Use a varnish or a polyurethane finish to seal the project. Most varnishes have a polyurethane base of some sort. Polyurethane forms a durable, water-resistant coat that can withstand the heavy traffic received by floors. These varnishes are available in matte, semi-gloss, and gloss finishes. In most cases, depending, of course, on the effect you are trying to achieve, the semi-gloss is the best choice. This finish will make the floor look clean, but not glassy. Also, unless you want the project to have a yellowish tint, buy a high-quality clear varnish. Use a wide, flat brush to apply the sealant and work with the grain of the wood, being careful to avoid brush strokes. Test a small portion of the stenciled area first to make sure that the paint is completely dry and the colors won't bleed. Two coats of varnish will result in a strong, durable floor that will last for years.

A floor stenciled in this manner can be sponge-mopped with a weak solution of soap and water. Avoid abrasive detergents and never use wax or wax-based cleaning products. Any buildup of wax will make future touch-ups difficult. You may eventually have to revarnish the floor if the finish begins to wear off.

## FLOORCLOTHS

Another option for decorating the floor of your house or apartment with stencils is to make a stenciled floorcloth. The floorcloth is one of the most charming manifestations of the revival in the art of stenciling. As with other types of stencil decoration, the painted floorcloth was a result of the New England colonists' attempts to beautify their homes using the minimal resources they had at hand.

The floorcloth, a decorated piece of heavy-duty canvas that has been primed with paint on one side then adorned with a stenciled pattern, has been virtually obsolete in both America and Europe since the nineteenth century. In recent years, however, this wonderful decorative piece, along

© Richard S. Mandelkorn

with other forms of eighteenth and nineteenth century interior design techniques, has been enjoying a renaissance. Floorcloths, forerunners of carpets and rugs, were the earliest floor coverings in both European and American homes. They were wide expanses of colorfully painted canvas, decorated with designs that simulated tile floors. Floorcloths served as both an inexpensive means of adorning plain wood floors and as an early means of insulating poorly built homes from drafts. Over the years, artisans began expanding the simple geometric designs of the early cloths into patterns of flowers, trellises, and vine borders.

Today, stencilers are exploring further the immense design possibilities of a floorcloth. Because the floorcloth is a well-defined geometric shape, it is the perfect medium for stenciling techniques. The final effect you achieve will depend largely on the motifs and color combinations you choose. Stenciling a floorcloth enables you to let your imagination and creativity run wild, because you are dealing with inexpensive canvas and not something permanent such as a wood floor.

By alternating squares, diamonds, triangles, and random patterns with striped borders in an array of colors you can create vibrant effects with simple geometric patterns. Traditional stencil motifs such as birds, flowers, vines, and farm animals work extremely well within the confines of a floorcloth. Quilts offer a fertile source of effective floorcloth motifs. The proportions of a quilt are often very similar to those of a floorcloth, enabling you to copy or accentuate the pattern of a quilted bed covering in a floorcloth for a bedroom or den.

Stenciled floorcloths also enable you to experiment using different application and painting techniques. You can blend the colors within a stencil to create a shaded effect. You can apply the stencil paints with a sponge to achieve a rustic, well-worn look. You can even glaze over the entire surface with a glossy varnish to create a deep, rich, dark color. Floorcloths work especially well on natural wood floors. The wood grain complements the rustic quality of the stenciled cloth.

# MAKING A FLOORCLOTH

A floorcloth can be made in any size to fit any room. I recommend using heavy #8 or #10 canvas, similar to the canvas artists use for oil painting. It is available at awning stores, or at sailcloth suppliers and comes in roll widths of 3, 4, 5, 6, and 10 feet (1 to 3 m). If 10 feet (3 m) is not wide enough for you, you can join two pieces of canvas together using a flat seam. Always buy authentic 100 percent cotton duck canvas and transport it in rolls. If it becomes wrinkled iron it with steam. It is important to keep it as flat and crease-free as possible.

## PREPARING THE CANVAS

Beautiful stenciled floorcloths can be made with both plain unpainted canvas, or canvas that has been treated with primer. If you choose to paint directly on the canvas the result will be a light neutral background and will, of course, require a lot less work. Priming, however, will enable you to control the background color. A simple off-white background will contrast nicely with dark stenciling

colors such as blue, red, and green. If you choose a dark background color, then you should rely mostly on light colors for your stencil motifs.

If you plan on priming the canvas be sure to allow up to two extra inches (5 cm) in both length and width since this will cause the floorcloth to shrink. Exact measurements, however, are only important in instances where the floorcloth is to be fitted tightly into a particular space. In this case, use a piece of canvas at least six inches (15 cm) wider and longer than the dimensions of the space. This will give you ample room for shrinkage and a hem. You can always trim down the canvas after it has been primed if necessary.

# PRIMING AND STENCILING THE CANVAS

Before priming or painting the canvas, clear out a large floor space and vacuum and mop it thoroughly. Dust or dirt will give the canvas a rough uneven surface and you can't sand it down and start over like you can when stenciling a wood floor. Lay down several layers of newspaper to soak up any excess paint that may soak through the canvas.

The best primer for floorcloths is flat, latex paint. Oil-based paint can also be used, but it is much more difficult to work with and takes much longer to dry. You will need two or three coats of primer to prepare the canvas adequately. Apply the first coat lightly, but evenly. This will prime the canvas for the second and third coats, which will provide a good working surface on which to stencil. Allow at least twenty-four hours between each coat for the paint to dry thoroughly. The number of primer coats you apply depends on the texture you are trying to achieve. The more coats of primer you apply, the smoother the floorcloth will be. Make sure to save some of the background paint to cover mistakes. If you make a mistake while stenciling you can always paint over it and start again.

Japan paints are the best for the actual stenciling. They are quick-drying and will last for years. Acrylics are also durable and are a bit easier to work with.

## HEMMING AND SEALING THE FLOORCLOTH

The easiest way to hem a painted floorcloth is with a hot-glue gun. Trim the corners to get rid of excess canvas and then turn the edges under and secure them with the hot glue. A good craft glue will also work, but a hot-glue gun is easier to use and the final hem will be more secure. Some of the paint around the edges of the hem may crack during this process. You can touch up the cracks with the extra background paint once the glue has dried.

The final step is to protect the cloth with a varnish. Apply two or three coats of flat or semi-gloss polyurethane varnish depending on what type of finish you desire. Varnish will make the surface water resistant, allowing you to sponge up spills and dirt. You may occasionally need to apply extra coats of varnish to extend the life of the floorcloth. A yellow-tinted varnish can be used to give the floorcloth an antique finish.

Courtesy Adele Bishop

# FURNITURE

There is a long tradition of stenciled and hand-painted furniture in every region of the world. In eighteenth-century France, the *gentelise* kept their clothing in large, ornate, gilt-laden armoires. In Provence, chests and commodes were decorated with simple stencils, using a vivid palette that echoed the Provençal countryside. The Scandinavians stenciled flowers and other natural motifs on their furniture, accenting the simple lines with soft, muted colors. In medieval England, churches and the homes of the rich were decorated with elaborately painted and stenciled screens and furniture. The Japanese have a centuries-old tradition of finely lacquered and painted furniture, adorned with patterns that echo the country's detailed wood prints.

Later, in nineteenth-century England, the proponents of the Arts and Crafts Movement turned their attention to the beauty found in design and color of the accessories of everyday life, such as chairs, chests, tables, and other practical adornments. In the workshop of William Morris, poet, artist, craftsman, and utopian socialist, artisans such as Dante Gabriel Rossetti, Edward Burne-Jones, and Morris himself began designing and painting extremely functional, yet aesthetically beautiful furniture of all types. These men and others were instrumental in changing the tastes of their countrymen from a heavy, gilded look to the simplistic charm of hand painted and stenciled oak furniture. Using rich basic colors and formal floral and heraldic patterns, these men not only designed exquisite chairs, chests, tables, and wardrobes, but also silk textiles, wall-hangings, and tapestries.

Another influential personality in the history of stenciled furniture design was Lambert Hitchcock. In the late 1820s, Hitchcock set up a small workshop in Hitchcocksville, Connecticut. There he designed and produced a small, elegant, dark-stained or black-painted chair that was adorned with ethereal gilt stenciling. Known as the Hitchcock chair, this delicately decorated piece of furniture remained extremely popular for well over a century. Hitchcock used bronzing powders and sizing compound—an adhesive that holds the grains of pigments—to achieve a shaded effect within the stenciled outlines. Many artisans still imitate the basic designs and methods developed by Hitchcock in his small Connecticut workshop.

As with other forms of country decoration, stenciled and hand-painted furniture was a large part of the American settlers' art. They had an appreciation for painted furniture that derived from their European roots, but developed it into a decorative style that is strictly American. Perhaps the Amish of Pennsylvania made the best use of stenciling and painting techniques in their furniture. In a style that almost betrays their otherwise spartan lifestyle, the Amish used bright, clear colors to embellish the modest lines and practical construction of their furniture. The bright reds, yellows, and greens of their furniture contrasts greatly to the blacks and dark purples of their clothing.

Today, there is a resurgence of interest in glazed, lacquered, stained, marbled, and stenciled furniture. The current fascination with country lifestyle and design has led many people to look at their plain wooden furniture in a different light. A very charming, yet sophisticated effect can be achieved with the addition of a simple outline or motif to a wood chair back or tabletop. Stenciling furniture requires an integration between the form of the stencil and the piece of furniture. The design must complement or enhance the characteristics and lines of the furniture. And, as with stenciled wood floors, the preparation of the wood and the finishing of the project are extremely important for a successfully stenciled furniture design.

A piece of furniture, particularly a small piece, is often a good first project for a beginning stenciler. The entire project—preparation, stenciling, and finishing—can be completed in a small work area, creating a minimum of mess. In addition, stenciling furniture entails working with a number of small, confined surfaces, somewhat limiting your design choices, but providing enough freedom to be challenging and to help you develop your skills. The best items of furniture to stencil are inexpensive pieces; either those bought cheaply at a secondhand store or new unfinished wood furniture. Never stencil on a genuine antique or a valuable piece of furniture because refinishing will detract from its value as well as its beauty. If you are a beginner and not very comfortable with your stenciling skills you may end up ruining a valuable piece of furniture. The monetary and aesthetic value of new, unfinished furniture and old, but not precious secondhand furniture, can be greatly enhanced with the addition of a well-designed and executed stencil motif.

Tables, armoires, chests, and dressers all respond well to stenciled designs. The extent of your design will largely depend on the lines and form of the piece of furniture you will be stenciling. Limit your stenciling to a specific surface rather than attempt an intricate overall pattern. Subtle borders and motifs work much better than an intricate gaudy pattern that may overwhelm the shape of the furniture.

Step back and look at the piece you are considering. Take note of the shapes and forms on the surfaces of the item. You may want to make sketches of the various surfaces you are planning to stencil, as is suggested in Chapter Three. Measure the various surfaces and carefully draw them to scale on graph paper. This will help you create a proportionate and integrated design, and will train you to look at each surface both as an individual component and as part of a greater whole. When breaking a piece down surface by surface it is important to keep in mind how the overall design will look. A well-integrated design that conforms with the lines of the various surfaces is extremely important when working on a confined space such as a chair, table, or chest.

There is a symmetry inherent in most pieces of furniture. This symmetry can be used to great advantage when designing your project. You may want to plan your design along the central axis of the piece with the remainder of

the pattern falling evenly to either side. Or, you may wish to work against the natural symmetry by placing more of the design on one side or the other. Be careful, though—working against a piece's symmetry can result in an awkward, unbalanced look.

It is also very important to consider any curvature the piece may have. It can be difficult to apply flat stencils to a curved surface, such as a turned leg or a rounded chair back. The stencil outlines you choose must conform to the shape and proportions of the furniture. Select stencils that fit in with and complement these curves so that they enhance the shape of the piece rather than detract from it. As a general rule, use small cutouts that don't have to be severely bent to conform with an extreme curve.

Ideas for motifs and designs can be found anywhere. Page through magazines and furniture catalogs. You may find the perfect element on which to base an entire design. Books on American and European folk art provide great examples of traditional color schemes and decorative effects. As with all stencil projects, printed and woven fabrics are great sources for design ideas. Perhaps the best place to look for ideas is in your own home, especially in the room where you plan to display the finished work. Look at the moldings, draperies, carpeting, and other furniture present. What elements can you pull from them and incorporate in your furniture design?

As stated earlier, the preparation and priming of the wood surface of the piece is just as important to the final result as the stenciling itself. As a general rule, stenciling on furniture is most successful when the surface has been treated with some sort of stain, glaze, paint, or gesso. Stenciling on raw, untreated wood will result in fuzzy, ill-defined outlines. This may, however, be just the rough rustic look you are striving for. On the other hand, if it is a clear, crisp effect you are after, then it is advisable to take advantage of the many paints, stains, and glazes available on the market.

Before doing any type of staining, painting, or glazing, you must be sure all of the surfaces are properly prepared. This is especially important if you are working with an old, secondhand piece of furniture. Completely strip off any old, damaged paint or varnish. There are a number of finish removers available on the market for this purpose. Many of these are extremely toxic, however, so always follow directions carefully and work with gloves in a well-ventilated area. Next, check the piece for any structural defects or damage. Be sure it is free of woodworm, glue together any loose joints, and fill any cracks or holes in the wood with wood filler tinted to match the color of the wood. Finally, sand the entire piece with a moderate grain sandpaper until it is smooth and then wipe it thoroughly with a tack cloth to remove all dust particles.

Glazing or staining produces a much softer, more translucent effect than paint. This soft effect will give the stencils great depth of color. A painted surface causes the stencils to stand out more; however, the color will not seem as vibrant. Depth of color can be achieved on a painted surface by applying a coat of tinted, semi-gloss varnish after the stenciling is completed.

Traditional stenciled furniture usually has a dark solid background color, such as deep red, black, charcoal gray, dark green, or blue. This adds weight and substance to the finished piece. A light floral motif, applied in gold or bronze paint to this dark background is added for a rich antique effect.

Conversely, a light, ethereal effect can be achieved by treating the bare wood with a light stain and then adding a light colored glaze. This stain and light glaze combination results in a thin base that enhances the wood grain, as well as any joints or routed edges the piece may have. Most glazes on the market are clear. They can be easily tinted, however, by adding a small amount of oil-based paint.

Be sure that all base coats of paint, varnish, or glaze are completely dry before you begin stenciling. If you use an extremely glossy or smooth primer, you may have to lightly go over the surface of the piece with very fine sandpaper or steel wool to create a surface that will hold the paint. Always wipe surfaces thoroughly after any sanding.

The basic techniques for positioning, measuring, and applying stencils to furniture is the same as it is for other stenciling projects (see Chapter Two). When attaching your stencil template to the surface to be stenciled, however, be careful not to use any tape that will damage the base coat. Masking tape generally works well without causing damage unless it is left on for a long period of time.

In addition to the traditional paints and colors used in stenciling, you may want to consider incorporating a metallic powder in your stenciled furniture design. Metallic powders create a rich, lavish look. To use metallic powder, apply a coat of clear gloss or satin varnish. Leave this until it is almost dry but still tacky. The tackiness of the varnish will hold the stencil in place. Place the stencil card over the surface. Then apply the metallic powder with a cotton swab or a foam eye-shadow applicator, working outward from the center of the design. Be sure to use a different applicator for each color of metallic powder you use.

Once your stencil, whether metallic powder or paint, is complete, it will be necessary to seal the project so that your design will last for years. Polyurethane varnish is easy to apply, will adequately protect the design, and will help to bring out its colors. As stated earlier, varnish is available in three different sheens. Matte varnish will protect but does not have a shine; a semigloss varnish will give a satiny glow; and gloss varnish will provide a hard, shiny effect. You can also add a small amount of oil-based paint to slightly tint the varnish if desired. Tinted varnishes are also available at art supply stores. The number of coats of varnish you apply depends on the type of varnish used and the amount of wear the furniture will be subjected to. Once properly sealed, the stenciled design should last for years. If some wear or chipping does occur, you may have to touch up the design and revarnish.

Courtesy Stencil Ease

# FABRICS

The decoration of fabrics with painted and dyed stencils dates back to the early nineteenth century. Canvas floorcloths (see Chapter Five) were the first stenciled textiles to become popular. These were soon followed by stenciled bed hangings and coverings, draperies, pillows, tablecloths and napkins, and even, to a lesser extent, clothing. Many times this decorative stenciling was combined with freehand painting.

Again, economic considerations as much as aesthetics led to the development of decorative stenciling on fabrics. The original stenciled fabrics were imitations of elaborate embroidered bed coverings and woven fabrics. The color choices were primarily basic greens, reds, yellows, and blues. The artisans meticulously sketched and cut out very intricate stencil designs based on the period's popular fabrics. They would attach the stencils to the fabric and use cotton balls soaked in dye to apply the colors. The dyes used were very difficult to work with and tended to run and blur in the printing process. In addition, they would quickly fade if the fabric was washed. Today, textile and acrylic paints have made the use of dyes in stenciling obsolete. Fabric stenciling became so popular in the 1820s and 30s that companies began mass producing preprinted stencils that imitated the popular textile prints of the time.

The popularity of this craft was extremely short-lived, however. Due to rapid advancements in the textile industry printed fabrics became widely available and increasingly inexpensive. Today very few examples of these early stenciled fabrics still exist.

The recent popularity in fabric stenciling can be largely attributed to the development of easy-to-use, water-based textile and acrylic paints. These paints produce beautiful, sharp outlines that are easy to shade, darken, and duplicate. Because these paints mix with ease it is not difficult to produce the same tone and shading with any number of stenciling impressions. Fabric stenciling is done with relatively thick paints so thinning is not usually required. If you do find it necessary to thin the paint, it can be done with water, unlike japan paints which require turpentine or mineral spirits. In addition, fabric and acrylic paints will last through repeated washings and will withstand substantial wear while remaining soft and pliable, making them ideal for clothing.

There are at least as many fabric surfaces in the typical home as there are hard surfaces. Look around your home. There are draperies, bed covers, hand towels, napkins, furniture covers, sheets, pillow cases, window shades, and more. All of these items offer inexhaustible possibilities for stenciling. Consider adding stenciled designs to T-shirts, children's clothes, plain white clothing, scarves, and handkerchiefs.

The fabric surfaces of a room should be the final step in your interior design project. They act as the unifier that completes a balanced design. If you have a stenciled wall in your bedroom, you can continue the patterns and borders you established there on your curtains, or you can just pick a motif from the wall and reproduce it sparingly on the curtains. The same pattern can then be continued on the bedspread, creating a well-integrated design. Another option is to create an entirely new motif for the fabric surfaces, one that complements or contrasts nicely with the other surfaces of the room.

Pillows and cushions are great objects for stenciled designs. Devise a pattern that creates a careful balance with the size of the pillow. Perhaps a thin hatched border around the pillow's edge with one or two small floral motifs that imitate a needlepoint applique. Again here, the pattern choices you make should be made with the themes and designs of the entire room in mind.

On chair seats and footstools, stencils can be employed in the same way that a piece of embroidery is used to decorate a specific area. Create a stenciled cover that fits the specific proportions of the chair and complements the fur-

niture's lines and forms. Floral and geometric designs work well on chair seats, footstools, sofa cushions, and padded outdoor furniture. You can even add new life to an old, beat-up cushioned chair by making your own throw cloth. Plain or colored canvas can be cut to size, stenciled, and then used to cover the worn printed fabric. Patterns can be as simple as single-colored checks, polka dots, or stripes, or as involved as elaborate multicolored floral or scrollwork designs.

Fabric paints today are relatively soft and pliable as well as durable; therefore, they are perfect for creating beautiful stenciled designs on bed linens and pillowcases, as well as on comforters, quilts, and bedspreads. If you use a patchwork quilt or a printed bedspread, you may want to pick up one or two elements from it and incorporate them into a design for your sheets. Some slight stiffness may occur on the painted surface, so be careful not to overdo a stenciled sheet pattern.

If you are adept with a needle and thread, you may wish to create yards of stenciled fabric for use in sewing. An article of clothing, a set of curtains, a bedspread—all of these home-sewn items are made even more personal when sewn with a fabric design you printed yourself. The fabric design, however, should be kept fairly simple so that it will not require difficult measuring and matching when it comes time to cut and sew. Also, if you are stenciling a great deal of fabric, the process will go much more quickly when using a simple repeated motif and only one or two colors.

Stenciling on fabrics is extremely simple; however, the basic techniques do vary a little from other types of stenciling. I briefly touched upon these and provided a number of pointers in Chapter Two. Review those pointers before beginning your fabric stenciling project.

Every room in the house has a number of fabric surfaces that could be stenciled. This is an easy and inexpensive way to put a personal touch on your overall design scheme.

# CHOOSING A FABRIC

Natural fibers are the best on which to stencil. Their smooth, absorbent surfaces are easy to stencil and create a durable bond with the paint. Fabric that contains some synthetic fibers can be used, but it will not take the paint as well as pure cotton, silk, or linen. The absorbency of even a natural fabric, however, will vary depending upon the weave of the cloth and the peculiarities of the specific paint you choose. So always test out a small piece of the fabric with various paint colors to see if they bleed. Fabrics with a tight, flat weave will also take the paint better. Loose, pliable fabric tends to move and shift during the stenciling process, creating a fuzzy, uneven look. Fabric with a raised weave, a nap, or knitted fabrics do not work well either. The paint rests on the surface of such fabrics and will wear off quickly. In addition, when this type of fabric stretches, the pattern also stretches, revealing the unpainted gaps in the weave.

Any fabric, new or old, should be washed before being stenciled to remove any trace of starch and sizing. You may wish to dye the fabric in the washing machine if you are looking for a specific background color. Once the fabric is dry, iron it thoroughly to remove all creases. Next, stretch it tightly and anchor it over a board or piece of cardboard. This will keep the fabric wrinkle free and prevent it from slipping while you are stenciling it. It is best to anchor the fabric with pushpins or dressmaker's pins; however, masking tape covering each edge of the fabric will also suffice. If you are printing a large piece of fabric, divide it into several working sections and then carefully align the grain and edge within each section and secure it. When stenciling a garment, place several layers of newspaper inside it to prevent the color from bleeding through to the back.

Use the same measuring and marking techniques outlined in Chapter Two. Register marks and guidelines, if needed, can be drawn using a tailor's chalk or a soft pencil. If using a pencil, however, draw lightly to ensure that marks can be easily removed.

© Robert Perron

The stencil brushes used for fabrics are the same as with any other project and the paint is applied using the same pouncing motion. For fabrics, it is best to use small amounts of paint at a time. Do not thin the paint at all, but use it directly from the tube or jar. If you use too much paint, or the paint is too thin, it will bleed through the fibers of the cloth. The fabric surface creates friction, making the application of the paint a little more difficult. It is always good to practice on a piece of scrap fabric before beginning.

Keep in mind that mistakes made on fabrics cannot generally be removed. Once the paint is applied, it is there to stay. Keep your work area clean and continually wash your hands to prevent any unwanted smudging. Also, periodically check the backs of your stencils to make sure they are free of paint. If you are creating a multicolored design, make sure the first color is dry before adding the second.

Once you complete the stenciling, allow the paint to dry thoroughly. This usually takes only about fifteen or twenty minutes for most textile paints; however, you may want to wait up to an hour just to be sure. Next, iron each side of the fabric with a dry iron for about ten minutes to set the paint. This heat sealing will bind the paint to the fibers of the fabric.

Stenciled fabrics can be washed in either a washing machine or by hand. The first washing should be done with a mild detergent in warm or cold water. After that you can wash it as you would normal laundry. **Caution:** Some textile paints cannot withstand dry cleaning. Check the label of the paint jar or tube for complete washing instrucions. The final stencil design will be extremely durable; however, some fading may occur with repeated washings or if the fabric is continually exposed to direct sunlight.

Courtesy Adele Bishop

# PART FIVE

COUNTRY

# KITCHENS

DECORATING, COOKING, AND ENTERTAINING

BARBARA RANDOLPH

# INTRODUCTION

# THE HEART OF THE COUNTRY HOME

**A**country kitchen begins with a frame of mind, not with a decorator's manual. By its very nature, a country kitchen is a comfortable place where family and friends gather to be a part of the household activity. A country kitchen is a busy place and its decor is born of the activities that are carried on there. It isn't a place where sticky fingers or messy projects are banned. Its sounds and scents are those of the foods that are created and shared there as well as the good times that naturally occur around its bountiful table.

Because a country kitchen isn't a decorator showpiece, it doesn't depend on a particular size or shape. Nor does it have to be in a home set deep in the woods or fields. A country kitchen, full of the aromas of fresh bread and pies in the oven, can be in a city apartment, the view from its windows a geometric skyline instead of the rounded green shapes of trees and distant hills.

While a large, roomy kitchen allows more space for bulky furnishings such as wood stoves, there is no one piece of furniture essential to a country kitchen. The wide farmhouse table can be replaced by a tiny breakfast table. Pick and choose those things from this book that will fit not only the space you have but your own style of living. Your country kitchen will not look or feel like anyone else's; it will be uniquely your own, and that is what makes it a real country kitchen.

Country kitchens can combine the best elements of modern and traditional decor.

*Image credit (vertical, left margin):* © Bill Rothschild/interior design by Jeanne Leonard

## BEYOND EARLY AMERICAN

Although the "look" that we think of as country is often based on the antiques and implements of the past, a country style is not the property of any one place. It is instead the combination of many influences, blended together in an infinite number of ways. One of the beauties of a country kitchen is that anything goes. Here you can mix the simple lines of Shaker furniture with the froufrou of Victorian cast iron. Bright and busy tile patterns from Portugal can live in the same kitchen with Pennsylvania Dutch pierced-tin designs. Braided straw ornaments from Scandinavia or England are comfortable with terracotta pottery from Central America.

## A WORLD OF COUNTRY STYLES

Just as American in its origins, although not reaching quite as far back into its history, the kitchens of the Southwest or Santa Fe style are among the most popular in country decorating. Like its Eastern counterparts, it relies on the traditional utensils and decorations of the area. Rich in terracotta tones and earth colors set against rough white stucco walls and highlighted with bright primary accents, this is a vital style.

The Southwestern kitchen is bright, airy, full of Native American motifs and lively Spanish decor. The colors spring from the deserts and skies: rich blues, sunset oranges, ocher, and russet sand shades. Pottery and baskets are used for containers, and a bright Navaho rug may cover the floor or a wall. Designs are solid and geometric, lines are clear, and the look is uncluttered.

Also born of a warm climate, where light and air are maximized in large open spaces, is the Mediterranean country kitchen. Primary colors predominate, set against creamy walls and dark wood tones. The furniture is rugged, and the work spaces are designed for a lot of use.

Bright designs are painted on tiles that may cover the walls, floors, or even countertops. Pottery is terracotta or painted, copper pots hang from hooks, and the ingredients themselves create decoration in the form of braided garlic cloves or bright purple onions. Like the Southwest, the cuisine and kitchen alike are enlivened by fiery bright red peppers hung in strings.

There are other variations. The French-Canadian country kitchen relies on time-worn implements, which are hung perhaps on a brick-fronted fireplace, but they are enlivened with bright pottery of Quimper or another whimsical design. The provincial touch is further provided in checkered linens and offset with plain white china. A Southern country kitchen welcomes the breeze with ruffled curtains of an almost gauzy white cotton, and a Midwestern farmhouse kitchen may add a freshly painted Hoosier cupboard to that look. In the northern Midwest, where the Scandinavian influence is strong, the cabinets may be painted in the bright, flowing designs of rosemaling.

The keynote of any country kitchen, whatever its particular style, is comfort, traditional designs, and the familiar warmth of home.

Tile countertops lend a Mediterranean flair to any kitchen.

© Lynn Karlin

# DECORATING IN COUNTRY STYLE

For the colonist of moderate means, the kitchen might well have comprised the whole house. But it was the first place to see "modernization." By the 1700s, conveniences such as the candle mold and roasting oven had made household chores less tedious, and the beds had moved from the kitchen to the bedrooms.

Prosperity brought China tea and porcelain cups to drink it from—at least when there was company. In the South, the kitchen of the more prosperous home was a separate building, used in the summer, to relieve the main living area from the added heat and danger of fire.

Later, the wood cookstove replaced the fireplace as a cooking place and source of heat, and it was better at both jobs. Slate or soapstone sinks replaced the washtub, and hot-water tanks attached to the wood stove replaced the ever-ready pot on the fire. Chairs replaced benches, and the table itself changed styles with the times.

By the early twentieth century, the black iron stove had become enameled in pale green or ivory, the pride of a housewife. Hoosier cupboards were painted to match. These minipantries had tin-lined bins for flour and sugar and a built-in flour sifter, as well as shelves for dishes, a pull-out work surface, and drawers for linens and bake ware. Today, these are among the most sought-after pieces of old kitchen furniture. They seem to represent American ingenuity, inventiveness, and the homely arts, all in one.

The pie safe, a cabinet with pierced tin doors and side panels that allowed air to circulate but kept flies off food, is another uniquely American piece of furniture. These were kitchen pieces, often painted and made of whatever wood was available, in whatever size struck the carpenter's fancy. They were often homemade, so their sizes, shapes, and styles vary enormously. (To replace tin panels, see tin piercing, page 286.)

The kitchen is probably the easiest room in your home in which to capture the wonderful country feeling. Homespun tablecloths and dish towels, crockery, wooden ware, glass canning jars, and baskets are all made in old styles and patterns. Old kitchen utensils are still available at flea markets and yard sales. Tin containers, cups, cookie cutters, and occasionally skimmers and apple corers are found, as well as gadgets from wooden-handled ice cream scoops to top-of-the-stove toasters.

Painted match safes from the 1940s blend with the nutmeg graters, wooden apple-butter paddles, stoneware crocks, and cast-iron waffle irons in a collection that can begin with whatever is available and grow in any direction. Some collectors specialize in one medium: tinware, cast iron, pottery, or wood. Others choose a specific purpose, such as nutmeg graters or implements and containers connected with herbs and spices.

Cookie cutters are still available and are fun to collect because of their varied shapes and designs. They are historically interesting as well, since it is easy to see their evolution and to spot those that were made of scrap tin by farmers. Aluminum ones from the 1930s and 1940s often had painted wooden handles, and modern ones represent current children's crazes, such as dinosaurs.

Old cookbooks are another useful collectible, and the recipes reflect the lifestyles of their time as well as the favorite foods. Along with the classics—original editions of *The Fannie Farmer Cookbook* and the handwritten "receipt books" full of homey tips—there are the advertisement cookbooks of the early twentieth century. These pamphlets came free with a product or could be ordered by sending a postcard or a box top.

Antique shops such as this one in Norton, Georgia, are a good source of kitchen decorations.

© Al Michaud/FPG International

© Robert Perron

**Old implements can be displayed on a beam or hung under a shelf.**

These small cookbooks are colorful, full of illustrations of smiling housewives in the day's popular hairstyles and pink-cheeked children reaching for another cookie. The recipes are the most innovative of their day, fresh from the test kitchens of Fleischmann's® Yeast, Baker's® Chocolate, Pillsbury® Flour, and other products. And they are so good that to this day these companies get requests for copies of a particular fudge or dinner roll that appeared in a booklet in the early part of this century.

Displaying these can be fun if you don't plan to use them, since they are colorful in small frames or grouped as a collage. Some collectors simply photocopy their favorite scone or cake recipe, then frame the original booklet.

Utensil collections can be hung from nails or hooks in a beam, or put in arrangements on the wall. Old mail-sorting cabinets make perfect display cases for these small items, since they allow you to frame each piece or group separately and keep them all visible.

Some of the pieces can be used for storage or for their original purpose. Clown-shaped lemon squeezers from the 1920s still squeeze lemons, and a big tin breadbox is a fine place to store cereal boxes, crackers, or bread. Old cookie jars can be kept full of cookies (perhaps those from a turn-of-the-century flour recipe booklet), and crocks can hold wooden spoons and whisks within easy reach of the stove.

Old glass-topped canning jars or new replicas are perfect for storing dried beans, nuts, grains, and pastas. Lined up along narrow shelves under the upper cabinets or on an unused wall, these are decorative and save cupboard space. Baskets can hold fresh vegetables, pot holders, garlic, and small utensils; and round, wooden Shaker-style boxes stack easily and close snugly for shelf storage.

# COUNTRY COLORS

Just as country decorating lends itself to many different styles—or to many combinations—nearly any color has its place here as well. While we think first of the warm rich tones of blue milk paint, dark red, old rose, and moss green, the bright primaries, russet earth tones, and pastels are all equally at home in a country kitchen.

There are no firm rules; your own eye will tell you how to mix and blend colors in a way you like. Comfort is the keynote.

Color is an inexpensive way to achieve a particular style—a coat of paint can change the mood or feeling in a room, even without making other renovations. Color is also a good way to tie together several different decorating styles. When planning colors, choose one to predominate and use it in 60 to 70 percent of your decorated areas (not counting the walls or floors, if these are plain wood, neutral white, or cream tones). That color might be used for wall or floor coverings or for a large piece of furniture. Then choose a secondary color that goes well with it, using it for curtains or other fabric coverings. A third accent color might be used to tie in small decorative items.

Your color scheme might be suggested by one major element used in the room, such as a rug, a chair or table, or curtains. You could choose two or three colors from it and repeat them elsewhere.

Rugs or other floor coverings are a good place to use your main colors together, since they provide a visual base for the room. Wallpapers can serve this same function.

Stenciling is a particularly good way to tie in different colors in a kitchen, since you can use whatever colors you like in your pattern. Stenciled walls can, for example, tie in the deep tones of painted wainscoting and door frames, pick up colors in the floor covering, or suggest new colors that could be echoed in table linens or towels.

The country kitchen need not be cluttered or filled with antiques to have a warm, homey feeling.

# WALLS

The kitchen lends itself to simple wall treatments. While vinyl wallpapers are quite durable as well as washable, it isn't necessary to cover walls completely. Plain painted walls are the choice of many people for their country kitchens. Sometimes these are enlivened by a simple stenciled border.

One problem in choosing the wall covering for a kitchen is that the room tends to be a busy one in terms of its furnishings. The country-style kitchen is often decorated with the implements that will be used there. As a background for displaying a collection of antique kitchen utensils, a plain painted or wood surface is best.

Wallpapers reproducing antique stencil designs do make good choices for a kitchen, especially if the colors are fairly pale. A simple stencil pattern that combines two light tones on a cream background is compatible with many kitchens.

Painted or natural wood is another option. Dark wood wainscot panels or entire walls offer a good contrast to white appliances, keeping the kitchen from appearing all white while adding a note of warmth.

## STENCILING WALLS

Stenciled borders have a timeless quality and an air of informal elegance that are particularly well suited to dressing up a kitchen. The best part about using stencils is that painting them requires absolutely no artistic talent.

Prepare the walls by painting them a neutral color (usually off-white). Choose a stencil design that fits the room and your decorating style—you can purchase ready-cut plastic film stencils in a wide variety of patterns. Brass stencils will last longer, but choose them only for larger designs without small patterns.

Acrylics are the best paints for stenciling walls. A jar holding less than one-eighth of a cup of paint can decorate a whole kitchen, and you are sure to have some left over. For more information on stenciling walls, see Part Four, Country Stencils, pages 236 to 241.

# DECORATIVE MOLDINGS

Even new kitchens can be given early American features with the creative use of inexpensive, precut molding strips from a lumber store. Chair rails, window cornice boards, boxed beams, and rich antique door frames can be put in place over a weekend.

These details add the finishing touch to an otherwise undistinguished kitchen, and when painted an antique color and combined with historic wallpapers and drapery fabrics, they can transform the entire room.

First, take careful stock of the room and be sure of how you want to dress it up. A very informal, small kitchen might look strange with elegant window and door-frame moldings, but a combined dining room and kitchen might be just the place for this touch of a fine old home. Consider

**A border of decorative molding highlights a set of shallow shelves.**

**If a kitchen does not have real beams to expose, these can be added below the existing ceiling.**

how wainscoting will visually alter the dimensions of the room. By cutting it in half crosswise, it will make the ceiling seem lower and the walls seem longer. If all the furniture in a room is table-height with no mantel or cabinet piece to give a vertical line, chair rails can also make the room seem cut in half.

To add chair rails, you will need only a simple narrow piece of molding to finish off the edge underneath a 1-inch-wide strip of plain board set at chair-back height. To border windows or door frames, you will want a fairly plain molding that's narrow enough so it won't stick out beyond the thickness of the frame boards.

## BEAMS AND RAFTERS

What would a country kitchen be without beams for hanging baskets, herbs, old tinware, and cast-iron pans? The beauty of these is that you can change the decorations to correspond with the seasons. Hang flowers to dry in the fall, herbs in the winter, and canning ladles and garden baskets in the summer. At Christmas, wrap beams in balsam roping or hang spicy pomanders there to dry.

If you haven't found any old square nails in your house, you can buy them at hardware stores. Blacksmiths will make you beautiful iron hooks with sharp ends that you can pound right into the beams.

While old beams aren't just lying around for the taking, they are available from salvage companies or from old barns and outbuildings that have been torn down. (In rural areas, it is sometimes possible to buy these directly from owners of fallen-in sheds.)

New beams can be purchased from lumber suppliers, but even with a coat of dark stain, they do not have the rough-hewn and weathered look of old wood.

To add a ceiling cornice, you can use either a wide strip of molding or you can make elegant ones for high-ceilinged rooms by placing a 2-inch strip of board along the upper wall next to the ceiling. Add two strips of molding: one against the ceiling and a narrower one along the wall below the board.

Cover these molding strips with primer before putting them in place. Use finishing nails, which should be set below the surface of the wood. Fill in the holes with wood putty before painting the molding to match the rest of the woodwork in the room.

Raised paneling can be created by using panels of wide boards and surrounding them with molding. These are particularly attractive on a wall above a mantel.

Instead of the more formal look of painted moldings and paneling, you may choose to use a chair rail of natural wood to finish off wainscoting of unpainted pine or cherry. Since new pine is often a very light color, you may wish to tone it down by rubbing it with a cherry or walnut stain.

# LINENS AND CURTAINS

Because of the natural informality of a country kitchen, there is a wide range of possibilities for the treatment of windows. Many people choose to let in all the light available and have no curtains at all in the kitchen. Another way to accomplish this is to have only a top ruffle or cornice curtain and narrow side curtains. These frame the window without cutting out light or a view.

Curtains of thin white fabric allow maximum light, and cut a not-so-country view. These also have the advantage of being easily washable, a necessity for any fabric used in an active kitchen. Unbleached muslin is a good fabric choice for a kitchen, combining washability with a homespun, informal appearance. Muslin also takes well to stenciling, with its slightly off-white surface, and can be used for table linens as well as curtains.

Silky damasks and other formal decorative fabrics are not generally suitable for the country kitchen, but there are some very attractive cotton "homespun" fabrics, especially in blue or old reds. These bring a distinctive aura of the past to a kitchen when used either as curtains or as tablecloths and napkins.

There is no rule that a kitchen table must have a tablecloth. In fact, if the table is used as a work area, a tablecloth may be a real nuisance. Bare wood lends warmth, and even at dinner it need not be covered.

## STENCILING TABLECLOTHS AND NAPKINS

Measure your table and add at least 18 inches of overhang on each side. Unless the table is very small, the resulting figure will be more than the normal 45-inch width of unbleached muslin. Since a single seam up the center of the tablecloth isn't attractive, you should make the tablecloth in four panels, joined by a crossed seam at the center.

To do this, begin with the measurements of the finished tablecloth as determined above. Divide each dimension by two, so that you have the measurement of one-fourth of the

**Brightly colored linens can add warmth and life to a light-colored kitchen.**

tablecloth. For example, if your table is 30 by 40 inches, you would add 36 inches to each dimension (18 times 2), giving you 66 by 76 inches for your finished tablecloth. Each of the four sections would then be 33 by 38 inches.

Cut the prewashed muslin to make four pieces this size. Using a half-inch seam, stitch these four pieces together into a rectangle. Press the seams of the first two sections open before you stitch the two halves together, so that you will have a perfectly flat seam. Be sure your seams are straight—any curve will show up as a lump in the tablecloth. It's a bit tedious, but you will have better luck if you baste the pieces together first.

Press all the seams flat and topstitch just the width of your sewing machine foot away from the seam (this makes it quite easy to keep the stitching straight). The topstitching will hold the rough edges flat and give a finished look to the seams. Be sure the thread matches the fabric perfectly. Hem the outer edges with a narrow hem and iron the tablecloth.

Choose a fairly simple stencil pattern with no more than three colors. The design can be a relatively large one, which you will stencil only in the four corners where the panels meet in the center and at the four outside corners. Or you could choose a border design that you stencil along each seam and the hem, just inside the stitching. This will give you a finished pattern of a border and a double row forming a cross at the center of the table.

Pad your work surface with several sheets of newspaper and cover it with a clean piece of fabric. (An old worn-out sheet works well, but a dish towel will do.)

Cut a scrap of the muslin or a similar fabric to use as a practice piece. Lay the stencil over the fabric and secure at the corners with masking tape.

Put a little smear of paint on a piece of glass or on the bottom of an old plate. Dip the brush into it just enough to pick up a tiny spot of paint. Rub the brush on a folded paper towel to remove most of the paint. All you want left is the color—there should be no paint on the brush.

Using short stabbing motions with the brush, rub the color into the fabric through the openings in the stencil. Do not rub back and forth or you will pull the fabric and change its position under the stencil. To make the color darker, keep working in the color with the brush. Add new paint only when you cannot get any more color from the brush. Be sure to rub the excess paint onto the paper towel before you apply the brush to the fabric each time.

When you have perfected the technique and can make a perfect design with clean edges, you are ready to stencil the tablecloth. Be sure to measure the placement of the designs carefully before you begin. You can mark these with tailor's pencils, which will come out of the fabric easily.

When the entire tablecloth is completed, iron the designs from the reverse side, using a warm iron. This will help to set the colors.

Cut the napkins and either hem or fringe the edges by raveling out the threads along each edge to a quarter-inch width. If the design you use on the tablecloth is a large one, you can repeat it in miniature or simply choose a single element from it to repeat on the napkins. If you choose a border, you can either repeat one element or, if it is a small design, you can stencil it all around the edge of the napkin as you did along the hem of the tablecloth.

© Bill Rothschild/interior design by Marilyn Rose

**All the comforts of this country kitchen make it an inviting room to work in.**

## FLOORS

There are a number of attractive, practical ways to cover kitchen floors. Plain floorboards need no coverings or may be accented with runners or small throw rugs. These should have a firm surface, such as hooked or braided, if they are to be used in heavy-wear areas. They are less suitable for floors directly in front of the sink and stove, where they are more likely to become stained. Woven grass mats or rugs can be used in living areas of the kitchen, but are not sturdy enough for a cooking area.

VALLEY HOME

DOG

© Lynn Karlin

Stenciled floor cloths have come back after a century of oblivion, and are especially well suited to kitchens. Easy to make and keep clean, they can cover an entire floor or protect a much-used area with a warm accent.

Commercial floor coverings come in a variety of styles, replicating Mediterranean country tiles, stones, brick, and other surfaces. These are easy to care for in work areas of kitchens. Real tile is good for entry areas and under wood stoves, where it is the safest floor covering. In warmer climates, tile can be used for the entire kitchen floor, but tends to be a cold surface to stand on in places with cold winters. Brick is too rough for kitchen floor areas, except for hearths, entries, and under wood stoves.

## BUILDING A WIDE-BOARD FLOOR

One of the most basic early American features, especially in a country home, is wide pine floorboards. But, sadly, the homeowner can't just rip up existing floorboards and lay an old wide set in their place. The main reason is that wide boards are not usually available, and when they are, they are usually so full of knots that they are unsuitable for floors.

The best place to look for wide boards is not at your local lumber store but at small lumberyards that treat each tree separately. These yards distinguish the big trees with fewer lower limbs and cut them separately.

Be sure that the boards have dried for at least four to five months and have them planed on one side only. It is the planing that makes a board you buy as 1-inch stock actually only three-quarters of an inch thick. By having the rough-cut board planed on only one side, you will have a seven-eighth-inch thickness, which cuts down on warping.

At this point, you must have at least the patience of Job, because the boards need to dry and season for a year. They should be kept indoors in a heated area, stacked with space between the layers and each board. A purist will turn the stack over about halfway through the year, changing the order and direction of each board. Pine boards shrink a lot for a long time, so you want them to be as close to their

final size as possible before you put them down.

Consider the visual effect of the direction of your floorboards. Lay them crosswise in a long, narrow room to prevent it from looking like a bowling alley. If the house is old and the floor joists uneven, you may have an occasional mound after you lay the subflooring. If this is the case, you

A well-sealed, false-grained floor finish will withstand wear in low-traffic areas.

will have to lay floorboards in the same direction as the lumps, not across them. Otherwise, the floor will bounce and board ends will pop up and become uneven after a while.

After seasoning, the widths of the boards will vary slightly, which makes it difficult to match them up end to end. If all the boards are the same length, begin each row from alternate sides of the room, so all the boards don't end in the same place, creating one long line running the width of the floor.

If you still have any patience left, leave the boards in place after you have laid them, but don't nail them down.

A wood floor, unbroken by rugs, adds a sense of space to a kitchen.

You want the wood to continue to shrink and move, and you want it to acquire a little character and a few scratches before you put a finish on it.

After a few months (but not in the summer if you live in a humid climate), tap the boards to close the spaces and fill in with more as needed. Nail the boards in place, keeping the nails at least 1 inch from the edges and 2 inches from the ends. Go back over them with a tool called a nail set to sink the heads slightly below the surface.

Sand the floor very lightly, just to even the edges and remove any rough places the planing missed. Vacuum and wipe the floor with a tack cloth to pick up all the sawdust.

Seal the floor with several coats of good finish, sanding between coats. Be very careful when choosing a stain, since nearly any one labeled "pine" will have a bright yellow tint that doesn't improve with age. Protect the finished floor with wax and clean it with Murphy's oil soap and warm water. Soon your floor will develop its own patina of age—and a few cracks between its boards. The vision of how wide those cracks would have been had you not let the boards season well will be the reward for your patience.

## PAINTED FLOOR CLOTHS

Painted canvas floor cloths were among the earliest American floor coverings, both protecting the soft pine floors and adding a layer of insulation underfoot. Because of their age (they were most common in the 1700s) and heavy use, very few survive to tell us what designs were used. But early descriptions and the few remaining examples suggest that designs were often geometric or "faux" finishes made to look like marble or granite. Since floor cloths were meant to be walked on, the colors were probably dark and the designs simple.

In a modern setting, any one of several styles and designs is appropriate. The pattern you choose can be enlarged or replaced with another stenciled design. Or geometric designs can be created with masking tape.

Your floor cloth is both durable and washable and can be used in heavy-traffic areas, such as in front of the kitchen

© Robert Perron

**Stenciling is the most common decoration for painted floor cloths.**

Designs for hooked rugs can be as fanciful as your imagination suggests.

sink and under the table. It can be washed with hot water and detergent. If the surface should begin to wear, another coat or two of polyethylene will restore it.

## MAKING A HOOKED RUG

There is considerable discussion over whether the early hooked rugs were made of yarn or strips of wool fabric, but for today's craftsman, wool flannel fabric gives the most durable and attractive results and is easier to work with. The finished rug is smooth, tight, and long-lasting.

While it is possible to hand-cut one-eighth-inch strips of wool fabric, it is also a difficult and enormous job to do for an entire rug. There is a small, hand-cranked machine that does this quite easily (it looks like the fettucine blade on a pasta machine), or precut strips may be purchased. The latter is sometimes the most economical if only a few strips of a color are needed for shading, but the cutting machine is a good investment if you are doing even a small rug.

Along with the cut strips, you will need a backing of good-quality burlap—about 8 inches larger each way than the final rug will be—a hook (which can be purchased at needlework shops), and a rug frame. If you do not have a frame, you can make a simple one of four sturdy strips of wood secured into a rectangle. An old picture frame will work if it is sturdy. Attach the burlap to this frame with pushpins.

Before attaching the burlap, it should have a pattern on it. Rug-supply houses sell these already printed, or you can draw your own. Designs of old rugs were often quite primitive, so don't worry too much about your artistic talent.

Patterns of squares or rectangles were common, sometimes with a flower or fruit design in each square, or sometimes alternating. These small designs are especially easy to draw. Measure the squares onto the burlap, marking along a yardstick with a soft lead pencil. Tack the burlap to a sheet of plywood or other surface to hold it even as you draw. The designs in each square can be drawn freehand or transferred with carbon.

The colors are your own choice. Checkerboard rugs often alternated black squares with gray-toned ones, with the designs in the gray squares. You could choose a solid color that suits your room, and bring out a secondary color in the flowers or fruit. When working the designs in each square, do the motifs first, then fill in the background.

To make the rug, hold the hook in the right hand and the strip of wool in the left. (Reverse this if you are left-handed.) The wool is used in pieces about a foot long, and is held underneath the pattern. Push the hook between the threads of the burlap with the smooth side going between the thumb and first finger of your left hand and the hooked side touching your thumb. It should slide under the strip of wool and catch it as you draw it up through the burlap again. A slight pressure on the smooth side as you bring it up will open the threads slightly and allow the hook to pass through easily.

When you begin, the end of the wool strip should be brought to the top and about three-quarters of an inch left loose (it will be trimmed later). Push the hook into the next space between the threads and bring up a loop about an eighth of an inch high. Repeat this step, going into the next space each time, unless the loops become too tightly

packed, in which case skip one occasionally to make them lie evenly. The loops should touch each other but not be so tight as to pucker the burlap. When you come to the end of the strip of wool, bring it through and trim both ends to the height of the loops.

If the previous loop slips when you pull up the next one, twist the hook away from you as you pull it through. With very little practice, you will find that the loops are of even height and the work smooth. If at any point you are not satisfied with a set of loops, you can simply pull out that strip and work it again.

When the rug is completely hooked, iron the entire rug from the back using the steam setting. On the sewing machine, zigzag stitch around the outside of the hooked area, about three-quarters of an inch away from the edge, or make two rows of straight stitching side by side. Cut off one-quarter-inch of excess burlap outside the stitching. Stitch rug tape to the burlap (don't use iron-on tape, since it tends to pucker the edges) and hand-hem the other edge of the tape to the back of the rug. Be sure to miter the corners by clipping them so they won't be too bulky.

## TIN PIERCING

Tin piercing, like most other folk arts peculiar to America, was born of necessity. Although it is now enjoyed as a decorative feature, in the past the beautiful designs of old pierced tin simply added an aesthetic note to the panels that were the forerunner of modern screening.

Pies and other baked goods attracted flies, so pie safes, or pie cupboards, were made with pierced holes that let air flow through, but kept bugs out. Lanterns were also made of pierced tin, which let the candlelight out while protecting the flame from breezes.

Since the purpose of the old panels was to let as much air through as possible, there were a lot of holes. Geometric designs worked well, with diamonds, stars, sunbursts, and, especially in Pennsylvania, hearts and tulips. We can use the pierced lines to carry out design themes in other decorative items, such as wallpaper or stencil designs.

Tinsmiths use a tool called a bar folder to turn neat edges on tin, thus strengthening them and eliminating sharp edges. Modern home craftsmen will probably want to frame pierced-tin panels for display, unless, of course, they are making them for use in a pie safe or to decorate the doors of kitchen cupboards. The easiest way is to choose the frame, then cut the tin to fit.

Trace the pattern on a piece of plain paper the size of the tin panel. Tape it in place over the panel. Do the piercing work on an old board, a piece of Sheetrock, or pad the work surface with at least a half-inch of newspaper. Use a sharp-pointed nail or an ice pick as the piercing tool.

Place the tool on the first dot and strike it gently with a hammer or a small wooden mallet. You will need to strike hard enough to pierce the tin with the point of the tool, but not so hard as to drive the entire shaft through it. When the design is complete, remove the pattern. You can rub the surface of the tin with vegetable oil to protect it from rust, but do so carefully, because the holes are like a grater.

If you wish to make an unframed panel, you can fold back the cut edge by hammering it with a wooden mallet along the side of a straight edge. It will not be as smooth as one done on a bar folder, but if done carefully the edges will look fine. Measure the panel 1 inch longer and wider than you wish the finished piece to be. Mark the panel a half-inch from each edge of the corner and draw a diagonal line. Cut off the corners along this line.

Place the panel on a board with a sharp square edge and hold securely in place with one edge of the tin extending a half-inch over the edge of the board. With a wooden mallet, gently tap the extended tin to bend it down. When you have formed a clean right angle, turn the tin over so the edge extends upward and tap it gently down against the tin sheet. Repeat with all the other edges. You can make holes for hanging just below the turned edge along the top. Be sure they are evenly spaced from the sides.

If you wish to create a design using straight lines instead of dots, use a sharp chisel. Be careful to keep these straight chisel punches parallel, not running in a line, since they will cause it to break apart along the indentations.

This pierced-tin panel is augmented with a hand-painted, geometric design.

© Mark E. Gibson

# DISPLAYING KITCHEN COLLECTIONS

**B**y their very nature, old kitchen utensils are at home hanging from kitchen rafters, stacked in corners, or arranged in display cabinets made from old store crates. They were made to be used in the kitchen and still belong there.

Hutches, spice chests, pie safes, quilt racks, thread cabinets, iceboxes, type trays, store crates, Shaker boxes, baskets, coatracks, and silverware trays are all good containers for collections as well as being collectibles themselves.

Stack crates or boxes to create an irregular set of shelves. Hang shallow ones on the wall as shelves. Type trays make shadow-box shelves for miniatures or a mixture of small objects. Quilt racks make perfect towel racks and are good for displaying linens.

Use old cubbyhole mail cabinets to display a collection of small kitchen utensils. Since many kitchen pieces were designed to hang, these look nice on handwrought nails or hooks against a wooden or plaster wall or along the end of a kitchen cabinet. A beam is a good place to hang larger utensils, baskets, cast iron, or graniteware.

Many country collectibles are containers that can be used for their original purpose and decorate your kitchen at the same time. Use old tins for storing dry ingredients in the kitchen or pantry, baskets to hold rolled kitchen towels, and wooden boxes to store cleaning supplies. Arrange boxes and baskets on open shelves as decorative containers.

# COLLECTING KITCHEN ANTIQUES

Assembling an assortment of old or unusual kitchen gadgets makes browsing in antiques shops, flea markets, and yard sales a real treasure hunt. Collecting can mean looking for things that are different in nature and use, or concentrating on items for a particular purpose or those from a certain era in history.

Instead of looking for just any kitchen utensil, consider collecting graters, or narrow the field even further and collect only old nutmeg graters. Search for obsolete kitchen implements such as a cork-sizer or a meat juice-extractor or cream separator. Try to find as many kinds of food choppers as possible. Since these were common, everyday items, there are still plenty of them to be found in flea markets and antique shops.

## WHERE THE TREASURES ARE

In your search for kitchen collectibles, be sure to tell your friends about your interest, and ask them to look in their attics and sheds. Other than the barn your grandmother stored things away in, there are several good sources of furniture and utensils.

**ANTIQUES SHOPS** vary greatly, but are usually the most expensive sources. Look for shops away from heavily traveled routes and tourist destinations, and remember the price range of the items you are interested in as you see them in various shops.

**ANTIQUES SHOWS** are gatherings of dealers that set up and display their pieces in one place for a day or a weekend. You will find a wide variety of small items at these shows and will have a chance to compare prices easily. Although most dealers bring smaller pieces and collectibles to shows, you may also find some furniture and larger items. A good tip for antiques shoppers is that early morn-

ing is the best time for rare items; late afternoon is best for bargaining.

**ANTIQUES MALLS** are permanent antiques shows where a number of dealers have space under one roof. Some malls have separate shops where each dealer sells his own merchandise, while others work on a cooperative basis with many displays and a central checkout. There is not much chance of discussing the prices in the latter type, but you should ask, since some use codes to show the lowest price they will accept.

**AUCTIONS** are excellent places to find country antiques, if you can resist the excitement that sometimes takes over during fast bidding. Best are house auctions, right on location, since they often bring out boxes full of unsorted treasures late in the day. Here's where you will be most likely to find the kitchen gadgets. If you are looking for rarer pieces or furniture, try to go early so you can look things over carefully and decide your top bid before the auction begins.

---

### HOW TO SHOP

Most flea markets, yard sales, and antiques shops are good places to ask for a better price. Larger or metropolitan galleries may have fixed prices, but most others are flexible. How you inquire about price policies depends on your own attitude toward bargaining. Usually the simple question, "Is this the best price you can give me on this?" will tell you whether there is any room for negotiation.

A less direct way is to indicate your interest in something, but hesitate and move on to look at other items. A dealer who sees you returning several times to look at the same item and is willing to bargain will usually suggest a better price at some point.

Poke about to see what's there before asking for a particular item. If you enter a shop or booth and immediately ask for ice cream scoops, you are placing yourself at a disadvantage in bargaining. But before you leave a shop, it is wise to ask, since the owner may have pieces that are not on display.

---

**FLEA MARKETS** are less formal than antiques shows, and often are held out of doors. A lot of secondhand and new items are mixed in, making it a real challenge to find the treasures. But if you go early, you can find some bargains, especially in kitchen utensils of the 1930s and 1940s.

**YARD SALES** can yield some very good finds and unbeatable prices, but you have to get to these before the antiques dealers do. You also may have to look for a long time, but you can find some surprising gems at prices that reflect a house-cleaning mood.

## SHOPPING FOR CRAFTS

The decorations and furnishings for a country home need not be antiques. The charm of the country style is that it is the perfect showcase for handcrafted or one-of-a-kind pieces, old or new. There are several good sources for fine handicrafts.

**ARTISAN'S COOPERATIVES** are run by art associations or groups of craftsmen, and offer a wide selection of crafts, often at lower prices than gift shops. The advantage, too, is that everything you find in these places is handmade, where gift shops tend to mix handwork with mass-produced items.

**CRAFTSMEN'S STUDIOS** are usually the best place to shop for larger items and those that need to be made on special order, such as wrought-iron utensils or handmade rugs. You can watch the craftsman work, see samples in progress, and discuss your special needs. Nothing beats dealing directly with the craftsman. But studio are often widely separated and off the beaten path. Whe you are traveling, ask the local tourist office for a map or listing of craftsmen's studios in the area. Many publish these and you can quickly check to see if there are any tha interest you along your route.

### COLLECTING OLD NAPKIN RINGS

Silver (and later silver-plate) napkin rings offer a glimpse into the lives of generations past. Since many were engraved with at least a first name, there is a personal touch to each one. They are enormously varied in style, size, and decoration, but they can be mixed on a table without looking untidy.

Some are finely patterned in baroque designs, light both in weight and style. Some have pierced scroll shapes on their surface. Others are wide and heavy, with designs and beaded edges. They are frequently engraved: Zebediah, Sarah, Abigail, and other old-fashioned names appear. Often there is a date and an additional inscription to identify it as a presentation piece: "To Hattie, from her boarders," or "Sophronia, born August 2, 1883." Some have only initials.

In the late Victorian era, silver plate became popular as napkin rings became larger, heavier, and more ornate. The figural rings became popular—birds and animals posed against plain rings, or a ring and a baby chick both attached to a wishbone. Many people collect only figural rings.

Silver and metals were not the only materials used for napkin rings. Wood was popular, and wooden rings with black etchings of hotels, landmarks, and vacation spots became favorite souvenirs for traveling Victorians. Niagara Falls, lighthouses, and scenes in the Catskills and White Mountains all show up on these wooden rings. They were inexpensive gifts to bring home at the time, and today are still less expensive than silver antiques.

**CRAFT SHOWS** are the next best way to meet the craftsmen and see their work. These vary greatly in size, quality, and style, so you are best to choose a large, well-established show or one that is run by an artists' or craftsmen's organization or art council.

**IMPORT SHOPS** usually have beautiful handmade items for sale, and some of these have just the right touch for the country kitchen. Terracotta and painted pottery, tiles, woodenware, tin lighting fixtures, brightly painted bowls, baskets, and a variety of informal and lively decorative items abound in these shops.

Hancock Shaker Village in Massachusetts is fortunate to have a craftsman who is an expert in box making.

# STENCILED SHAKER
# SPICE SET

Round Shaker boxes make good storage containers in the kitchen, where their tight lids keep contents clean and dry and their flat tops make them easy and attractive to stack. Although they may be used plain, they are even more decorative if they are stenciled.

Choose any stencil pattern that fits your kitchen or make a simple design like the one pictured on the opposite page. Trace onto mylar stencil paper and cut carefully, using an X-acto knife and working on a sheet of glass. Trim any rough places so all the edges are smooth.

If your box is made of unfinished wood, cover the surface with a coat of clear sealer or a medium-toned stain. (Be careful of pine stains, since they often give a yellowish cast

Plain, unfinished surfaces of boxes and baskets are just right for decorating with simple stenciled designs.

to light wood. Cherry is a nice shade.) When the box has dried thoroughly, lightly buff with fine sandpaper to smooth the surface.

Decide where you will put your stencil, and mark the box lightly with a pencil to center a single design. If you are using a smaller motif repeated as a border, determine how far from the edge you want it and mark the stencil at that point so you can line the mark up with the edge each time and keep the border straight. Trace the outline of the box onto paper, cut it out, and fold it in pie-shaped wedges to get even measurements for placement.

Using a small stencil brush, put a tiny dab of stencil paint on the tops of the bristles and rub back and forth on a paper towel until no wet paint rubs off, and only dry color is left. Tape the stencil to the box. Working from the outer edge of each stencil opening to the center, rub the color from the brush, creating the pattern. To make color tones deeper, go over a section several times. Do not be tempted to hasten the process by applying more paint, since this will cause the paint to run under the edge of the stencil.

When the design is completed you can coat the box with a clear satin finish spray, sanding lightly between coats, or you can leave it as is. The finish coat will protect the stenciling if the boxes are washed.

# COUNTRY COOKING

## WOOD STOVES

A wood stove is the heart of a country kitchen—in fact, of the country home itself. On a frosty evening it is a gathering place; its warmth and the aromas from its oven seem to draw everyone closer to it and to each other. While some stoves are there just for appearances, if yours is in working order (and most are), it would be a shame not to cook and heat with it.

Using a wood stove is mostly a matter of common sense and a few principles of physics. If you remember that fire requires oxygen, smoke rises, and small wood burns faster, you will be able to build and maintain a good fire.

The dampers (the vents that allow air into stoves and chimneys) vary from stove to stove, but most have one beside the firebox (the chamber where the fire is), one on the back of the top above the oven, and one on the stovepipe near the wall. The trick is to adjust these so the fire gets enough air to burn without letting all the heat go up the chimney.

To start a fire, open all three dampers as far as possible. Put three or four sheets of crumpled newspaper into the firebox, then a few sticks of thin split kindling, then two larger pieces of wood, also split. Don't stack these solidly, but put them at enough of an angle so air can circulate between them. Light the paper with a match and close the door. The fire should be burning merrily in a few minutes, after which you can open the door and add some larger pieces of wood.

## WOOD STOVE SAFETY

A wood stove in your home presents certain problems not associated with an electric range, and it is *essential* that you consider these before installing or using one. Brick, tile, stone, or other fire-resistant surfaces must be underneath the stove and extend out several inches on all sides. Failing this, an insulated metal "stove board" can be used to keep it off the floor. The stove should *never* sit on wood, linoleum, or carpet.

The stove should sit at least 24 inches from the wall unless the wall is made of brick or stone. The area where the stovepipe connects to the chimney must be fireproof; any portion of the stove or pipe should be at least 18 inches from an unprotected surface.

Since each state has its own regulations, it is best to call your local fire chief or contact your insurance company for a brochure with exact specifications.

Be sure to inspect the inside of your chimney and stovepipe regularly for creosote, which causes chimney fires. Have them cleaned whenever there is buildup. Always check chimneys before their first use in the fall to be sure they haven't become homes to nesting birds during the summer!

Never feed a fire through the top of the stove—it is dangerous and allows smoke to escape into the room. When the fire has caught well, close down the dampers, always starting with those at the bottom. You will soon learn how to regulate these to give you the heat you want. To prevent smoking, close the bottom damper and open the chimney damper a little more. For safety, the chimney damper should always be open when the bottom damper is open.

To cook on the stove, you move a pan and adjust the damper instead of turning a dial. The surface above the firebox is the hottest; over the oven is cooler.

The many surfaces of a wood stove each have their uses for cooking, warming, drying, and setting bread to rise.

# BAKING BREAD IN A WOOD STOVE

There is no scientific reason why bread should taste better baked in a wood stove, but everyone seems to agree that it does. Bread is also the easiest thing for a new wood-stove cook to try, since it is forgiving and can withstand irregular and uneven temperatures. It may get a little crusty or brown on one side, but it will still be delicious. As a showoff piece, nothing beats homemade loaves of bread fresh from the oven.

A little basic understanding of the wood-stove oven will be helpful before you start to bake. Check its heat with a thermometer and see if the dial on the door is correct. If it isn't, you need to know how far it is off and in which direction, or you will have to regularly use an inside thermometer. Be sure the oven damper is in the right position to let air circulate around it. The fire should be burning well ahead of baking time.

Hardwood is best for baking because it burns slowly and evenly, as well as hotter. It also makes a good bed of coals, which helps to keep the oven temperature even.

## LIGHT WHEAT BREAD

¾ cup sugar

3 teaspoons salt

¼ cup vegetable oil

4 cups lukewarm milk

2 packages dry yeast, dissolved in ½ cup lukewarm water

4 cups whole-wheat flour

8 cups white flour

Combine sugar, salt, and oil with milk and add yeast. Stir in flour a cup at a time, beginning with the whole-wheat, then alternating between the two, until the dough is stiff. Turn dough out onto a well-floured board and knead for 15 minutes, adding remaining flour to the board as necessary.

Place in a large greased bowl, cover with a towel, and let rise on the warming shelf of your stove until doubled in bulk. Punch down with a floured fist and let rise again. Punch down, divide into fourths, and shape into loaves. Place these in greased pans and let rise again. Bake in a 350°F oven for 45 minutes or until the bread feels crisp and hollow when tapped with your finger. During the baking, move the loaves around twice to make sure they bake evenly. This recipe makes four loaves, but may be easily cut in half for two loaves.

## BRUNSWICK STEW

This Southern classic is perfect for slow simmering on the back of the wood stove or in a cast-iron kettle over an open fire, as it was originally made.

1 chicken (about 6 pounds), cut into pieces

2 tablespoons cooking oil

10 small onions, peeled

5 carrots, cut in chunks

Boiling water

Sprig of fresh thyme or ½ teaspoon dried

3 cups fresh or frozen lima beans

3 cups fresh or frozen corn

Salt (to taste)

Pepper (to taste)

Brown the chicken pieces in oil in a heavy skillet, then remove to cooking pot. Sauté the onions until light brown in the same skillet and add to the pot, along with the carrots. Cover with boiling water and add thyme. Simmer slowly until the meat is tender. Stir in beans and corn and cook until beans are done (if both vegetables are fresh, the beans will take longer than the corn, which is why you should use them as a test).

**Makes 6 servings.**

## INDIAN PUDDING

Few people are so extravagant in these days of rising energy costs as to bake a dessert for three hours in a gas or electric oven. But the wood-stove oven is warm whenever the stove is busy heating the kitchen, and requires only an occasional small log to maintain the temperature needed to bake Indian Pudding. No wonder it is a favorite!

3 cups milk

3 tablespoons yellow cornmeal

⅓ cup molasses

1 teaspoon ginger

¼ teaspoon cinnamon

¼ teaspoon salt

1 egg, beaten

1 tablespoon butter

1 cup cold milk

Heat the milk in a heavy saucepan and slowly stir in the cornmeal, molasses, spices, and salt. Continue stirring over low heat until the mixture begins to thicken, about 10 minutes. Remove from the heat and stir in the egg and butter. Pour into a heavy, well-greased baking dish. Bake at 300°F for about 30 minutes. Pour cold milk over the top, and do not stir. Bake, uncovered, at 250°F for 2 hours or until all the milk has been absorbed and the pudding is thick and dark. If the pudding seems to be scorching at the edges, add a little more milk. Serve hot with cream or a scoop of vanilla ice cream.

**Makes 4 servings.**

# KITCHEN FIREPLACES

In early homes, the fireplace was not merely a place to cook, it was the center of the home's activity, especially in winter. It was the only source of heat and often light as well. Suspended strings of fruit dried over its mantel. Fireplaces were huge—the openings often tall enough to stand in—and with their ovens and hearths they took up an entire wall. In the winter, most of the household activities were carried out within the radius of its warmth.

Whatever the size of your fireplace, building a fire is much the same, as is its basic equipment. You will need andirons or a fireplace grate, the purpose of which is to support the wood and let air circulate from underneath. You should also have a fire screen to place over the opening while you are not actually using the fire. This is a simple but necessary safety precaution to keep flying sparks and falling logs contained. A pair of long-handled tongs and a poker are useful, too.

**This fireplace in a Virginia restoration shows samples of early American implements.**

To build a fire, be sure the damper is open and begin with a few sheets of tightly twisted newspaper. Lay these on the hearth between the andirons or underneath the grate. Over these lay several pieces of split kindling, then two or three small split logs. Light the newspaper. After the kindling is burning well and the larger pieces have caught, you may want to add a little more wood.

A small fire is all that is needed—a roaring bonfire is unsafe and sends too much heat up the chimney. Most cooking is done with hot coals, not the flame, so a cooking fire should be built well in advance and with good hardwood so a bed of coals will form in the fireplace.

## FIREPLACE UTENSILS

Unique tools were created for use in and around the fireplace and some of these are still available to collectors. Because of renewed interest in fireplaces, Dutch ovens are being manufactured again, and S-hooks are still made by blacksmiths.

Harder to find are old ash peels—long-handled, flat, shovel-like implements used for scooping up and raking out ashes and hot coals. Shorter-handled wooden bread and pie peels were used to remove baked goods from brick ovens beside the fireplace.

Wafer irons were like waffle irons, but made flat wafers that could be rolled and filled with berries and fresh cream. They are rectangular with long tonglike handles. Also of cast-iron were toast racks that held bread above the coals for browning. Hanging pots with wire or perforated metal insert baskets that can be suspended over the pot by a hook on their bales are sometimes found. These were for straining and removing cooked vegetables steaming over a boiling pot.

Unusual pierced-tin drums on long wooden handles were for roasting precious coffee beans, and long-handled pans, much like bed-warming pans but with holes in the bottom, were for roasting chestnuts.

Perhaps the most interesting of all were the reflector ovens, half-round tin boxes that stood in front of the fire,

Fireplace and utensils at the Bonney House in Historic Bath, North Carolina.

**An interpreter demonstrates various fireplace cooking implements at Tryon Place in North Carolina.**

© Mark E. Gibson

caught its heat, and reflected it onto the meat or baking foods on the rack inside. Fancier models even had a little sliding door in the back so the cook could check the progress of the roast or baste it without lifting and turning the whole oven around to look in the front.

Pots, Dutch ovens, and frying pans are still being manufactured in cast-iron and can make an interesting collection in themselves if the antique examples are not available.

Fireplaces are often equipped with some built-in means of suspending a pot over the fire, either an iron rod set into the sides and running the width of the masonry or a crane that swings out on a hinge. Pots are suspended from these on S-hooks.

Soups, stews, and water for boiling can be hung from these hooks. The more likely the contents of the pot are to burn and stick in the pot, the farther they should be pushed to the side and away from the direct flame. Water can hang right over the flame as long as the pot doesn't boil dry.

The mainstay of fireplace cooking is the Dutch oven, a heavy cast-iron pot with a flat bottom and a lip around the edge that extends about a half-inch beyond the lid. Older Dutch ovens sometimes had rounded bottoms and three short legs that held them off the hearth and allowed the coals to be raked under them.

These ovens are used for baking biscuits, pies, and cakes as well as for roasting potatoes and meats (they're perfect for pot roast) or stews.

The oven is first heated by setting it over a layer of hot coals raked to one side of the hearth. The lid can be suspended by an S-hook over the fire to heat.

Biscuits, rolls, pies, or cakes are set inside the oven in round pans. Batter breads, such as corn bread, can be poured directly into the oven. After the lid is in place, hot coals are scooped onto the top of the oven, where the lip holds them in place. Fresh coals are raked underneath. Since the bottom of the pot is directly on the coals, these should not be as hot as the top layer.

To fry food in a fireplace, rake a layer of hot coals out onto the hearth and set the frying pan directly on top. Or, if you have a "spider," a little frame with short legs, you can set that over the coals and cook with the frying pan on it. There are also cast-iron frying pans made with little feet attached for this purpose.

Broiling is the easiest method in terms of equipment, but it requires a good bed of coals without a high flame. Small meats such as sausages can be roasted on long forks held over the fire. Larger roasts and poultry are hung beside the fire or suspended over it on spits.

Potatoes can be roasted by burying them in hot ashes on the warm bricks where the fire has been burning. Corn, a fireplace favorite, can be stripped of its silks without removing the husks, soaked in cool water for about 10 minutes, then re-covered with the husks and placed directly on the hot coals to steam.

## DUTCH-OVEN CORNPONE

1 cup flour

¾ cups stone-ground cornmeal

2 tablespoons sugar

½ teaspoon salt

1 tablespoon baking powder

1 cup buttermilk (or substitute ½ cup milk and ½ cup sour cream)

1 egg, beaten

2 tablespoons salad oil

Grease the entire inside of a Dutch oven with oil and preheat it and the lid by placing directly on the hot coals.

Sift the dry ingredients together. Add buttermilk, egg, and oil to the dry ingredients and mix well, but do not beat.

Sprinkle a little dry cornmeal inside the preheated oven, making sure to coat both the sides and bottom lightly, and pour the batter in. Replace the lid and cover with coals. Check it in about 15 minutes, at which time the cornpone should be done. If not, carefully replace the lid and coals and bake for another 5 minutes.

**Makes 8 servings.**

## DUTCH-OVEN POT ROAST

A heavy, cast-iron Dutch oven set over the coals provides just the right combination of fast and slow cooking required for a tender, juicy pot roast.

4 pounds thick chuck or other roasting cut of beef

10 small onions, sliced

2 cups canned tomatoes and their juice

Salt (to taste)

Pepper (to taste)

Heat the Dutch oven over the coals until quite hot, add a little oil, and quickly sear the meat on all sides. Remove the meat and add the onions, stirring until slightly soft. Add the meat on top of the onions, then the tomatoes with their juice, and salt and pepper. Add whatever herbs you like and cover the oven. Place in the coals and rake a few coals over the top. The oven should not sit in a deep bed of very hot coals, since the meat needs to cook slowly. Check the meat after an hour and add more liquid if needed (you can use water, beef broth, or more tomato juice). As the meat cooks, the onions will help make it tender. The roast is done when it is easily pierced with a sharp-tined cooking fork.

**Makes 8 servings.**

© Mark E. Gibson

© Robert Perron

# CHAPTER FOUR

# USING YOUR COUNTRY KITCHEN

## THE FRAGRANT KITCHEN

No potpourri can match or even imitate the warm and wonderful aromas that come from a busy kitchen. The fragrance of herbs growing on the windowsill, hot bread or spicy cookies in the oven, tinged with a hint of woodsmoke, are among the most memorable sensory delights that a country kitchen can offer.

But even without the potted herbs and the unmistakable note of a wood stove in the air, you can bring the country to your kitchen with a few well-chosen spices simmered on the back of your stove or placed in an open jar near the sink. The materials for a kitchen potpourri are right on the spice shelf.

For a blend to simmer, choose hard, sturdy spices. Mix any combination of whole allspice, cloves, coriander, cardamom, cracked nutmeg, broken cinnamon sticks, and pieces of gingerroot. Add bits of dried orange and lemon peel. This same mixture can be reused often and revitalized periodically with a handful of fresh spices. To package this blend as a gift, put it in a glass-topped canning jar or an apothecary jar with an instruction tag that says to add a quarter-cup of spices to a quart of water and simmer slowly on the stove.

Dried herbs can be added to this blend or mixed without the spices for a potpourri as fresh as a spring breeze blowing in the open window. Whole bay leaves, lemon verbena, sprigs of thyme and savory, bee balm, marjoram, oregano, or basil can be mixed with spices or used alone. Or make bouquets of fresh rosemary and any or all of the herbs above and put them in a vase on the kitchen table. Here they are as useful to the cook as they are fragrant.

## SETTING A TABLE

Fortunate indeed are those whose kitchen is large enough to allow for the traditional family table. The very center of household activity, the table can nevertheless be set for dinner with all the grace of a dining room. Pottery plates in spatter or redware, curved flatware based on old pewter patterns, or wooden-handled utensils set on a homespun tablecloth make a gracious table setting, rich in country tradition. A wooden or crockery bowl or toleware dish of fruit would be a good centerpiece, or in the fall, an arrangement of dried grasses in a tin coffeepot. Candles for this setting could be placed in old tin "hog scraper" push-up candlesticks; the candles themselves could be bayberry.

Use stenciled napkins of unbleached muslin, too informal for the dining room but just the right touch for a dinner in the kitchen. Or use brightly colored napkins in a variety of colors. Use unmatched plates and different settings, but with coordinating napkins for each.

For a Victorian family touch, use silver napkin rings, again unmatched and this time historically accurate as well. Napkin rings were given as gifts or "presentations" and were usually unmatched or engraved with names so each person could return his napkin, neatly rolled, to the proper ring for future use.

For a Western touch, use bandannas for napkins, pulling these from the center into napkin rings. Country table settings shouldn't be stodgy, and unusual additions can add a touch of surprise to table accessories and decorations.

## MAKING YOUR OWN CANDLES

Even though candles are no longer a necessity, they are welcome for their soft, warm light. In a kitchen, their glow is reminiscent of firelight.

To make candles, use candle wax, not paraffin, which has a lower melting point and will not burn properly. Likewise, use woven wicking; do not substitute wrapping string. Both wax and wick are available at craft stores.

You will need a container as deep as the length of the candle (such as a large juice can). Set the can of wax inside a kettle of boiling water and heat it to 165 to 170° F. Wax that is too cool will thicken and make dipping difficult, while wax that is too hot will melt off the previously dipped layer. Once the wax is hot enough, you can remove the pan from the stove and work until the wax cools.

Cut a wick twice the length you want your candles to be plus 3 inches. Tie the wick around a stick, looping it in two half-hitches so the wicks hang down about 2 inches apart. Dip both wicks into the wax, lift them out, and let the excess wax drip back into the container until the candles are cool enough to touch. Pull each wick straight after the initial dipping. After that, the candle will keep its shape without pulling. Continue dipping, letting the wax cool a little between dips, until the candles are the desired thickness. You will soon learn just how long to leave the candle in the hot wax each time. If you leave it too long, the heat will melt the previous coat and the candle will get smaller instead of larger. If you are making thin tapers, be sure they are sturdy enough to stand firmly.

Allow the finished candles to harden overnight before trimming their bases with a sharp knife. Leave them in pairs until they're used and hang them on pegs or hooks.

If you have a lot of old candle ends, you can reuse the wax to make new candles. Before melting, sort the candle stubs by color and combine only those that are compatible. Blues and greens can be mixed, as can reds and yellows. Do not combine red and green or you will get a dull brown color. White candles can be mixed with any color.

**Fancy-shaped candles such as these are made in molds, not by dipping.**

# STOCKING THE PANTRY

Filling the pantry or jelly cupboard with neat and glistening jars full of the fruits of the harvest is not a tradition reserved only for those who live in the country. Farm housewives aren't the only ones who can turn out beautiful jellies, preserves, chutneys, and pickles. The tiniest backyard garden can produce fruits and vegetables for preserving, and those without a backyard have an abundance of produce as close as the nearest farmers' market.

There are very few tricks to fine preserving, but a few safety precautions are essential. Be sure that all your jars and utensils are clean and sterilized. Boil the lids and jars for ten minutes just before filling them. Process sealed jars for fifteen minutes in boiling water to ensure a perfect seal.

Although most older recipes do not say to do this, modern research has proven it to be necessary. You should add this step to all recipes. Paraffin seals are not safe; all products should be put in jars with rubber-lined lids.

The only other general rule is to use fresh, perfect produce. Jam is not the place for old, bruised fruit or berries. Cucumbers for pickles should be very fresh and firm.

In pickling, vegetables are cut or sliced, sometimes soaked in ice or salt water, and cooked briefly in a brine made of vinegar, sugar, and spices. The vegetables are removed, packed into hot jars, and the brine poured over them. The sealed jars are then processed in boiling water to seal. Follow the same procedure for relishes, but use finely cut or ground vegetables instead of large chunks.

For preserves and jams, fruit is combined with sugar, then boiled until a small amount of the hot mixture slides from a large spoon in a sheet instead of separate drops. Use whole or large-cut fruit for preserves, and use crushed fruit for jam.

Jelly is made by cooking the clear juice strained from cooked fruit and boiling it until it reaches the jelly stage, as above. Some fruits, such as peaches, which lack pectin, can be made into jelly by adding pectin-rich fruit or by using a commercial pectin. Each of these products is used differently, so always follow the directions that are enclosed in the pectin package.

Conserves and chutneys are similar to jams, but have added ingredients such as nuts and raisins. Use vinegar and less sugar than jam for chutney, which is used as a condiment with meats and main dishes. Fruit butters are made from pureed fruit, which is cooked very slowly until it is dark and thick.

### CRABAPPLE JELLY

Cut crabapples in half and simmer in water to barely cover. When the crabapples are soft, mash and continue cooking for 5 minutes. Pour into a jelly bag and allow to drip overnight. Do not squeeze. Measure the juice and combine with an equal amount of sugar. Boil to the jelly point, which will probably take only a few minutes unless the apples have been stored for a long time. Skim froth from top and ladle into hot, sterilized jars. Seal and process for 15 minutes in boiling water.

### PEAR CHUTNEY

*5 pounds pears (Bosc or Anjou)*

*½ pound raisins*

*2 large onions, chopped*

*1 lemon, thinly sliced*

*2 cups vinegar*

*3 cups sugar*

*½ cup fresh lemon or lime juice*

*¼ cup fresh ginger, sliced*

Peel, core, and chop the pears. Combine the remaining ingredients and cook until thick, stirring often. Seal in hot, sterilized jars and process 15 minutes in boiling water.

**Makes 3 pints.**

### PICKLED CHERRY PEPPERS

*Red cherry peppers*

*Cider vinegar*

Wash peppers well and pierce in several places with the tip of a knife. Pack the peppers as snugly as possible in hot, sterilized jars. Bring the vinegar to a boil and add to the jars. Seal and process 15 minutes in boiling water. To use in recipes calling for fresh peppers, simply rinse in cold water first.

### PICCALILLI

*6 green tomatoes*

*4 green bell peppers*

*2 sweet red peppers*

*1 hot pepper*

*5 onions*

*¼ cup salt*

*2½ cups brown sugar*

*1 teaspoon celery seed*

*1 tablespoon mustard seed*

*1 teaspoon whole cloves*

*1 tablespoon whole allspice*

*1¾ cups cider vinegar*

Slice all the vegetables very thinly, toss with the salt, and let rest overnight. Rinse in cold water and drain well. Combine in a large pot with the other ingredients, bring to a boil, and simmer 15 minutes. Seal in hot, sterilized jars and process 15 minutes in boiling water.

**Makes 3 pints.**

# ONION BRAIDS, PEPPER STRINGS, AND SCHNITZ

In a Mediterranean country kitchen, long braids of onions, shallots, and garlic, and strings of bright red peppers decorate the walls and serve as handy ingredients for the cook. Strings of hot peppers are also a familiar sight in the Southwest. Strings of drying apples are a common sight in Pennsylvania Dutch farmhouses, while ears of popcorn or grinding corn on an iron "drying tree" can be seen in homes from New England to the Southwest.

The purpose in hanging onions and garlic is not to dry but to store them in an airy place where they will keep well and be handy for use. Hot peppers, corn, and apples are left hanging only until completely dry, then may be stored in containers.

To make braids or strings, use onions, garlic, or shallots with their tops still attached. When these tops are dry but not brittle, tie six of them together and begin braiding. Add more onions as there is room. When the string is long enough, tie the braid and cut off the remaining ends.

Hot peppers, such as chilies or the long, red, Italian variety, can be strung on long threads to dry, or you can braid jute cord tightly, slipping pepper stems into the braid as you work.

Popcorn, seed corn, or varieties that will be ground for meal may also be braided by their husks or tied into bundles for drying. Corn is especially attractive displayed on a wrought-iron "drying tree," which holds the corn ears separately and hangs from a rafter or flat against a wall.

To dry apples, peel, core, and slice firm apples into thin rings and drop them into a bowl of water with a few drops of lemon juice. Remove the apples within ten minutes and pat dry. Thread these on a long string and hang in a clean, airy place, separating the rings. They are dry when they become leathery, and should then be stored in a tightly closed jar. Dried apples make excellent pies.

© Jules Zalon/FPG International

## SCHNITZ UN KNEPP

*2 cups dried apples*

*3 pounds ham hocks*

*1 egg*

*¼ cup milk*

*2 tablespoons butter*

*2 cups flour*

*3 teaspoons baking powder*

*¼ teaspoon salt*

Soak the dried apples in water to cover overnight. The next day scrub and dry the ham hocks and simmer in water for about 3 hours. Add the apples and soaking water. Boil together for 45 minutes to make the knepp.

Beat the egg and add milk and butter. Sift and add the dry ingredients. Mix well, but don't overbeat. Drop by spoonfuls into the boiling knepp. Cover tightly and steam for 15 minutes without raising the lid. Serve at once.

**Makes 4 servings.**

© S. Metz/FPG International

CHAPTER FIVE

# SHARING AND ENTERTAINING

## A YANKEE BEAN SUPPER

In New England, a bean supper is more than just a meal. It is a social occasion and a major source of revenue for churches, fire departments, and a variety of other organizations.

But bean suppers don't have to be community events. As a way to entertain a group of friends informally in your own kitchen, the bean supper is perfect. The cooking is comparatively easy and nearly everything can be done ahead of time. A supper can be cooked by a single hostess or a group of friends working together. Individual guests can bring food, already prepared, or friends can gather to cut the slaw and make the corn bread as a group. But one person easily can give a bean supper alone.

The corn bread (or corn sticks, which will not dry out or crumble) can be baked a day or two early and stored in large plastic bags. The bread is better if it is reheated, covered with foil, shortly before serving. You can pile it in a large pan and put it in the oven when you take out the beans. This will warm and also crisp it.

The coleslaw can be cut and refrigerated for assembling on the day of the supper. The ham can be arranged on its platters in advance and refrigerated if it is to be served cold for the supper.

Although it is a bit more work, it is better to buy and bake hams instead of serving the canned versions. The hams can be cooked, cooled, and then sliced for serving cold or for rewarming on the griddle before serving. If your oven is big enough or the group a fairly small one, you can even bake a ham at the same time as the beans and serve it whole, letting guests do their own carving.

If you are using home-cooked ham and want to serve it cold, you can pre-slice it quite easily. Bone it while it is still warm, tie it firmly, and chill it. Then you can slice it with a sharp carving knife.

Everyone has a favorite recipe for baked beans and you will probably want to use your own. If you have them, soldier beans bake beautifully, but navy beans are more readily available. The following recipe will serve about twenty-five people and you can bake it in a large pan.

© Rogers Associates

The oven of a wood stove is more economical for the long hours required to bake beans than a modern kitchen range.

Red kidney, soldier, Jacob's cattle, navy, pea, yellow-eye, and several other bean varieties work well for baking.

## BAKED BEANS

8 cups dry soldier or navy beans

8 small onions (scored with a cross on the bottom)

1 pound salt pork, cut in 1-inch cubes

1 cup brown sugar

⅓ cup molasses

2 tablespoons salt

2 tablespoons dry mustard

1 tablespoon powdered ginger

1 tablespoon thyme

Cover the beans with cold water, bring to a boil, and boil for 2 minutes. Cover the pot, remove from the heat, and let stand 1 hour. Return to heat and slowly bring to a boil. Reduce the heat and simmer about an hour, or until the skins wrinkle and peel away when you blow on a few beans.

Drain (saving the liquid) and put the beans in a large baking pan with the remaining ingredients. Mix the ingredients among the beans evenly, then add the bean liquid to cover. Bake at 300°F for about 8 hours. Check every hour to make sure that the liquid isn't boiling away, and add more of the reserved liquid or hot water if needed. The beans can stay in the oven until you serve them, as long as you check the liquid level. Toward the end of baking, let the liquid level drop a little so the beans will not be too juicy.

No matter how many corn sticks you make, there will not be any left over. Plan to serve at least two apiece. Some people won't take two, but many will take five! The best way to prepare a lot of them is to line up all of the ingredients in order of use and keep several batches going at once. Since cast-iron corn-stick pans should be used hot, this "assembly line" method saves heating the pans each time. Brush the crumbs out with a stiff natural bristle brush and apply a fresh coat of oil with a paper towel before pouring in the next batch of batter. If you can't get cornstick pans, this same recipe can be used to make corn muffins.

By mixing the ingredients for one batch as you bake the previous one, the whole process takes surprisingly little time. You can keep three batches going at once with a little practice. Each batch makes a dozen.

### CORN STICKS

1 cup yellow cornmeal

1 cup flour

2 tablespoons sugar

¾ teaspoon salt

1 tablespoon baking powder

1 cup sour milk (sweet will do)

1 egg, beaten

2 tablespoons melted butter

½ teaspoon crumbled rosemary or sage

Sift the dry ingredients together, then add the remaining ingredients to the bowl. Mix well and pour into greased muffin tins. Bake for 20 minutes at 425°F, check, and continue baking until they are golden but not dry.

For coleslaw, shred a large head of cabbage for each dozen people. Once shredded, it can be stored in the refrigerator in plastic bags. Make the dressing in a large jar and refrigerate. Mix 2 cups of dressing to 6 cups of shredded cabbage, and let stand at room temperature for 3 hours before serving.

### COLESLAW DRESSING

4 cups sour cream

1 teaspoon dry mustard

1 teaspoon black pepper

¾ cup sugar

1 cup cider vinegar

1 teaspoon celery seed

2 teaspoons salt

Put ingredients in a jar and shake to blend.

### A WREATH OF DRIED APPLES

A circle of dried apple slices, their red peels left intact, is attractive in the kitchen at any time of year. Slice apples about a quarter-inch thick and dry as described on page 95. Or, if you have a wood stove, place the circles of apple on wire racks and dry in a slightly warm oven (leaving the door open) for several hours until they are leathery.

For the wreath, choose only the perfect center slices of uniform size and shape. Glue these in an overlapping row to a single crinkle-wire wreath ring. A glue gun will work best for this, since the glue dries quickly and remains pliable enough to secure the leathery apples. This simple wreath does not need a bow.

For dessert, you can ask guests to bring their favorite pie. Serve it either plain or with vanilla ice cream. Another possible dessert, which can be prepared in advance and placed into the oven just as you sit down to eat, is baked apples. Stand them in rows in cake pans to bake, and serve them hot with fresh cream poured on top.

As a variation, leave out the maple syrup, use 1 ½ cups of sugar, and add a cup of fresh whole cranberries to the nuts and currants. You will have to pile this mixture on top of the apples and possibly sprinkle the leftover berries around the pan between the apples.

## MAPLE BAKED APPLES

*12 firm, tart apples*

*½ cup chopped walnuts*

*½ cup dried currants*

*½ cup sugar*

*1 teaspoon cinnamon*

*Pinch of nutmeg*

*¼ cup maple syrup*

Core the whole apples, but do not peel. Stand them in baking pans. Mix the nuts, currants, sugar, and spices and spoon a little into the cavity of each apple. Spoon just a little maple syrup over each apple and bake in a 350°F oven for 30 to 45 minutes, or until the apples are soft. Carefully remove the apples with a large spoon and serve hot, with a spoonful of the syrup that has accumulated in the bottom of the baking pan poured over each apple. Pass a pitcher of cream.

© Jerry W. Myers/FPG International

**Firm apples are best for baking whole, but nearly any tart apple works well.**

No room in the house is more fun to decorate for the holidays than the kitchen.

© Hanson Carroll

# HOME TO THE
# CHRISTMAS KITCHEN

In a country home, the kitchen is always the busiest place, but at Christmas it seems as though everything is happening there at once. Children are making gifts for their grandmother at the kitchen table, the counters are spread with racks of cookies to be packed into gift boxes, and the top of the stove has full cookie sheets waiting for space in the oven. A bowl of apples and a jar of whole cloves sit handy in case anyone has a spare moment to turn them into fragrant pomanders, and a string of apple slices is drying over the wood stove.

With all this activity, there is hardly any need to think about how to decorate the kitchen for the holidays. The very busyness of the season decorates it for you! Let the kitchen be your workshop (and Santa's) by standing rolls of bright-colored gift wrap in a basket, along with tape, scissors, tags, and ribbons, ready for anyone who needs to wrap a present. Create a seasonal tablecloth from a length of calico in a Christmas print—you don't even have to hem the ends if you cut them neatly. Use red or green napkins and put a few extra Christmas tree ornaments in a wooden salad bowl as a centerpiece. Tuck a few sprigs of greens between the ornaments or mix in large pinecones.

Make a quick arrangement of evergreen tips and spice it up with a few dried red peppers on florists' wire. If you have access to bright red berries such as bittersweet, add a few sprigs to the peppers and greens. Be careful, however, to keep any fresh evergreens—arrangements, roping, swags, or wreaths—away from the stove or fireplace.

**Add decorations of bright fresh fruit to your holiday wreaths.**

## A WILLIAMSBURG WREATH
## OF FRESH FRUIT

A welcoming circle of glossy broad-leaved evergreens and shining fresh fruit is a Southern tradition perfect for the kitchen door. If the weather is too severe to use fresh fruit outdoors, hang this wreath on a protected porch or use it indoors, replacing the fruit as necessary.

The base is a doughnut-shape, cut from plywood. It can be any size, but the ring itself should be at least 3 inches wide. (If the outer diameter is 12 inches, then the inner cutout diameter would be 6 inches.) Paint this base dark green and let it dry thoroughly. Stud the center with 2-inch nails, pounded all the way through so the surface has a row of pointed nails on one side, but is perfectly flat on the other. Wrap a loop of florists' wire around the frame for a hanger.

Impale bright red or green apples, oranges, lemons, limes, crabapples, or other bright fruit on the nails. These can be a mixture, balanced for size and color, or they can be a simple row of matching apples or crabapples. Cover the rest of the frame by tucking magnolia leaves and sprigs of boxwood or other greens between the fruit. You may have to wire or glue some of these in place if their stems will not hold securely under the fruit.

# A BREAD WREATH

What better way to welcome your friends to your country kitchen than with a decoration that combines two ancient symbols of hospitality—bread and the wreath. Mix half a batch of the bread recipe on page 297, substituting white flour for the whole wheat. Let it rise once as directed, then divide it into three equal parts. Let the dough rest for 10 minutes and knead it to remove as much air as possible.

Roll each of the three sections into a long rope. On a well-greased baking sheet, braid the three ropes of dough, forming them into a circle. Tuck the ends into the braid so it forms a continuous pattern. (If you cannot get a perfect join, don't worry. You can always cover it with a bow of red-and-white gingham.)

Brush the entire surface with lightly beaten egg white and let rest 10 minutes. Carefully brush the wreath with egg white again and bake in a 350°F oven for 45 minutes or until it is golden brown. Remove to a wire rack to cool.

You can either use this as an edible centerpiece on your table or hang it on the wall as a decoration. It will keep well outdoors as long as it is kept inside the storm door and out of the rain. When you are through with the wreath, hang it outdoors for the birds to enjoy.

Fresh breads, especially in wreath shapes, add to holiday decorations.

# PART SIX

COUNTRY

## CHRISTMAS

RECIPES, CRAFTS, AND MORE

BARBARA RANDOLPH

# THE ESSENCE OF A COUNTRY CHRISTMAS

**A** country Christmas delights all the senses. Its essence hangs in the air with the pungency of balsam, the smell of pies in the oven, the hint of wood smoke, and the scent of drying mittens. It is the bubbling sound of laughter, caroling, sleigh bells, church bells, and the stamping of snow from boots. Its look is simple, homespun, and natural. It is deep greens accented in red, bright primaries tempered in warm earth tones.

A country Christmas stirs the remembrance of Christmases past, and on it are built the memories that will endure a lifetime.

© Thomas Lindley/FPG International

# PREPARING FOR CHRISTMAS

The easy atmosphere and relaxed pace tinged with anticipation that characterize Christmas in the country are not accidental. The country year is, perforce, one of seasons and to each belongs its own activities. If the time before Christmas seems more relaxed than others, it is possibly because it follows one of the year's busiest seasons.

The harvest that begins with the first pink chive blossom in the spring lasts until the snow lies deep upon the garden. And as the fruits and flowers of summer are all carefully preserved, so begins the preparation for Christmas. The most sparkling jar of pickles is set aside for Christmas dinner, glowing jellies and herb-rich vinegars are put away to fill gift baskets, and the everlasting flowers that will grace wreaths have been a part of that harvest all through summer and fall. By December they are collected and ready. Now all that needs to be done is to prepare the fruits of your labor—making the wreaths, pickling the cucumbers—most of which can be done at your leisure throughout the summer and fall months.

# PLANNING AHEAD

In the well-ordered country home there will always be at least a few homemade gifts ready and tucked away in the closet under the eaves—wool mittens knit in February and March, sachets made from the needles saved from last year's tree, jars of potpourri made from June's roses, packets of the summer's herbs picked at their prime.

More than conscious planning, this is perhaps just the normal response to the offerings and opportunities of each season. The feel of wool slipping between knitting needles was comforting in February, the roses and chives were in bloom in June, and the cucumbers were just the right size for pickling in July. And so the well-stocked pantry and eaves closet was filled.

But even with these preliminaries accomplished, there are many things that must be done in those busy weeks before December twenty-fifth. The trick is to do these without feeling pressured or as though you are running at full speed only to always remain a few paces behind. Some serious planning is a must.

It helps to begin with a few lists of those things you feel must be done: gifts to assemble, decorations to make and display, cards to send, cookies to bake, packages to mail and deliver. Sort these into several lists in order of priority. Put those things you simply must do on the "priority one" list, the next most important on the "priority two" list. List these on separate pages of a small notebook. The rest of the notebook is a good place for noting what you plan to give to whom and other essentials it will be handy to have in one place.

If you sort these activities by priority, you are less likely to find yourself doing less important things first and rushing around at the last minute to do the essentials. Add a page of rewards—those things you love to do before the holidays, but seldom have a chance to do, like taking the children to see the animated windows, having a few friends in for an impromptu Sunday brunch, making everyone's favorite (but time-consuming) dinner or dessert. Resolve to do one of these whenever you cross a certain number of tasks off your list.

Keep it easy, fun, and manageable. Working the extra chores of the holidays into an already full schedule is never easy, so don't expect to do it all yourself. Christmas is not a one-man (or woman) show with you doing it all, nor is it a monthlong party thrown for the rest of the family by mother. Let everyone take part. Look carefully at your lists and share those chores that suit the schedules and talents of others.

Let a child wrap the gifts. So what if they are not exactly the way you would have done them—grandmother will be delighted at the original wrappings and the proud grandchild who created them. Give errands to others, have an older child address the envelopes for cards, leaving them for you to sign and add personal notes. Or don't send cards at all this year and write short notes after Christmas to faraway friends. Set your own priorities.

Make things more convenient by keeping materials handy. Put wrapping paper, ribbon, tags, scissors, and tape in a large basket next to the fireplace or under an end table. As gifts are finished or purchased, wrap them or give them to someone else to wrap, without having to haul out all the materials each time.

If you have children to wait for after school, or carpools to drive, carry your Christmas cards, a pen, your address book, and stamps with you in a little basket.

Along with lists of things to do, make lists of things to buy—gifts, wrappings, materials, ingredients—well in advance and pick them up as you see them instead of spending an exhausting day shopping or making separate last-minute trips. Begin stocking your pantry in the fall with those things you'll need extras of—nuts, chocolate chips, dried and candied fruits, sugar, and flour.

# KEEP IT SIMPLE

Few things are fun if done in a hurry or under pressure. By simplifying your plans, you can leave yourself and your family time to enjoy Christmas. Keep your house uncluttered, too—it will save you time and give you a sense of space and calm instead of frenzy. Clear away other decorative items as you unpack and set up the crèche sets and other Christmas decorations, storing the year-round knick-knacks in the boxes that held the holiday treasures. After Christmas, swap back. Instead of crowding the furniture together to make room for the Christmas tree, try removing a chair and storing it on an enclosed porch that isn't used in the winter or placing it in a bedroom or guest room.

Cook twice as much stew as you need for supper and put it away in the refrigerator to have two or three nights later. There is no law that says you can't have the same dish two nights in the same week. That leaves your kitchen and your time free for an evening's baking or relaxing by the fire to read a favorite story together. Plan more simple one-pot menus for the weeks before Christmas.

Think ahead to some of the dishes you will need for holiday meals and cook them ahead. Cranberry sauce keeps in the refrigerator for weeks and cornbread for stuffing can be frozen. Pâtés and cheese spreads for entertaining can be made a week in advance.

Group your activities together to avoid repeatedly getting out and putting away your half-finished projects. If you have a guest room or other place you can spare for a few weeks, use it as a Christmas studio and keep all your materials there. That will save cleanup time and allow you to leave works-in-progress where you can resume them.

If you must work on the kitchen or dining room table, collect all the supplies for one type of project in a basket to make cleanup and preparation faster and easier. If you are making several stenciled gifts, for example, keep paints, brushes, stencils, tape, paper towels, and other supplies together. Or, if you are making homemade cards, keep scissors, paper, and other accessories together.

Don't plan to make *all* your gifts (unless you begin very early). Choose a few projects and finish one before starting the next. Otherwise, you may end up with all half-finished projects. Group similar activities together—cutting fabric and machine stitching, for instance—but be sure you are not beginning more projects than you can possibly finish.

By trying only a limited number of new crafts or techniques in one season, you will avoid getting your plans so

**This wide variety of sugar cookies came from one basic recipe.**

complicated that you can't complete them all. If a project turns out to be more difficult and time-consuming than you had expected, put it away until after Christmas when you will have more time and energy. You'll have a good start on next year. Gift-giving, like parties, should be fun for the giver, too.

Simplify your Christmas entertaining as well. Plan informal get-togethers instead of full-course, sit-down dinners. Buffets are easier to plan, as are brunches. Invite everyone for "Just Desserts" in the evening or have a late party after a school concert or other evening event.

Plan cooperative social events: an old-fashioned potluck supper or a cookie swap where everyone brings a few dozen of their favorite cookies and goes home with a grand assortment. Or clear the decks and invite friends to join you in decorating sugar cookies you've baked ahead.

# ALL THROUGH THE HOUSE

**E**ach season has its own decorations—a swag of bright dried corn on the front door, a jack-o'-lantern grinning from the window, a bouquet of spring flowers on the table—but only Christmas fills the house with them.

Decorating the house for Christmas is a labor of love. It isn't a project you set about purposefully one day and complete on the spot.

Fresh greens appear an armful at a time and gradually fill the house with the scent. Baskets of ribbon and wrapping and greeting cards creep in, a big bowl of bright potpourri appears, and a row of pomanders is drying above the wood stove. Decorating for Christmas is more fun this way, instead of being an obstacle to overcome.

Throughout this chapter are suggestions and ideas for filling your home with Christmas. There are special sections on quick tricks you can do with greens, special ways to scent your home during this season, and decorating with candlelight. Use these ideas as a starting point and let your imagination run wild.

# GATHERING WILD MATERIALS

Long before the snow falls, it is time to gather the cones, pods, dried grasses, and seeds that will become wreaths and ornaments. An early snow may cover these, making collection difficult or impossible, so it is best to do this early in the season.

While not everyone has their own "back forty" from which to gather materials, there are many alternatives. Since you won't be cutting wild greens or plants, nearly any open piece of land, except public lands established as nature reserves, will do. Friends' gardens, fields, wood lots, vacant lots, backyards, and roadsides will provide ample seeds, cones, and grasses. On a Sunday drive in the country, armed with scissors and paper bags, you can collect plenty of material for your decorating projects.

Always cut or break off dried plants such as grasses and seed pods on stems. Never pull on the plant hoping that it will break off, since many of these have shallow roots and you could easily uproot the plant.

Look along roadsides and streets for cones and seeds from trees: the winged seeds of maple, beechnuts, buckeyes, acorns, and sweet gum pods are all beautiful on cone wreaths. Collect different varieties of cones. Even the large, ungainly ones can be used as bases or broken into lovely rosettes. Tiny cones such as hemlock and balsam make good fillers in potpourri as well as being the right size for miniature wreaths. Keep your eyes open; no matter where you live, you will find good material.

## GATHERING GREENS

To gather greens in the woods (with the landowner's blessing, of course), use a pair of stout clippers or pruning shears and cut each branch at an angle. Never strip the branches from the tree. You will soon notice, if you are gathering balsam, that the branches at the top have fuller, more three-dimensional needle growth than those at the bottom, which are fairly flat. Both are good for wreaths and other

uses, but the top greens make a fuller wreath with more depth.

Collect the boughs into bundles and tie them near the stem end for easier carrying. Remember that whatever jacket and gloves you wear are very likely to get pitch on them. A layer of newspapers will protect car seats from both pitch and falling needles. If you do not plan to use the boughs immediately, store them in a cool place, standing them up in a large bucket of water. Be sure to get them into the water as quickly as possible, before the cut ends seal over and prevent water intake. If this happens, cut the stems again, and put them in water immediately. If the greens are kept standing instead of being stacked they will maintain a more natural shape. Standing them also avoids crushing and breaking the needles.

Unused boughs should be discarded outdoors when they are no longer needed. They can become a serious fire hazard, particularly in a garage, if left to dry out. The same is true of wreaths after they are taken down.

# EVERGREENS AND WREATHS

Evergreen boughs, either formed into wreaths or tied in swags, bundles, bouquets, or ropes, are the favorite Christmas decoration. For many, even those who live where evergreen is not plentiful, it simply is not Christmas without an evergreen wreath on the door.

**Balsam** is the favorite green to use during Christmas. Its pungent fragrance grows more intense as the season progresses, and its rich green color, short needles, and outstanding keeping qualities have earned it first place. In addition, it is often available already cut from Christmas tree sellers, who trim branches from trees or have damaged trees that they must discard. Balsam is also the best material for evergreen roping, since it holds its needles well even when cut into short sprigs.

Other greens work almost as well for wreathmaking and other decorations, and each has its own special qualities.

© Anita Sabarese

**White pine**, with its long, soft needles, makes a nice, full wreath, especially if you use a larger wreath frame as a base. On very small frames, its long needles tend to fill in the center. White pine is the preferred branch for door swags and baskets or vases of standing boughs. It is full, pliable, and mixes well with other greens as well as with berries such as bittersweet and alder.

**Cedar** has interesting foliage, unlike the needles of the pines and firs, and is a good green on its own or mixed with others, where its texture is a fine contrast. Its foliage is flat, making it a good base for combinations of fresh and dried materials.

**Spruce** and **hemlock** both have short needles that make handsome wreaths, but tend to begin losing their needles very quickly. They can be used in vases or arrangements where their stems can be kept in water. It is possible to make wreaths on a base that holds moisture, and this is the only method suitable for these two. **Blue spruce** is especially attractive, and contrasts well with the deeper greens of others.

**Scotch pine** would make a good wreath, but it is so stiff that it is nearly impossible to work with. In a swag it lacks the graceful flexibility of white pine or cedar.

**Juniper** can be used alone, but its needles are so short that it is best used in combination with other greens. Its pale color and white berries contrast well to darker greens, and its narrow, stiff shape works well in standing arrangements.

**Monterey pine** has shiny, bright green needles nearly twice the length of white pine needles, and a bit stiffer. A wreath of these would have to be quite large, but the branches are fine for standing arrangements.

## A BASIC EVERGREEN WREATH

*A crinkle-wire single-wreath frame*

*A spool of green florist's wire*

*Plenty of evergreen boughs*

*Clippers or strong scissors*

Clip the tips of the boughs into sprigs, each about the same length. The larger your wreath, the longer these can be, but they should be uniform. Six to eight inches is a good length if you are making a small wreath. Be sure that there are no cut ends showing —all the tips should be natural ends. Assemble a large pile of these sprigs before you begin tying them into bundles. Although many wreathmakers simply tie the sprigs to the wire frame without tying each bundle first, beginners will find it less time-consuming in the long run to add this step. Wrap the wire two or three times around the stems of each group of three or four sprigs, and collect up a pile of these before beginning the wreath itself.

Lay the first bunch of greens alongside the top of the frame, stems pointing to the right (reverse this if you are left-handed). The stems should be parallel to the wire of the frame, not perpendicular to it. Tie the end of the wire securely to the frame and begin wrapping it around the frame and the stems of the greens, using two or three wraps of wire. Add a second bunch, this time inside the frame, but with the stems still facing to the left. Again, secure with a few wraps of wire.

Continue to add bunches of greens, each one covering the wrapping on the one before it, working around the frame and alternating between the inside and the outside of the frame. You may also need to place some bundles directly in the center to keep the wreath full. When you come full circle to the place where you began, you will have to pull back the ends of those first greens and work underneath them. Finish with several tight wraps of wire and leave a long tail for a hanging loop if desired.

Stand back from your wreath and look at it from a distance to be sure it is even. If there are bare places, or those where the greens are a little thinner or the wreath a little narrower, you can usually simply tuck a bundle or two of greens into the wreath, under the wire that is already there or between other stems.

The shape of your wreath will be determined by the length of the tips you cut. Longer ones will make larger, more open wreaths, while short ones will make narrower, more compact wreaths.

If you choose to mix the greens in your wreath, it is best to mix each little bunch. To make a double-faced wreath, one with greens on both sides, flip the wreath over after each bundle is added and wire one to the other side. Double wreaths are full and luxurious, but are sometimes too thick for the

© Hanson Carroll

space between the door and storm door.

When you have made a number of wreaths, you may wish to skip the step of tying the little bundles first, simply adding the bunches of sprigs and tying them on with the wire. Use whatever method gives you the best finished wreath.

You will most likely get pitch on your hands, so to clean your hands after working with evergreens, use lard or vegetable shortening. These are much easier on your hands than turpentine or most hand cleaners and you will not have to scrub—just rub it on and wipe it off. Then wash your hands with regular hand soap.

© Hanson Carroll

## EVERGREEN SWAGS

The soft, pliable nature of white pine makes it perfect for the base of door swags, but any evergreen that lies fairly flat will do.

*Medium-gauge florist's wire*

*Evergreen boughs 10 to 18 inches long, preferably a mix of several, such as white pine, cedar, balsam, juniper, and boxwood*

*Pinecones, one very large or three medium-size*

*Red all-weather ribbon*

Lay three long sprays of white pine or other flat evergreen on a work surface. Lay three more medium-length boughs over them. Wrap their stems together with wire, spreading the greens gracefully.

Arrange shorter boughs (about half the length of the first group) of the same varieties of evergreen so they form a spray facing the other direction. Push the two groups together so the cut ends of each one are partly buried in the other. Wire the second group of stems to the first with several wraps.

Wire the pinecones together into a group (or use a single large cone) and place them over the long boughs, near the place where the stems meet. Wire the cones in place and fill in around them with shorter sprigs of evergreen to cover the stem section. Tie the ribbon into a bow—a multi-looped wire bow is usually best for these—leaving long streamers. Wire the bow to the swag, just above the pinecones, so it covers the wire. If necessary, add a few short sprigs to balance the design or cover any bare places. Trim the ribbon ends diagonally or with a notch, making them a little shorter than the long pine boughs.

Hang the swag on the door at a slight angle, with the longest boughs facing down. If the swag is in the sun, some of the needles may fall. If there are bare branches, simply pull these out carefully (put the swag on a flat surface first) and replace them with fresh ones pushed into the arrangement.

## ROPES OF EVERGREEN

Long strings of evergreens are lovely and graceful when draped around mirrors, mantels, doors, and windows or spiraled around a banister or newel post. Although time-consuming, these ropes are not difficult to make. Cedar and white pine are the easiest greens to work with because they are flexible and long-lasting, but balsam makes a more fragrant rope and lasts quite well.

*Soft cotton clothesline cord (stiff cords do not drape well)*

*Fine-gauge florist's wire*

*Short sprigs of evergreen*

Measure the length of roping needed and mark it on the cord, but do not cut. Leave 2 feet of cord for tying before starting to measure. Tie one end of the cord to a fixed object: a table leg if you are working on the floor, or a doorknob.

Cut greens into 5 to 6 inch lengths and wrap three or four together into little bundles, their stems tied with wire. After a while you may decide to wire individual sprigs directly to the cord, but at first this extra step makes the job a lot easier.

Wire the bundles to the cord so that each bunch covers the stems of the previous one. Work around the cord in a spiral so the evergreen covers the cord evenly. Make a half knot in the wire after every few bunches to keep them from coming unwrapped when you set it down. You can make the rope thicker or thinner by increasing and decreasing the bundles used per foot of cord.

After you have finished the length needed, go back to the beginning and cover the stems of the first few with very short sprigs wired in the opposite direction. Push their stems into the main part of the roping and hide the wire under the needles.

These ropes can be highlighted by spiraled strings of cranberries or unbuttered and unsalted popcorn. Cranberries should only be used close to the holidays or they will need to be replaced, since they become soft quickly. Do not string cranberries and popcorn together, since the cranberry juice will run all over the popcorn and ruin it. Use a strong thread and a heavy needle to string either of these. Run the needle through the popcorn slightly to one side in order to avoid any hard kernels in the center.

# POINSETTIAS

The bright red flowers of poinsettias are actually leaves, not blossoms. The true flower is the cluster at the center of the rosette of red upper leaves. Whatever their technicalities, they are the favorite Christmas plant. Over 25 million of these decorate homes each year during the holidays.

Use them alone or in groups. A cluster of them in a corner of the front hall—one elevated on an upturned flowerpot in the corner and two or three in front of it sitting on the floor—creates a bright accent. Or use a larger grouping in the same way in the corner of a large room.

Since poinsettias should not be in direct sunlight for more than an hour or so a day, a sunny windowsill is not the best place for them. But poinsettias do need light. A good test of the correct natural light is whether a person of normal eyesight can read fine print. If they can, the room has enough light to keep a poinsettia healthy. Water them frequently, whenever the soil feels dry to the touch, but do not let them stand in water.

© Thomas Lindley/FPG International

Contrary to popular myth, the poinsettia is not poisonous. The United States Department of Health and Human Services' Bureau of Product Safety reports that despite numerous reports of children having eaten various parts of the plant, there was no poisoning. Ohio State University conducted laboratory tests and failed to find any evidence of toxicity. While children should not eat any houseplant or Christmas green, the poinsettia is no worse than any other plant and no one seems to know how this rumor started or how it got its dangerous reputation. So the next time you hear that poinsettias are poisonous, you can reply "Bah, humbug," and continue to brighten your Christmas with these beautiful plants.

## IVY TOPIARY TREE

A live ivy plant can be trained into the shape of a Christmas tree over the course of a few months. Begin with healthy, fairly full plants.

*3 small English ivy plants*

*1 10-inch plastic flowerpot filled with potting soil*

*Chicken wire cone with a base 8 inches in diameter (see instructions for making a tabletop tree, page 43)*

*1 12-inch terra-cotta plant pot*

Plant the ivy close to the edges of the plastic pot, with the plants equally spaced. Place the wire cone carefully over the pot, pushing the wire very gently into the soil. Pull all the ivy stems to the outside. Entwine the ivy through the wire just enough to hold it so it covers the outside. It will probably not cover the entire cone.

Place the plant in a well-lit window and keep it watered.

As the ivy grows, continue to entwine it into the wire frame, winding it around, if necessary, to cover all the bare places. Turn the plant frequently so it grows evenly on all sides. In a few months, the ivy will cover the entire cone, forming a solid green "tree." Display the completed tree in the terra-cotta pot, setting the plastic one inside it. Tie a red bow around the top of the pot during the holidays.

## WINDOWSILL GREENS ARRANGEMENTS

Windowsills are the perfect place for sprays of evergreen, but are often too narrow to support a vase. This arrangement uses a long, narrow basket designed to hold crackers, just the right shape for a windowsill.

*A long, narrow cracker basket*

*Oasis® or other floral foam to fit the basket*

*Toothpicks or wooden skewers*

*A sheet of plastic wrap large enough to line the basket*

*Assorted evergreen sprigs, such as white pine, balsam, spruce, juniper, cedar, and boxwood*

*Red berries such as bittersweet or sumac, or rose hips*

Soak the Oasis® in water and let it drain. Line the basket with plastic wrap and put the Oasis® in it. Secure at the ends and edges with toothpicks or skewers, pushing them through the holes in the basket and into the Oasis®. Put these skewers near the top rim of the basket so they will not puncture the bottom of the plastic.

Begin with the larger sprigs and push their stems into the basket near the center of the back. Continue to work to the edges, inserting the stems at more and more of an angle until the final sprigs drape over the sides onto the work surface. Soft, flexible greens such as white pine are best for these edges, since they drape gracefully. When the back layer is full, defining the shape of the arrangement, fill in the center and front with shorter sprigs, mixing them for variety. Add accents of holly or other red berries if they are available. Fresh flowers may be added to this arrangement, since the Oasis® will be kept moist. Red or white carnations, small red roses, or white mums provide a nice contrast to the dark greens.

Water the arrangement frequently but lightly, keeping the Oasis® moist at all times, but not enough to allow water to leak through the plastic.

## A TABLETOP TREE

Finding a small tree for the center of a table or a buffet is not as easy as it may seem. Real trees rarely achieve that perfect a shape: That comes with age and shearing. Most of the tabletop trees sold at Christmas tree farms are really the tips of larger trees. Even these are sometimes a little bare.

They do allow a lot of space for ornaments, but if you prefer a fuller, perfectly shaped centerpiece tree, the best way to get it is to make your own. Unlike a natural tree, your manmade tree can have a variety of greens and can be any size. For an unusual and fragrant tree, try creating it from branches of rosemary.

*1 piece of small-gauge chicken wire, 18 by 36 inches*

*Wire cutters*

*Florist's tape*

*Sphagnum or other floral moss*

*Branches of white pine, cedar, boxwood, rosemary, or other fairly flexible evergreens*

Cut the chicken wire screening into a semicircle with wire cutters. Fold the straight side in half to form a cone, overlapping more for a narrower tree and less for a wider one. Twist the cut wire ends into the mesh to fasten the edge and hold the cone in shape.

Wrap the bottom edge with florist's tape, stretching the tape as you work to make it stick. Check the tree to be sure it stands straight. If it does not, you can pull it into shape or fold up a little wire on the longer side. Soak sphagnum moss in water and drain so it is moist but not dripping. Fill the cone lightly with the wet moss and set the tree on a platter or a round tray.

Beginning at the bottom, push short lengths of evergreens into the cone, with their stems pointing upward inside the cone and the tips curving downward like the branches of a fir tree. Continue working up the sides of the cone, using slightly shorter stems as you work. At the top, you will run out of space inside.

Choose one straight sprig and push it straight down into the point of the cone to form the tip of the tree. With very short sprigs, fill in the top of the tree, pushing the evergreens in so they face outward and upward. Heavily branched sprigs that cover a lot of surface without many stems are best for this part. If there are places you simply cannot cover, you can fill them in with small ornaments, but you can usually manage to cover the top neatly by forcing stems into the wire.

Keep the moss moist by turning the tree over very carefully whenever it seems dry and pouring water through it. Let it drain lying on its side and stand it up again. If you have ornaments on the tree, you can water it by pouring a thin stream of water from a sharp-spouted watering can into the very top of the tree and letting it drip through. Even without water, the tree will last for several weeks.

# CHRISTMAS TREES

**E**veryone has a favorite Christmas tree. The most popular is the **balsam**. It looks and smells like the quintessential Christmas tree and is easy to decorate, being neither bushy nor prickly. Best of all, you can strip the tree of its needles after Christmas and use them for balsam sachets and pillows. Also fragrant is the **Douglas fir**, a native of the Rocky Mountains and Northwest. The **Fraser fir** grows in the Southeast and looks much like the balsam.

**Spruce** also has a classic Christmas tree shape, though it tends to be fuller than balsam. This makes it difficult to decorate with large ornaments that need to be placed farther into the tree rather than on the ends of branches. But if you favor smaller ornaments and garlands (popcorn strings, tinsel, and the like), a spruce tree is just right.

In shape, the **Scotch pine** is more spherical than conical, and its branches are so thickly furred with spiny needles that it is nearly impossible to put lights or ornaments deep into its foliage. In addition, it scratches.

# CHOOSING AND CARING FOR YOUR CHRISTMAS TREE

If you are buying a tree that has already been cut, remember that a fresh tree not only lasts longer but is safer and less prone to combustion. If it is possible, get a recently cut tree. When shaken, the tree should lose few, if any, needles. If you can easily bend a needle without breaking it between two fingers, then the tree is likely to be fresh. Storing an early-bought tree in water until Christmas is much better than buying a dry one later.

Be sure to measure from floor to ceiling before you choose a tree. Surrounded by its giant neighbors, a tree looks much smaller in the woods or tree lot than it will in your living room. Also, think where you will put the tree and look at it from all sides. If it is to go in a fairly small room, you might look for a tall, thin tree. If it is to sit right against a wall, try to find an otherwise perfect tree with one flat side.

Cut your tree as late in the season as possible and keep its base in water at all times. Cut the trunk at a slight angle so it will have a larger absorption area. When you are ready to put the tree in the stand, cut it straight so it will stand better. Use a firm stand with a large water basin. If you purchase a tree that's already cut, immediately saw a piece off the base to give it a fresh start, and keep it in water. To prolong the "life" of any tree, put it in hot water to begin with; thereafter, tap water can be used to keep the basin filled.

Your tree stand should be wide enough at the base so that the tree cannot easily tip over. This is especially important if you have small children or pets. If your floor is thickly carpeted, it is wise to put a large sheet of plywood or other firm material under the tree stand to stabilize it.

A living Christmas tree has many advantages and requires little care while you have it in the house. The ball of roots should be put in a plate or shallow bowl that's deep enough so dirt or water won't spill on the floor or rug. Place the tree away from any sources of heat and be sure it stays cool. Keep the ball moist, but don't soak it. Keep the room well ventilated and let in plenty of light to keep it in good condition until you plant it outside. Observe the safety precautions as if it were a cut tree. Even though live trees' needles are not as likely to catch fire, it is still a good idea to be careful.

When Christmas is over, take all the ornaments, tinsel, and other decorations off the tree. Pick a spot in the yard where your tree can grow without interference. Don't pick a place too close to wires or to the house, because the tree will need plenty of room to grow and spread out. If you cannot replant your tree it can be used as kindling for a wood stove or fireplace, but not as firewood, since its needles will cause too many sparks if used in large quantities.

# TRIMMING THE TREE

Second only to opening presents, trimming the tree is a highlight of the Christmas season. It is a time of renewal and of memories as all the familiar ornaments are unpacked, each one a piece of some Christmas past.

While every family seems to have its own ritual for trimming the tree, there is a vague order of business that makes it easier. The tree should be set up at least a few hours before you are ready to trim. This gives it a chance to warm up, stretch, and have its limbs fall to their natural levels.

Because it is difficult to place lights on a tree hung with ornaments, the lights should go on first. The lights' heavy cord helps weigh down or hold up branches to fill in bare spots. If you use tiny lights they will balance easily since there are so many, but larger lights may need quite a lot of moving about to keep them from all being in one place. Look at the tree from every angle to make sure they are well positioned.

Although some (tall) people manage to "crown" their tree with a star as a grand finale, practicality suggests that on a large tree with fragile ornaments, crowning is best done right after the lights.

If you are hanging garlands or chains, they should come next. Your garlands may be tinsel, chains, strings of beads, candy, popcorn, or cranberries. Professional decorators who do those perfect trees in store windows have a few tricks with garlands that help bring the tree together and frame the other ornaments. Begin draping garlands on the bottom branches and loop a heavy garland once around each branch that supports it. Leave plenty of drape—you don't want the garland to appear to tie the tree up like a bundle. Hang your largest and showiest ornaments in the places where garlands intersect and frame smaller ornaments in the spaces between. Plain glass balls should hang inside the branches, near the trunk, to reflect lights and give depth to the tree.

Hang the smallest ornaments at the very tips of branches where they can be seen. Or have a separate tabletop tree for these tiny treasures.

© Paul T. McMahon/Heartland Images

© Cezus/FPG International

# TREE TRIMS TO MAKE

## CALICO HEARTS

Bright old-fashioned prints, especially in Christmas colors and designs, bring a traditional look to the Christmas tree. These hearts may also be hung in windows or be made in different sizes. Add whole spices or potpourri to the filling for fragrance.

*Calico scraps at least 5 inches square*

*½ yard narrow, gathered, lace trim*

*Cotton or fiberfill for stuffing*

*½ yard narrow grosgrain ribbon in a matching or complementary color*

Cut two hearts from calico fabric, using the pattern provided. Stitch lace around the outer edge of one heart, ¼ inch from the edge. Stitch it to the right side of the fabric, with the ruffle facing in.

Place second heart face down over the first, over the lace, so that right sides are facing and the edges of the two hearts match. Pin in two or three places to secure. Turn hearts over and stitch around the edge, following the first line of stitches exactly. This assures that the lace will show evenly when the hearts are turned right side out. Leave a 2-inch space unstitched along one straight edge.

Turn to the right side, pushing with your fingers to smooth the edges under the lace. Fill with stuffing and blind-stitch to close the seam.

Cut a 5-inch length of ribbon and fold it to make two loops with ends meeting in the center (*see diagram, page 342*). Secure ends with one or two stitches, leaving thread attached. Wrap one end of the remaining ribbon around the center to look like the tie on a bow; secure with a stitch, but do not cut. Fold loose end into a 3-inch hanging loop, cutting off remaining ribbon. Secure the ribbon to the heart with a few stitches; knot and end thread.

## CALICO HEART (CUT 2)

## PAPER CUTOUTS

**Miniature wreaths can be used on a tree, to decorate presents, or stand on their own.**

## MINIATURE CANE WREATHS

Miniature wreath bases of entwined cane or vines can be purchased in craft and hobby stores. There is almost no end to the ways in which you can decorate these for tree ornaments.

*Miniature cane or vine wreath base*

*Narrow red ribbon*

*Small wooden hearts, ribbon roses, flocked animals, or other decorations*

*Quick-drying glue or glue gun*

Wrap the ribbon around the wreath in a spiral and tie into a bow at the top. Make a small loop of ribbon for hanging at the back of the wreath behind the bow.

Glue hearts or animals to the wreath, placing these over the ribbon and arranging them in a balanced design. If you are using the ribbon roses, put them in groups of three.

These are good ornaments to mail as small gifts or package decorations, since they are fairly sturdy.

## BEESWAX ORNAMENTS

Nothing adds warmth to a tree like the honey tones of beeswax. These are especially nice in the shape of teddy bears.

*Beeswax*

*Double boiler for melting*

*Plastic candy molds in appropriate shapes: bears, animals, stars, etc.*

*Narrow red satin ribbon*

Melt wax in the double boiler over low heat. A metal pitcher suspended in a pot of boiling water is even easier to use, since it has a pour-spout. Cut ribbon into 3-inch lengths.

Carefully pour melted wax into the plastic molds. Quickly imbed the ends of a ribbon in the top of each one as a hanger. Place molds in the freezer, taking care to keep them level. In a few minutes they will be firm enough to pop out, so you can reuse the mold.

Be sure to store these in a cool area, since they will melt if kept in a hot place.

© Lynn Karlin

**Molds are available in many holiday designs.**

# COUNTRY DECORATIONS

N owhere is the warm, homespun style of country decorating more appropriate than in a home decked in its Christmas finery. Warm colors and designs drawn from the farm, nature, and folk art give any home, however small or urban, the look and feel of a gracious country home.

There are so many crafts you can do to make your Christmas a country Christmas. Again, the projects included in this chapter should just be the starting point. Take ideas from the things around you and from things you have seen elsewhere. Nearly anything you see can be made your own—to become a tradition in your home.

## PAPER CUTOUTS

Taking a hint from the strings of paper dolls children often make, these paper cutouts are a simpler version of the delicate and detailed paper cuttings made in Switzerland and Germany. They add a festive touch to door frames, mantels, and cabinets. Or use them as the Pennsylvania Dutch do, to line the edges of shelves.

A variety of papers can be used: parchment for a slightly more formal look or brown paper grocery bags for cutouts that are the color of gingerbread boys.

*Brown paper bags or parchment paper*

*Sharp paper scissors*

*White tempera or acrylic paint (optional, for brown paper)*

Measure a length of paper to fit the area you wish to decorate. You may need to do several strips and tape them together for longer spaces. The width of the paper will depend on the size of the design, but for the gingerbread boy shown (*see diagram, page 343*), it should be about 4 inches wide.

Fold the strip of paper accordian style, leaving ½ inch extra on either end if several pieces will have to be joined together. The width of the fold will also depend on the size of the design, but 3 inches will make the gingerbread boys.

Fold the stack of paper in half lengthwise, or, if this will make it too thick to cut, omit this last fold. If you are unsure of your freehand cutting, trace half the design onto the folded paper as shown (or the whole design if the paper was too thick to fold again). Cut through all thicknesses and unfold. It is sometimes necessary to trim the edges of the figures at one end of the string, since they become fatter toward the outside of the fold.

Press the paper so it will lie flat or, if you are making short strings to go on bookcases or cabinet doors, you can leave them in their accordian shape to stand up.

If you have used brown paper, you can add little dots of white paint to look like frosting, making eyes and buttons down the front, even a little bow tie at the neck.

## GINGERBREAD VILLAGE

Even five- and six-year-olds can master the construction of simple gingerbread houses made from graham crackers, with the help of a few extra adult hands. Ages seven and up will need considerably less help.

*Cardboard for a base, about 8 by 11 inches*

*Small candy canes, Necco® wafers (for the slate roof), gumdrops, candy mint leaves, peppermint drops, licorice sticks, miniature marshmallows, and other small candies*

*Graham crackers*

*Royal icing*

*Note:* When you are working with the icing, put a small amount out in a small dish and keep the rest tightly covered, since it dries out quickly. Also, each house requires eight squares of graham cracker, but you will want to allow plenty of extras in case some break.

Using a sharp knife, separate one of the crackers along the center scored line to make two squares; this will assure that they break evenly.

Lay one double cracker flat near the center of the cardboard. Spread frosting along two opposite edges and stand another whole cracker at each edge, outside the base cracker, so that their edges are standing on the cardboard. Hold or prop them upright for a couple of minutes until the frosting is stiff. Be sure they are straight.

Spread frosting on three edges of one of the half (square) crackers and carefully place it *inside* the two standing walls, with its bottom on top of the base. It should fit just inside the two end walls, and will stand a tiny bit higher. Allow a minute or two for this frosting to set, before repeating this with the fourth wall. Your house should now be able to stand up by itself.

Cut a cracker diagonally with a very sharp knife, first perforating it in a straight line. If the crackers are very brittle, hold them over a pan of boiling water to soften them slightly before cutting.

Spread frosting along the long (cut) edge, and carefully stand the triangle on the top of one end wall. You will have

to hold this in place until it is dry. Repeat with the other end wall.

Frost three edges of a whole (rectangular) cracker and lay in place on the top of the house. Repeat with a second cracker to complete the roof.

Wait about twenty minutes before starting to decorate the house. Frost the roof and then lay rows of Necco® wafer "slates" beginning at the bottom edge and overlapping slightly with each row. Or simply cover the roof with icing snow. Add a broken piece of candy cane for a chimney, or build one out of small squares of cracker.

Entryways or even front porches can be added with candy-stick pillars. Licorice laces, clipped into short lengths with scissors, are perfect for outlining windows and doors. Gumdrops or peppermint drops lined along the ridge pole help to define the shape of the roof, and the rounded tops of candy canes are splendid fan windows over front doors.

When the house is finished, spread a light coating of frosting snow around the base and make a front walk from Necco® wafers or flat mints. You can landscape the yard with trees made of spearmint candy leaves or large marshmallows, which look like snow-covered shrubbery. A candy-cane lamppost might add just the right touch for the front yard.

You can make a whole village of these houses for a mantel or tabletop arrangement, varying their size, decor, and landscaping. Make smaller houses by using single (square) crackers for side as well as end walls. Doghouses can be made by cutting these squares into fourths (easier if you steam the crackers briefly). Once you have mastered cutting, you can even make barns with hip roofs.

## ROYAL ICING

*3 egg whites*

*1 pound confectioner's sugar, sifted*

*1 teaspoon vanilla*

*½ teaspoon cream of tartar*

Combine all ingredients in a mixing bowl and beat with an electric mixer until the frosting is stiff. This may take up to ten minutes. Keep frosting in a covered container or at least covered with a damp towel, since it dries very quickly.

**Makes 3 cups.**

## CORN HUSK DOLLS

One of the earliest of American craft materials, corn husks were used by Native Americans to make dolls and baskets. They taught these skills to the early settlers, who also made doormats from the husks.

Make corn husk dolls in a variety of sizes. Small ones are good tree decorations and package ornaments.

# PREPARING CORN HUSKS FOR CRAFT USES

You don't have to live in the country to make these dolls. Fresh corn on the cob from the grocery store provides enough husks for this project. You can dry the husks yourself by cutting the stem end off the corn, close to the point where the kernels begin. Slip the husks off, discarding the tough, coarse, dark green outside husks. Spread the softer inside husks on a screen or newspapers to dry. They will do this faster in the sun, but a shady place will do very well, too. If you dry them outdoors, be sure to bring them in at night. When the husks are stiff and crisp, you are ready to make your dolls. Do not try to use the husks fresh from the corn. They must dry and then be softened in water before they can be used in crafts without curling and twisting, which would ruin your dolls.

*12 to 15 dried cornhusks*

*A bowl of warm water, large enough to hold the husks*

*Sturdy white or beige thread or raffia*

*Scissors*

Soak the husks in water for about ten minutes. Take them out only as you need them, leaving the others in the water.

Stack five or six long husks with all the narrow ends at the top and tie them into a bundle, about 2 inches from the top.

Roll the narrow ends down in a tight roll, as far as the place where you have tied them. Turn the husks so this part is at the bottom and hold this roll between your left thumb and index finger.

Pull the husks, one by one, down over the rolled part, as if you were peeling a banana. Catch each one under your left thumb as it is pulled down. They should be as smooth and tight as you can get them, and spread around the rolled husks from side to side. Tie the husks again, right under the lump formed by the rolled husks, to form a neck.

To make the arms, take three narrow husks (or split

wider ones by pulling them apart lengthwise) and tie them together at one end. Braid these and tie at the other end. Or, you can take a wider husk and roll it into a long pencil shape and tie in the center to hold it together.

Hold the doll facing you—the smoothest side of the head will be the face—and lift the two top husks away from the others. Push the rolled or braided arms right up against the tied neck, under these two husks and fold them back down over the arms. Tie just below these to form a waist.

With another narrow husk, make a shawl over the doll's shoulders and bring the ends down, crossing them in front at the waist. Tie the waist again.

Take one perfect, wide husk and lay it, wide side up, over the front of the doll, so that the widest end is over the face and the pointed end is about halfway down the skirt. Tie once more around the waist, securing this husk over the rest. Pull the husk down and smooth it over the skirt to make an apron.

Trim the skirt evenly so the doll will stand, and trim the arms to a natural length.

While the doll is still wet, you can shape the arms to hold something or turn them up or down. Tie them in the position you like. After the doll is completely dry (overnight, at least), cut these threads away and the arms will remain in place. You may have to trim the skirt again slightly after the husks are dry.

The dolls' heads may be covered with scarves made from triangles of husk, and bonnets can be made by folding a rectangular husk over the top of the head and folding it like the ends of a package wrapping in back. Hold the bonnet in place by tying it with thread. When the husks are dry, the bonnet will hold its shape and can be held in place with a drop of white glue.

Corn husk dolls traditionally had no faces drawn on them, but there is no reason why you can't add more detail to yours. Be sure the doll is completely dry and use colored pencils to draw the face. Ink will spread, so don't use markers or paints.

## CONE WREATHS

The varying shades of brown and the unusual textures of cones and seed pods give the wreathmaker the opportunity to create any number of original arrangements. A cone wreath can be exuberant or restrained. It can be any size, depending on the size of the cones and seeds available. And, unlike evergreen boughs, pinecones can be purchased by mail if they do not grow locally.

While it is not essential, many people are more comfortable storing these seeds and cones in their home after they have been baked in a slow oven to kill any insects that might be harbored there. In the case of the white pinecone, which tends to be covered with spots of pitch, baking melts the pitch and evens the color.

Wreathmakers strongly disagree on whether it is better to wire or to glue the cones on. Traditionalists use wire, but many people are perfectly happy with glue now that the glue gun has been created. Whatever method you choose to use, it must allow for the significant movement of the cones due to changes in humidity. Cones continually open and close enough to break the bond of any but a flexible glue. Also, if you choose to use a glue gun, be very careful not to leave any glue showing, and to cut off all the little threads of glue that form when the gun is moved from one place to another.

Some seeds and nuts are almost impossible to wire to a wreath without drilling, so even if you wire the basic wreath you might want to use glue to attach the final pieces.

*A double-wire wreath frame*

*Fine florist's wire*

*Scissors*

*A glue gun*

*A quantity of white pine or blue spruce cones*

*An assortment of other cones and seeds of various sizes*

Soak the white pine or spruce cones in warm water for a few minutes until they close. Wearing gloves or using a cloth to protect your hands, push these larger cones between the upper and lower layers of wire on the wreath frame. You can either have them all facing out or you can alternate. If they all face out, the outer edge of the wreath will look more solid. But if you alternate, you can fill in the spaces with other cones for a less regular effect.

Allow the cones to dry overnight or put the wreath in a slow oven until they dry and open (about an hour). While you are doing this, wire the other cones, preparing a selection of several different kinds.

Beginning with the larger cones, attach them along the center, covering the wires of the wreath frame completely. Push the wire tails through the wreath and twist them together at the back, securing each cone tightly.

Don't cut these wire tails until you are finished. This allows you to find them again if you decide to rearrange the cones, and it also gives you spare wire for fastening the other cones.

One of the major advantages of the wired wreath is that you can move cones around after they are in place by simply untwisting the wires. Experiment with different arrangements of the larger cones, since these will set the tone of your wreath.

Fill in the spaces with the next smaller cones and seeds, ending with hemlock cones and other tiny ones to fill in any space where wire or frame shows. These should be glued in place by touching the stem end to the point of a hot glue gun. It is better to put the glue on the seed and then the seed on the wreath than to try to get a dot of hot glue onto the wreath.

## ATTACHING WIRES TO CONES

Since wires for attaching cones to the wreath must be flexible enough to hide inside the cones as well as tie and twist easily, a fairly fine wire is the best. Cut it in lengths of 8 and 12 inches, the longer ones for larger cones.

Slip the middle of a piece of wire under the top row of petals (scales) on a cone and pull it tightly. Twist the ends together, securely, so the wire does not slip. There should be two tails of nearly equal length. By placing the wires under the top line of petals, the tails can be pulled up toward the stem to attach the cone so it points directly up, or it can be left to come out the side so it attaches flat.

## CINNAMON SWAGS

Long sticks of fragrant cinnamon tied with ribbon and decorated with cones and greens make attractive centerpieces for a buffet or small table. Their long, narrow shape also makes them perfect for windowsills or mantelpieces.

*10 to 12 cinnamon sticks, at least 10 inches long*

*Sprigs of dried flowers in deep reds, such as plumed celosia or clusters of sumac berries*

*Pinecones*

*Florist's wire*

*Taffeta ribbon, 1 to 2 inches wide, in deep red or red-and-green plaid*

Tie the bundle of cinnamon sticks together at the center, using the florist's wire. Spread the sticks a little so they are not in a tight clump at the ends.

Attach wires to the pinecones (see above) and set aside. Wire the dried flowers or sumac to longer stems, if necessary. Tie the ribbon around the center of the cinnamon, covering the wire, and tie a large bow. Add decorative sprigs of dried flowers, pinecones, even sprays of evergreen to complete the arrangement.

**Fir, pine, juniper, cedar, and holly combine to form this festive swag.**

# THE FINE ART OF GIVING

**G**iving gifts is one of the oldest Christmas traditions, beginning with the arrival of the three Wise Men at the first Christmas. Choosing gifts for family and friends can either be a chore or it can be part of the fun of the holidays. For many people, the crowded stores and traffic snarls are not a treasured part of the holidays; it is here that another country tradition solves a great part of the problem. From the days of the first Sears Roebuck catalog, people who lived in rural areas have ordered things by mail. Catalog shopping has now become common to people all over, and it is still one of the best ways to find really unusual gifts and decorations. But you have to know which catalogs to shop from.

The usual run of gift catalogs begin to look very much alike after a while—full of gimmicks and plastic do-dads that grow more expensive each year. Clever shoppers begin to look in the less common places for quality country gifts. There are several kinds of catalogs that are not sent in a mass mailing to everyone whose name appears on a list. Small mail-order companies, often family-run cottage industries or craftsmen's cooperatives, send catalogs only to those who ask for them, often charging a modest fee to cover the printing and mailing. But for a dollar or two, you can save hours of time and gallons of gasoline, and find interesting gifts that your friends won't have seen before.

Museum shops are an especially nice place to shop before the holidays. If you have a large museum or reconstructed historical site near you, these shops offer beautiful and carefully selected gifts. Many smaller restorations have modest brochures describing some of their offerings, and nearly all of them specialize in historic replicas and hand-

**Brightly wrapped Christmas gifts can decorate your home.**

made items. Along with finding gifts that are interesting, beautiful, and unusual, you will have the satisfaction of knowing that the profit from these shops goes into the museum's treasury to acquire new collections and protect and preserve the treasures they have. It is really like giving two gifts in one.

Another catalog that nearly always offers gifts that you would never find elsewhere comes from the many small herb businesses throughout the United States and Canada. These are usually small, family-run farms, with modest catalogs and very personal response to their customers. The gifts they offer are designed right there, made by family members and friends. Instead of mass-produced wreaths, theirs will be one-of-a-kind, often made to order. Bouquets of dried flowers, pottery balls filled with potpourri, gift baskets of packets of farm-grown herbs, and the personal favorite herb blends of each family fill these catalogs.

Hartman's Herb Farm in Massachusetts offers a lovely herbal calendar designed and drawn by Lynn Hartman. Betsy Williams, also in Massachusetts, creates beautiful wreaths of herbs and dried flowers (hers is one of the few of these catalogs that has full-color photographs). Rosemary House in Pennsylvania has a large selection of herb-related gifts, plus recipe collections based on years of experimenting with these delicious flavors.

Other herb farms offer "gifts that give twice." Instructional booklets on gardening and herb crafts as well as kits containing the materials and instructions for lovely and fragrant sachets, tea cozies, scented mug coasters, and catnip mice are offered by Herbitage Farm in New Hampshire. The pleasure of these gifts is that the recipient will enjoy creating the product enclosed in the kit, while learning a new skill at the same time. Appledore Gardens in Michigan sells a kit for making your own beeswax-based hand cream (as well as beeswax nativity sets). Western Reserve in Ohio has a catalog of antique furniture kits. Arctic Trading Co. in Manitoba has kits for such unusual Indian crafts as moose-hair tufting (along with lovely examples of Indian handicrafts).

For the gardeners on your list, look in the garden catalogs. Smith and Hawken in California show fine terra-cotta planters as well as garden hats, gloves, and tools that would delight any gardener. Mrs. MacGregor's Garden Shop has carved garden decorations and teakwood window boxes, while The Gardener's Collection in Ontario creates stoneware garden markers. Swinging Bridge Pottery in Virginia also makes garden markers, plus stoneware herb jars and attractive bird feeders.

There are a number of craftsmen's cooperatives that offer fine handcrafted gifts. These are professionally managed groups that offer those craftsmen who work in rural areas a chance to market their products. These artists often produce only a few pieces of any design. Berea College (Kentucky) Student Craft Industries is one of these, as is Kentucky Hills Industries. Montana Exclusive has a full-color catalog of handmade and homemade gifts ranging from coatracks in the shape of moose heads and horses to country sausage and chocolate chip cookies.

Food gifts are always welcome at Christmas, and these need not be limited to those made in your own kitchen. Unusual and hard-to-find items such as Vidalia onions and a Country Cornbread kit with cast-iron cornstick pans are shown in the catalog from Bland Farms in Georgia. Meadowbrook Herbs in Rhode Island sells their own original herb tea blends as well as utensils for making tea, and Smith and Hawken will send a dozen perfect Oregon pears.

As well as the foods themselves, cooks will appreciate kitchen accessories, which often can be found in the end pages of seed catalogs. Johnny's Selected Seeds in Maine shows a natural-fiber vegetable brush and fine kitchen knives, while Gurney Seed and Nursery in South Dakota has utensils any cook with a garden would treasure: corn cutters, vegetable slicers, and parers.

City friends without gardens can always find a place for indoor plants, and these make welcome gifts in the winter. Rhapis Gardens in Texas specializes in lady palms and other tropical exotics; Applewood Seed Company in Colorado has herb garden kits in planting sacks printed with the name of the herb. The Natural Gardening Company

Gifts of food, homemade or purchased, are always welcome.

kits are designed for children. The American Girls' Series of books is full of activities from America's past, based on the stories of girls growing up in different places and periods of history. Klutz Books offer children lively and entertaining introductions to everything from juggling and blowing bubbles to cooking. These are available at bookstores and by mail from Hearthsong in California. Their catalog is filled with similar high-quality gifts for youngsters.

Although cookbooks are not an unusual gift—they are, in fact, among the most popular—you can use a cookbook as the basis for a uniquely personal gift. Combine a book on herb cookery with several packets of herbs, a wooden spoon, and a bottle of herb vinegar (see page 80). A book on growing and using fresh herbs could be grouped with simple garden tools, gloves, and a pair of garden scissors, all placed in a harvesting basket.

All-time classics of foreign cuisines can be grouped with seasonings or utensils used in that cooking style. *Come With Me to the Kasbah*, the beautifully illustrated cookbook on Moroccan cuisine, could be combined with a bag of couscous and a package of dried mint from your garden. *Cuisines of Mexico* offers a number of put-together possibilities, including your own pickled jalapeños (see page 371) or a string of dried red chili peppers (see page 371). *The Complete Book of Greek Cooking* could be combined with tahini, prepared grape leaves, or a package of pignoli nuts. A book on Chinese cooking suggests a pairing with an Oriental chopping knife or a selection of Joyce Chen's stir-fry sauces and oils.

Other how-to books are good bases for gift packages or baskets. *Natural Fragrances* would make a lovely basket combined with a potpourri jar, fragrant oils, and a bouquet or packet of dried flowers.

Think about the special interests of the people on your gift list and you will have enough ideas to last you for several Christmases. In fact, some of the best ideas often come after you have already wrapped the gift for that person, so it is wise to jot down the idea in your Christmas notebook where you'll have it ready next year.

Decorations made from dried plants are a "natural" at Christmas.

carries terra-cotta herb planters. White Flower Farm in Connecticut ships narcissus bulbs ready for forcing into flowering plants and jasmine plants in stoneware pots ready to burst into bloom in January.

When looking for children's gifts, don't limit yourself to the standbys of toys and clothes. Craft kits and supplies and do-it-yourself toys and books will hold a child's interest long after Christmas. Several of Herbitage Farm's folk craft

# TREASURED GIFTS TO MAKE

You don't have to be an artist or skilled craftsman to create original gifts. And the nicest thing about a handmade gift is that the recipient knows you've cared enough to give them the gift of your time. The smallest handmade gift brings a personal warmth that no purchased gift can equal.

Think first of the skills and materials you have on hand. Do you sew or knit? Do you have stencil brushes and paints left from some long-ago project? Do you have woodworking tools?

If you have no tools or supplies on hand, begin with projects that do not require a major investment beyond the materials. Simple hand-sewn gifts, a small basket, old-fashioned stocking dolls, or potpourri are good starting projects that require neither expensive equipment nor special tools. Other projects require only a modest outlay, so that if you discover that you enjoy the craft, you will reuse the supplies many times. Stenciling is one of these crafts.

Other gifts can be created from nature's bounty. You don't have to live in the country to collect the dried seeds, cones, and grasses for most of the projects listed earlier in the book, any of which would make a welcome early Christmas gift. Especially for friends in the city, a balsam wreath or a box of fresh greens for decorating would be a priceless treasure. These are not fragile, they are easy to ship, and by sending them early in December you can even avoid the rush at the post office.

## WOVEN RIBBON PILLOW

Little sewing is required for this elegant pillow made of satin ribbon. For variety, try mixing different types and widths of ribbon, but be sure always to use those with woven edges. Cut edges are not as durable and will not withstand the process of weaving, let alone the use of the pillow.

*A 15-inch pillow form*

*16 yards of 1-inch-wide satin ribbon in two contrasting colors*

*18-inch square of velvet or other fabric in matching color*

*18-inch square of white muslin*

*Masking tape or transparent tape*

*Corrugated cardboard, at least 18 inches square*

*Straight sewing pins (common pins)*

Place muslin on cardboard. Cut ribbon into 18-inch lengths and lay sixteen of one color parallel over the muslin, their edges just touching. Push a pin through each piece of ribbon into the cardboard, ½ inch from the ends of the ribbons. Press a strip of tape over the raw ends to keep them from fraying. Remove the pins and carefully stitch the ribbons to the muslin, just below the tape. Keep the ribbons straight and in line, with edges still touching. Pin to the board again through the tape, using only enough to hold the ribbons and muslin flat (you do not need a pin in each piece of ribbon this time).

Beginning close to the stitched edge, weave the remaining ribbons through the first set. Pin each cross ribbon to the cardboard at each end and be sure that each one lies close to the preceding one.

When all the ribbons have been woven, tape and stitch the remaining sides as you did the first one. Remove the tape. Place the velvet backing face down over the front of the woven square and pin them together. Stitch them together on three sides, just inside the stitching in the ribbon. This is easier if you stitch from the ribbon side, where you can always see the first stitching.

Turn the pillow right side out, squaring the corners. Pull cover over the pillow form and make sure the corners fit neatly. Turn the open edges inside and blind stitch the pillow closed.

## POTPOURRI CLOTHES HANGERS

Use a purchased potpourri blend or make your own from the recipe in this book or fill these hangers with freshly dried lavendar or cedar shavings.

*Wooden clothes hanger without a pants bar*

*2 pieces floral-print fabric, each 6 by 12 inches*

*1 yard matching⅜-inch satin ribbon*

*2 pieces cotton or polyfiber quilt batting, each 8 by 12 inches*

*½ cup potpourri with extra oils and orrisroot added*

Fold one fabric piece in half, with right sides facing, and stitch the long sides together to make a tube 12 inches long. Gather one end together and tie firmly with thread. Turn to the right side and repeat with the other fabric piece.

Lay the quilt batting flat and sprinkle each piece with half the potpourri. Wrap these around the wooden arms of the hangers, adjusting the tightness of the roll so they will fit inside the fabric tubes. Secure with a few wraps of thread. Pull the tubes over the batting and blind stitch together at the center. Pull the fabric toward the center so that it is shirred slightly and the ends of the fabric meet the ends of the hanger arms. Secure the ends in place with a few stitches.

Beginning at the end of the metal hook, wrap the ribbon around the metal to cover it neatly. Use the remaining ribbon to tie a bow around the base of the hook, where it meets the fabric.

## CHRISTMAS POTPOURRI

Most potpourri should be kept in a container that can be covered at least half the time so that the blend can regain its strength each night and be fragrant in the daytime. This blend, however, is rich in spices and balsam sprigs, which will remain fragrant throughout the entire season even if kept in an open bowl or basket. Be sure to keep the little sprigs and needles left over from the wreaths, arrangements, and roping as well as the whole cloves that are not large enough for pomanders. Any fragrant or colorful blossom, even fallen holly and bittersweet berries, can be added to this blend.

Note: All these measurements are approximate; use more or less, or leave out ingredients that are unavailable. All plant material should be thoroughly dry.

*¼ cup lemon verbena leaves*

*¼ cup red rose petals*

*½ cup balsam tips and needles*

*¼ cup cedar chips or tips*

*¼ cup dried orange peel*

*¼ cup coarsely broken cinnamon sticks*

*2 tablespoons whole cloves*

*2 tablespoons whole allspice*

*2 tablespoons rosemary leaves*

*2 tablespoons mint leaves*

*¼ cup mixed dried flowers*

*10 bay leaves*

*10 hemlock or other tiny cones*

*3 tablespoons orrisroot chips (not powder)*

*4 to 5 drops rose oil*

*4 to 5 drops balsam oil*

*2 drops cedar oil*

Mix well in a large plastic bag or glass jar that will hold the potpourri, leaving plenty of air space. The jar or bag should be no more than half full. Stir or mix each day for two weeks. You can decorate the top of this blend with larger cones, sprigs of holly, or even small glass ornaments.

## COVERED PICTURE FRAME

Dress up the school portrait of a child in a custom-made frame to match the bedroom of a grandmother or favorite aunt. After you have tried this project in a cotton fabric, you may dare to make one in satin, velvet, or moire taffeta.

*Mat board, at least 12 by 18 inches*

*Matte knife or X-acto™ knife*

*White fabric glue (Sobo™ is preferred, since spilled drops can be wiped off with a damp cloth and it dries without staining)*

*Clip clothespins*

*Ruler*

*Calico fabric, at least 9 by 20 inches*

*Quilt batting, 6 by 8 inches*

*12 inches narrow satin ribbon in matching color*

Cut two pieces of mat board 6 by 8 inches. Cut a rectangle from the center of one, measuring 3½ by 5 inches. To center this, measure 1¼ inches from either side, 1⅜ from the top, and 1⅝ from the bottom. Cut a 5 by 1½-inch stand from the piece cut out of the center piece.

Cut two fabric pieces, each 7 by 9 inches, then another piece 4½ by 6 inches, and another 3½ by 6 inches. Glue batting to the frame-cut mat board and let it dry before cutting out the center piece of batting.

Place frame front, batting side down, on the wrong side of one piece of fabric and center it. Mark a dot on the fabric at each of the corners of the frame opening. Remove the frame and carefully cut out the center of the fabric, leaving 1 inch inside the frame and clipping at an angle almost to the dots in each corner.

Return the mat frame front, padded side down, to the wrong side of the cut fabric. Center it carefully. Put a line of glue around the edge of the frame opening and fold the fabric to cover the edge. Be sure not to make the fabric crooked as you do this. Hold in place with clothespins. Repeat this with the outer edge, mitering the corners. Secure with clothespins. Check the right side and adjust the fabric if necessary, while the glue is wet. Take particular care with the inside corners, clipping a little farther if they do not look neat.

Cover the solid piece of mat board with the remaining large piece of fabric, using the same method. Cover the stand, using the smallest piece of fabric and folding it over to cover both sides. There will be a rough edge, but it will be glued down and on the inside where it will not show. Glue the remaining piece of fabric to cover the center of the solid mat board. The edges of the fabric do not have to meet, but be sure this piece fills the entire space, which will show when the front and back of the frame are put together.

From the remaining piece of mat board, cut three narrow strips for spacers. When the glue on the frame pieces is completely dry, remove the clothespins and glue the spacers to the top and sides at the outer edges. Glue the front of the frame over the back with the wrong sides facing. Leave the center 4 inches of the bottom without glue, and be sure to keep the glue toward the outer edges of the sides and top so the picture will slide in easily.

Spread glue on the upper third of the back side of the stand (the side with the seam)

and center it on the back of the frame. Be sure it is facing the right way and that its bottom is exactly square with the bottom of the frame, so it will stand straight.

Place the entire frame under a flat, heavy weight, such as a book, and leave overnight. When it is dry, place the ruler over the top third of the stand, and pressing down on this firmly, lift the bottom of the stand to form a neat crease. Make a bow of the ribbon and glue it near the inside corner at one side of the top on the front of the frame.

## STENCILED SACHETS

Choose a stencil design that fits in a very small space for these homey little sachets. For filling, use the dried balsam needles that are left from other projects. Be sure to save the needles from this year's tree and wreaths, or you can purchase balsam needles from a supplier in Maine (see sources, page 382). You can purchase ready-cut stencils or cut your own from stencil paper. Brass stencils will last longer but are harder to use if the design has small openings.

*Stencils of your choice*

*Stiff stencil brushes, one for each paint color*

*Acrylic stencil paints*

*Drawstring bags of unbleached muslin or 5-inch squares of unbleached muslin and narrow ribbon*

*Balsam needles or potpourri*

*A piece of cardboard small enough to fit inside the drawstring bags*

If you are not using ready-made drawstring bags, fold the muslin in half and stitch around the long side and one short side. Turn bags to the right side and press flat.

Put a little acrylic paint into an old dish or piece of glass and dip the brush in it lightly. On a folded paper towel, wipe most of the paint from the brush, until it appears almost dry. Lay a stencil on a scrap of heavy paper and paint over the openings of the

stencil using an up and down circular scrubbing motion to push the bristles onto the surface of the paper. Remember to keep the brush dry; the smallest smear under the stencil means you are using too much paint. For deeper shades, go over an area several times, but don't use more paint.

When you can control the paint flow on your practice paper, you are ready to stencil on the fabric.

Slip the cardboard into the bag to protect the other side from paint and center the stencil on the bottom half of the bag. Stencil the designs, using a different brush for each color.

Clean stencils frequently with warm water. A little nail polish remover on an old toothbrush is good for removing paint buildup on brass stencils. Cleaning is important to keep paint from filling in the holes and making your design shrink as you work. Always clean on a flat surface. Be sure to clean brushes well with soap and warm water before storing them.

If you are using drawstring bags, fill them with potpourri or balsam and pull strings tight. Tie them in a double knot. If your bags do not have drawstrings, fill them a little over half full and tie with ribbons, using a bow knot.

These sachets can be piled in a basket and given to holiday guests as they leave. Or, a small basket of them makes a very nice gift.

APPLE
BUTTER

CRANBERRY/
PINEAPPLE/
ORANGE
JAM

# CHAPTER SIX

# GIFTS FROM A COUNTRY KITCHEN

**N**o gift is as welcome, especially at the holidays, as one you've created in your own kitchen. If you have made your own harvest—or that of a farmers' market—into preserves during the fall, you already have a good beginning. But even closer to Christmas, pumpkins, oranges, lemons, limes, cranberries, and other products are at their peak so don't forget to include them when you are making preserves.

By combining preserves, vinegars, and herb blends, which you can make ahead, with a loaf of tea bread and a few decorative cookies as a finishing touch, you can give elegant food baskets without overcrowding your holiday season. These personal gifts will be enjoyed and appreciated all through the winter.

## LEMON NUTMEG COOKIES

*1 cup sifted flour*

*½ cup cornstarch*

*¼ teaspoon salt*

*½ teaspoon freshly ground nutmeg*

*½ cup plus 2 tablespoons unsalted butter, softened*

*½ cup confectioner's sugar*

*1 tablespoon freshly grated lemon rind*

Sift together flour, cornstarch, salt, and nutmeg. Cream butter with sugar and lemon until fluffy. Add dry ingredients and beat until smooth. Roll teaspoonfuls of dough into balls and place on ungreased cookie sheets. Flatten with the bottom of a glass that has been dipped in confectioners' sugar. Bake at 325°F for 15 minutes, or until cookies are golden at the edges. Cool a minute or two before removing from cookie sheets and continue cooling on racks.

**Makes approximately 3 dozen small cookies.**

## BRANDIED FRUIT

*Fresh or canned peach halves*

*Fresh or canned pear halves*

*Canned pineapple rings*

*Thinly sliced lemon*

*Peach or apricot brandy*

Layer fruit carefully in a French-style canning jar with a hinged lid. Pour peach or apricot brandy over the fruit to fill the jar and seal. Let stand one week before using. Whole dark cherries or apricot halves may be added or used to replace other fruits.

## MINCEMEAT BARS

*½ cup margarine*

*½ cup sugar*

*1 egg*

*⅓ cup molasses*

*2 cups flour*

*½ teaspoon baking soda*

*½ teaspoon baking powder*

*¼ teaspoon cinnamon*

*¼ teaspoon allspice*

*¼ teaspoon salt*

*1 cup well-drained mincemeat*

Cream margarine with sugar. Add egg and molasses and beat until light. Sift together flour, baking soda, baking powder, cinnamon, allspice, and salt and add alternately with mincemeat, stirring until well blended. Pour into a well-greased 13-inch × 9-inch pan and bake at 350°F for 30 minutes or until center is firm and springs back when touched. Cool and cut into squares. Seal in a tightly covered container to store.

**Makes about 32 bars.**

## PUMPKIN COOKIES

*1 cup shortening*

*1½ cups sugar*

*1 egg*

*1 cup mashed cooked pumpkin*

*1 teaspoon baking soda*

*3½ cups sifted flour*

*½ teaspoon salt*

*½ teaspoon cinnamon*

*½ teaspoon nutmeg*

*½ teaspoon ginger*

*1 cup raisins*

Cream shortening with sugar and add egg. Mix well and add pumpkin. Stir to blend. Sift together baking soda, flour, salt, cinnamon, nutmeg, ginger, and raisins and add to blended mixture. Drop by teaspoonfuls on greased cookie sheets. Bake at 400°F for 8 to 10 minutes. These cookies stay moist and keep very well.

**Makes approximately 6 dozen cookies.**

## SUGAR COOKIES

½ cup butter

¾ cup sugar

1 egg

½ teaspoon vanilla

1 tablespoon milk

1¼ cups flour

¼ teaspoon salt

¼ teaspoon baking powder

Cream butter and sugar until light. Add egg and vanilla, beat again, and add milk. Sift together flour, salt, and baking powder and stir into butter mixture to make a smooth dough. Chill well and roll out on floured board. Cut in shapes and bake cookies until lightly browned. Cool on racks.

Decorate with red- and green-colored sugars or with decorator's frosting, which can be purchased in tubes complete with cake decorating tips. Small, colored candies, such as cinnamon hots and gum drops may be pressed into the center of the cookies before baking. Brushing the dough with egg white will make the surface of the cookie glossy.

**Size may vary, but yields 2 cookie sheets.**

## MOLDED GERMAN CHRISTMAS COOKIES

3 cups flour

½ teaspoon cloves

1½ teaspoons cinnamon

1 teaspoon ginger

½ teaspoon nutmeg

½ teaspoon allspice

Pinch of baking powder

Pinch of salt

1¼ cups margarine or butter

3 tablespoons milk

¼ cup ground almonds

1 cup firmly packed brown
    sugar

Combine flour, cloves, cinnamon, ginger, nutmeg, allspice, baking powder, and salt and cut in butter until the mixture is fine and crumbly. Add milk, almonds, and sugar.

Dust the carved side of wooden cookie molds with flour. Grease the cookie sheet lightly. Roll dough ½ inch thick and cut into rectangles the size of the molds. Lay a piece of dough over the carved side of a mold and roll firmly with rolling pin until the dough is pressed into the carved design. Remove dough carefully and place, design side up, on cookie sheets. Trim edges if necessary. Dust mold again with flour before reusing. Bake 25 minutes in a 350°F oven. Remove from sheets and cool on racks.

**Makes approximately 2 dozen cookies.**

## APPLE-CRANBERRY BREAD

*½ cup margarine*

*1¼ cups sugar*

*2 eggs, beaten*

*1 tablespoon buttermilk*

*2 cups flour*

*1 teaspoon baking powder*

*1 teaspoon baking soda*

*1 teaspoon salt*

*1 cup finely chopped, peeled apple*

*1 cup coarsely chopped cranberries, drained*

*1 tablespoon grated lemon peel*

*½ cup chopped pecans*

*1 teaspoon vanilla*

*½ teaspoon cinnamon*

*½ teaspoon allspice*

Cream margarine and sugar, then beat in eggs and buttermilk. Sift together flour, baking powder, baking soda, and salt and add alternately with fruit. Add remaining ingredients. Pour into greased loaf pan and bake 50 to 60 minutes at 350°F.

**Makes 1 large or 2 small loaves.**

## DATE NUT TEA BREAD

*1 pound chopped dates*

*1½ cups boiling water*

*2 teaspoons baking soda*

*2¼ cups flour*

*½ teaspoon baking powder*

*1½ cups sugar*

*½ teaspoon salt*

*1 egg*

*1 tablespoon vegetable oil*

*1 teaspoon vanilla*

*1 cup chopped walnuts*

Combine dates, water, and baking soda. In another bowl combine flour, baking powder, sugar, and salt. In a third bowl, beat egg and add oil and vanilla. Add egg and date mixture alternately to dry ingredients, stir in walnuts, and pour into two small loaf pans lined with waxed paper. Bake 1¼ hours or until springy and firm. Remove from pans immediately after taking the loaves from the oven and peel off waxed paper while still hot. When cool, wrap in waxed paper and then in foil. This sturdy bread ships well and can be kept for several weeks.

**Makes 1 large or 2 small loaves.**

## CHARLESTON BENNE WAFERS

¾ cup raw sesame seeds

¾ cup unsalted butter

1 cup brown sugar, packed

1 egg

1 cup flour

½ teaspoon baking powder

1 teaspoon vanilla

In a dry frying pan, lightly toast seeds over low heat. Pour them from the pan the minute they begin to toast and allow to cool.

Cream butter and sugar until soft, add egg, and beat until fluffy. Combine flour and baking powder and add with vanilla and sesame seeds. Mix well.

Drop by spoonfuls onto greased cookie sheets about an inch apart. Bake 12 to 15 minutes at 325°F until they are lightly browned. Leave on the sheets for a minute after removing them from the oven, then remove them to racks to cool. These may be stored in tightly sealed tins.

**Makes approximately 3 to 4 dozen wafers.**

## PRALINES

3 cups sugar

1 cup light cream

Dash of salt

1 cup light brown sugar

3 cups pecan pieces

Combine sugar, cream, and salt in a heavy saucepan and cook to 234°F. Meanwhile, melt brown sugar in a saucepan over very low heat. Add to the syrup with the pecans. Bring to a rolling boil and cook for two minutes, stirring constantly. Drop by teaspoonfuls onto waxed paper squares and allow to cool. When they are firm and cold, wrap each in its paper square and store.

**Makes about 1½ dozen pralines.**

## TAFFY KISSES

1 cup sugar

2 tablespoons cornstarch

¾ cup light corn syrup

½ cup water

2 tablespoons margarine

½ teaspoon salt

1 teaspoon flavoring (orange, lemon, mint, or other)

Mix sugar and cornstarch in a large, heavy saucepan. Stir in remaining ingredients, except for flavoring. Cook over medium heat, stirring constantly, until sugar is completely dissolved. Continue cooking without stirring until temperature reaches 260°F. Remove from heat, and after all boiling has stopped, stir in flavoring. Pour onto lightly greased cookie sheets and let stand until it is cool enough to handle. Grease hands and pull taffy, stretching it, doubling it over, and stretching it again until it is glossy and pale colored. Form into ropes about ½ inch in diameter and cut with scissors into 1-inch pieces. Wrap individually in waxed paper, twisting ends like firecrackers.

**Makes about 1 pound.**

## LEMON OATMEAL BARS

⅓ cup margarine

⅔ cup brown sugar, packed

1 egg

1 cup sifted flour

¼ teaspoon baking soda

1¼ cups rolled oats

½ cup milk

6 ounces butterscotch chips

Blend margarine and brown sugar together; add egg and mix well. Sift together flour and baking soda and add to butter with oats and milk. Stir in butterscotch chips and pour into a greased 10-inch × 5-inch × 3-inch pan which has been lined with waxed paper. Bake at 375°F for 35 to 40 minutes. Meanwhile, make lemon syrup (see recipe below). Pour hot syrup over immediately after removing from the oven. Cool thoroughly and cut into bars.

**To make lemon syrup:**

¼ cup sugar

1 tablespoon lemon juice

1 tablespoon grated fresh lemon peel

Bring sugar and juice to a boil, stirring constantly. When sugar has dissolved, remove from heat immediately and add peel.

**Makes 2 dozen 2-inch × 1-inch bars.**

## PENNSYLVANIA DUTCH CHOW CHOW

*2 cups very small green tomatoes, quartered*

*2 cups very small cucumbers (4-inch maximum), cut in ½-inch slices*

*2 cups tiny pickling onions, peeled*

*2 cups firm, fresh cauliflower, broken into florets*

*2 firm green peppers, cut in 1-inch squares*

*2 firm, sweet red peppers, cut in 1-inch squares*

*2 cups fresh-picked green beans, cut in 1-inch lengths*

*1 cup pickling salt*

*¾ cup white flour*

*¼ cup ground mustard*

*1½ teaspoons turmeric*

*1½ cups sugar*

*6 cups cider vinegar*

Mix the vegetables in a large glass bowl or stainless-steel pot and sprinkle with the salt. Cover with very cold water and let stand overnight. Drain, cover with cold water, and bring just to the boiling point. Drain well.

Combine the remaining ingredients with a wire whisk to make a smooth sauce; cook over moderate heat, stirring constantly until thick and smooth. Add the vegetables and slowly bring just to the boiling point. The vegetables should not become soft. Stir often to prevent the sauce from scorching the bottom of the pan. Spoon into hot, sterilized jars and seal immediately. Process for ten minutes in boiling water.

**Makes ten half-pint jars.**

## PUMPKIN PICKLES

*2½ cups sugar*

*2½ cups white distilled vinegar*

*3 cups water*

*4 cinnamon sticks*

*1 tablespoon whole cloves*

*4 pounds pumpkin*

Combine sugar, water, vinegar, and spices and boil for ten minutes to make a syrup. Peel the pumpkin and cut into 1-inch squares. You will have about 6 cups. Boil in the syrup for five minutes, then cover and let stand for one hour. Simmer slowly about one hour until the pumpkin is transparent. Remove the spices. Spoon the pickles into hot, sterilized jars and cover with the syrup. Seal and process in boiling water to cover for fifteen minutes.

**Makes six half-pint jars.**

## PICKLED JALAPENOS

*Fresh jalapeño peppers*

*Cider vinegar*

Wash the peppers and prick each in two places with the tip of a paring knife. Pack in hot, sterilized jars as snugly as possible. Meanwhile, heat the vinegar just to the boiling point. Fill the jars with hot vinegar and seal. Process ten minutes in boiling water to cover.

## DRIED PEPPER STRINGS

*Fresh red hot peppers*

*Jute cord*

*A heavy needle*

Thread the cord into a needle and make a large loop in the free end. String the peppers onto the cord. Tie the cord around the final pepper and knot firmly. Hang the peppers in a dry, airy place until crisp.

## SPICED GRAPE JELLY

*3½ cups grape juice*

*½ cup cider vinegar*

*1 cinnamon stick*

*10 whole cloves*

*7 cups sugar*

*½ bottle liquid fruit pectin*

Combine the grape juice, vinegar, and spices in a saucepan and bring just to the simmering point. Turn off the heat and allow to stand, covered, for ten minutes. Remove the spices.

Add sugar to the juice and mix well. Place over high heat and bring to a boil, stirring constantly. Stir in the pectin all at once, bring to a full, rolling boil, and boil hard for one minute, stirring constantly. Remove from the heat, skim off the foam, and pour into sterilized jars. Seal immediately.

**Makes nine half-pint jars.**

## KITCHEN METRICS

For cooking and baking convenience, use the following metric measurements:

### SPOONS:

1/4 teaspoon = 1 milliliter
1/2 teaspoon = 2 milliliters
1 teaspoon = 5 milliliters
1 tablespoon = 15 milliliters
2 tablespoons = 25 milliliters
3 tablespoons = 50 milliliters

### CUPS:

1/4 cup = 50 milliliters
1/3 cup = 75 milliliters
1/2 cup = 125 milliliters
2/3 cup = 150 milliliters
3/4 cup = 175 milliliters
1 cup = 250 milliliters

### OVEN TEMPERATURES:

200° F = 100° C
225° F = 110° C
250° F = 120° C
275° F = 140° C
300° F = 150° C
325° F = 160° C
350° F = 180° C
375° F = 190° C
400° F = 200° C
425° F = 220° C
450° F = 230° C
475° F = 240° C

## WEIGHT AND MEASURE EQUIVALENTS

1 inch = 2.54 centimeters
1 square inch = 6.45 square centimeters
1 foot = .3048 meters
1 square foot = 929.03 square centimeters
1 yard = .9144 meters
1 square yard = .84 square meters
1 ounce = 28.35 grams
1 pound = 453.59 grams

# SOURCES
## NORTH AMERICA

### GARDENS, FLOWERS, AND HERBS

Alberta Nurseries and Seed, Ltd.
P.O. Box 20
Bowden, Alberta
Canada T0M 0K0
*(Plants and seeds, vegetables, and flowers)*

Andre Viette Farm and Nursery
Route 1, Box 16
Fishersville, Virginia 22939
*(Hard-to-find perennials)*

Applewood Seed Company
5380 Vivian Street
Arvada, Colorado 80002
*(Indoor herb garden kits)*

The Gardener's Collection
Deline Lake, P.O. Box 243
Sydenham, Ontario
Canada K0H 2T0
*(Stoneware garden markers)*

Herbitage Farm
Old Homestead Highway
Richmond, New Hampshire 03470
*(Herb books and kits, corn-husk doll kit)*

High Altitude Gardens
P.O. Box 4619
Ketchum, Idaho 83340
*(Flowers, vegetables, herbs, and grasses for high altitudes)*

Jackson and Perkins Co.
P.O. Box 1028
Medford, Oregon 97501
*(Rose specialists)*

Johnny's Selected Seeds
Foss Hill Road
Albion, Maine 04910
*(Vegetable, flower, and herb seeds)*

Mrs. MacGregor's Garden Shop
4801 First Street North
Arlington, VA 22203
*(Teak window boxes and accessories)*

Native Gardens
Route 1, Box 494
Greenback, Tennessee 37742
*(Native flowers)*

The Natural Gardening Company
217 San Anselmo Avenue
San Anselmo, California 94960
*(Terra-cotta planters)*

Nichols Garden Nursery
1190 North Pacific Highway
Albany, Oregon 97321
*(Herb and flower plants and seeds, vegetable seeds)*

Owens Farms
Curve Nankipoo Road
Route 3, Box 158A
Ripley, Tennessee 38063
*(Trees, shrubs, perennials)*

Rhapis Gardens
P.O. Box 287
Gregory, Texas 78359
*(Lady palms, exotic plants, and pots)*

Robeson Farms
P.O. Box 270
Hall, New York 14463
*(Seeds for butterblossom squash)*

Shepherd's Garden Seeds
6116 Highway 9
Felton, California 95018
*(Unusual vegetable, herb, and flower seeds, container vegetable varieties)*

Smith and Hawken
25 Corte Madera
Mill Valley, California 94941
*(Garden accessories and gifts)*

Swinging Bridge Pottery
S.R. 2, Box 395
Criglersville, Virginia 22727
*(Herb feeders and garden markers)*

Taylor's Herb Gardens
1535 Lone Oak Road
Vista, California 92084
*(Herb plants and seeds)*

White Flower Farm
Litchfield, Connecticut 06759
*(Narcissus bulbs and forcing bowls)*

### FOOD AND KITCHEN ACCESSORIES

Bland Farms
P.O. Box 506
Glennville, Georgia 30427-0506

The Chef's Catalogue
3915 Commercial Avenue
Northbrook, Illinois 60062

The Crate and Barrel
190 Northfield Road
Northfield, Illinois 60093

Cuisinart
120 Top Gallant Road
Stamford, Connecticut 06912
*(Strainer attachment)*

Glashaus, Inc.
415 W. Golf Road
Suite 13
Arlington Heights, Illinois 60005
*(Rubber rings)*

Gurney Seed and Nursery Co.
Yankton, South Dakota 57079
*(Kitchen utensils)*

Johnny's Selected Seeds
Foss Hill Road
Albion, Maine 04910
*(Unusual kitchen utensils and knives)*

Joyce Chen Products
411 Waverly Oaks Road
Waltham, Massachusetts 02154
*(Nonstick woks, Chinese sauces, and cooking utensils)*

Meadowbrook Herb Garden
Route 138
Wyoming, Rhode Island 02898
*(Herb teas and blends)*

Sears, Roebuck and Co.
Telecatalog Center
9390 Bunsen Parkway
Louisville, Kentucky 40220
*(Pressure canners)*

William Glen
Mail-Order Department
2651 El Paseo Lane
Sacramento, California 95821

Williams-Sonoma
Mail-Order Department
P.O. Box 7456
San Francisco, California 94120

## CRAFTS AND CRAFT SUPPLIES

American Indian Archaeological
   Institute
P.O. Box 260
Curtis Road
Washington, Connecticut 06793
*(American Indian crafts)*

Appledore Gardens
Box 36125
Grosse Pointe Farms, Michigan
   48236
*(Beeswax kits and gifts)*

Arctic Trading Company
Kelsey and Bernier Streets
Churchill, Manitoba
Canada R0B 0E0

Berea College Student Craft
   Industries
CPO 2347
Berea, Kentucky 40404
*(Folk arts and mountain crafts)*

Betsy Williams/The Proper Season
68 Park Street
Andover, Massachusetts 01810
*(Herb and dried flower wreaths)*

The Fort at #4
Route 11, Box 336
Charlestown, New Hampshire
   03603
*(Colonial items and blacksmithing)*

Hartman's Herb Farm
Old Dana Road
Barre, Massachusetts 01005
*(Calendars and herbal gifts)*

Hearth Song
P.O. Box B
Sebastopol, California 95473
*(Creative and unusual children's gifts)*

Herbitage Farm
Old Homestead Highway
Richmond, New Hampshire 03470
*(Herb and folk craft kits)*

Maine Balsam Fir Products
P.O. Box 123
West Paris, Maine 04289
*(Fragrant balsam needles, small cones)*

Montana Exclusive
29 Border Lane #1
Bozeman, Montana 59715
*(Pottery, wood, foods, and toys)*

Old Sturbridge Village
One Old Sturbridge Village Road
Sturbridge, Massachusetts 01566
*(Early American crafts and gifts)*

Pleasant Company
8400 Fairway Place
Middleton, Wisconsin 53562
*("American Girls" books and activity portfolios)*

Rosemary House
120 South Market Street
Mechanicsburg, Pennsylvania
   17055
*(Potpourri supplies)*

The Western Reserve
Box 206A
Bath, Ohio 44210
*(Reproduction furniture kits)*

# AUSTRALIA

## GARDENS, FLOWERS, AND HERBS

The Garden
Dickson Place
Dickson, ACT
*(garden equipment)*

Greenery Garden Leisure Centre
4 Banksia Street
Heidelberg, VIC
*(garden supplies, plants, gifts)*

Harmony Nursery
450 South Arm Road
Lauderdale, TAS
*(plants, supplies)*

Irwin's Nursery
216 Geldart Road
Chandler, QLD
*(seedlings and herbs, flowers, and vegetables)*

Mansfield Garden Centre
533 Mt. Gravatt
Capalaba Road
Wishart, QLD
*(plants, garden supplies)*

Michele Shennen's Garden Centres
44 Old Barrenjoey Road
Avalon, NSW
*(plants, garden items, landscaping)*

Queanbeyan Nursery
68 Morrissett Street
Queanbeyan, ACT
*(plants, irrigation supplies)*

Sherringhams Nurseries
299a Lane Cove Road
N. Ryde, NSW

Swane's
490 Galston Road
Dural, NSW

Sully's Garden Centre
210 Beach Road
Christie Downs, S.A.
*(rare and exotic plants)*

Waldecks
Karrinyup Road
Osborne Park, W.A.

## FOOD AND KITCHEN ACCESSORIES

BBC Hardware
195-197 Marion Road
Richmond, S.A.

David Jones
310 Bourke Street
Melbourne, VIC

David Jones
194 Queen Street
Brisbane, QLD

David Jones
44 Rundle Mall
Adelaide, S.A.

Grace Brothers
Canberra Civic
Akuna Street
Canberra City, ACT

Grace Brothers
Corner George and Market Streets
Sydney, NSW

Mitre 10
*(canning and preserving items can be purchased from selected stores in each state throughout Australia)*

Myer
Forest Chase
Perth, W.A.

Myer
98-108 Liverpool Street
Hobart, TAS

## CRAFTS AND CRAFT SUPPLIES

Crafty Birds
24a Glenrose Shopping Centre
Belrose, NSW
*(local handmade crafts, pottery, and paintings)*

Crafty Cottage
Shop 5, Swan Street
Revesby, NSW
*(handmade crafts and pottery)*

Emily's Crafts
277 Rode Road
Wavell Heights, QLD
*(craft supplies, gifts)*

Hobart Craft Supplies
(Behind 63) Salamanca Place
Hobart, TAS
*(baskets, paint, and glitter)*

Peek-Inn-Inn at Ringwood
42c Wantirna Road
Ringwood, VIC
*(arts and crafts)*

Peggy Rose Cottage
507 North Beach Road
Gwelup, W.A.
*(gifts, silk, and dried flowers)*

Queanbeyan Cottage Crafts
Millhouse Gallery
49 Collett Street
Queanbeyan, ACT
*(handcrafts, ribbon and lace, patchwork fabrics)*

Spotlight
11 Beach Road
Christie's Beach, S.A.

Terry's Crafts & Ceramics
Shop 1, 12–14 Hunter Street
Parramatta, NSW
*(craft and ceramic classes)*

# INDEX

# Y

# Z